Service-Learning
in Higher Education

Service-Learning in Higher Education

Concepts and Practices

Barbara Jacoby and Associates

Foreword by Thomas Ehrlich

Jossey-Bass Publishers • San Francisco

Jossey-Bass books and products are available through most bookstores. To contact Jossey-Bass directly, call (888) 378-2537, fax to (800) 605-2665, or visit our website at www.josseybass.com.

Substantial discounts on bulk quantities of Jossey-Bass books are available to corporations, professional associations, and other organizations. For details and discount information, contact the special sales department at Jossey-Bass.

 Manufactured in the United States of America on Lyons Falls Turin Book. This paper is acid-free and 100 percent totally chlorine-free.

Credits are on p. 381.

Library of Congress Cataloging-in-Publication Data

Service-learning in higher education : concepts and practices /
Barbara Jacoby . . . [et al.]. — 1st ed.
    p. cm.—(The Jossey-Bass higher and adult education series)
    Includes bibliographical references and index.
    ISBN 0-7879-0291-8 (cloth : acid-free paper)
    1. Student service—United States. 2. Student volunteers in
social service—United States. 3. Community and college—United
States. 4. Education, Higher—United States—Curricula.
5. Experiential learning—United States. I. Jacoby, Barbara.
II. Series.
LC220.5.S45 1996
361.3'7—dc20   96–10047

FIRST EDITION
HB Printing   10 9 8 7 6 5 4 3

The Jossey-Bass
Higher and Adult Education Series

Contents

Foreword

Not long before the start of World War II, two great public intellectuals engaged in a bitter war of words. The issue was the nature of a liberal education. One protagonist was Robert Maynard Hutchins, president of the University of Chicago, who was on a crusade to transform the undergraduate curriculum around a canon of "Great Books." With the support of his friend and colleague Mortimer J. Adler, Hutchins claimed that the study of texts written by major Western intellects would lead to a set of immutable first principles covering all aspects of human life. On the other side, the renowned philosopher John Dewey argued that this claim was dangerous nonsense—dangerous because the notion of fixed truths requires a seal of authenticity from some human authority, which leads away from democracy and toward fascism; and nonsense because purely intellectual study should not be separated from practical study or from the great social problems confronting society. Such separation can only weaken the intellect and undercut the resolution of those problems. Study Aristotle, Plato, Aquinas, and the others, Dewey urged, but recognize that contemporary learning from their writings requires the application of their insights to contemporary issues. Dewey was the most important public intellectual of his day, and no other American philosopher has ever had more impact outside his own discipline.

At the time of the debate, and for most of the next half century, leaders in higher education generally concurred that Hutchins won the argument. The premise of service-learning, and the premise of this book, is, however, that Dewey was right and Hutchins was wrong. *Service-learning* is the various pedagogies that link community service and academic study so that each strengthens the other. The basic theory of service-learning is Dewey's: the interaction of knowledge and skills with experience is key to learning. Students learn best not by reading the Great Books in a closed room but by opening the doors and windows of experience. Learning starts with a problem and continues with the application of increasingly complex ideas and increasingly sophisticated skills to increasingly complicated problems.

This book is an important gathering of insights on why service-learning makes sense, and on the best ways to implement a service-learning program that is integrated into the academic life of a college or university. Barbara Jacoby is a splendid service-learning leader. She is in charge of a growing service-learning program operating in a state that has been among the most creative in encouraging service-learning. Jacoby does not suggest that service-learning is appropriate for all academic subjects or for all teachers, but she does make clear that service-learning ought to be part of the education of every undergraduate. Many paths are possible for delivering service-learning, and the various authors of the book's chapters are extremely helpful in suggesting concrete approaches while emphasizing flexibility. I learned a great deal from this book, and I am sure that both experienced practitioners and newcomers to the field will as well.

Service-learning is a long way from academic center stage in higher education, but it is moving in that direction with increasing speed. The growth of Campus Compact, a national organization of college and university presidents established a decade ago to promote student public service, reflects the rapid expansion of service-learning across the country. Campus Compact was started by a dozen presidents in the mid-1980s because they thought that the labeling of the "me" generation was a bum rap and that students were genuinely eager to help others and to be part of something larger than themselves. The presidents acted out of a mixture of sincere belief and desire to create a self-fulfilling prophecy. The result was successful beyond their dreams. Students in institutions across the country engaged in thousands of different service projects that linked campuses to communities. In some cases, those communities were close by; in others, they were in foreign countries. Students came to judgments about who their neighbors were and about what obligations they had toward those neighbors.

By the 1990s, it became clear to Campus Compact leaders that although community service by students was expanding, it was in danger of remaining a marginal campus activity. Years ago, when I was a Harvard student, undergraduates had to swim twenty-five yards as a degree requirement. Even at institutions that required some community service, that service was often as unrelated to the academic enterprise as the swimming requirement. At the same time, the work of the National Society for Experiential Education, and its predecessor organizations, together with the efforts of thousands of interested faculty members, renewed John Dewey's call to tie academic study to practical experience, using community service as the focal point for that experience. Campus Compact turned its primary attention to the integration of service into the curriculum. It grew to an organization of more than five hundred colleges and universities. Most of those institutions have physical centers where community service is facilitated and links with the curriculum are supported. Most also have community-service directors with responsibilities for enhancing service-learning throughout their campuses. Faculty members involved in service-learning are now joined through the Internet and in scores of coalitions around the nation, some by discipline and some by technique.

Service-learning is one of several trends in pedagogy that together mark a shift in undergraduate education from an emphasis on teaching to one on learning. Among the other trends are a focus on problems rather than disciplines, an emphasis on collaborative rather than individual learning, the use of integrative technology, and careful articulation of learning outcomes coupled with assessment of learning success. As a complementary trend, service-learning is a technique of learning, a way to strengthen learning. It enhances academic learning, enabling students in political science or philosophy courses, for example, to learn more political science or philosophy. Community service linked to academic study can also promote civic learning on the one hand and moral learning on the other. Benjamin Barber, of Rutgers University, has made the case persuasively in *An Aristocracy of Everyone* (1992) that a democracy depends on an involved citizenry, and that civic learning demands the same kind of academic attention as calculus, as well as the field experiences that are involved in service-learning. And Robert Coles, in *The Call of Service* (1993), makes a similar case with extraordinary eloquence for the impact on moral character that derives from community service in conjunction with guided reflection, a necessary ingredient of service-learning in the view of all contributors to this book. Finally, service-learning can enhance interpersonal skills that are key in most careers—skills such as careful listening, consensus building, and leadership.

So what took so long? If service-learning is as good an idea as Barbara Jacoby, her fellow authors, and Tom Ehrlich say it is, why did Dewey not win the argument? Perhaps most obvious to anyone who has tried to read Dewey, his prose is not easy. In many areas, it is virtually impenetrable. For a man who could write clearly, powerfully, and persuasively, two things amaze me: one, that he did not much of the time; and two, that in spite of his thick-textured prose, he was the country's most widely read, as well as influential, intellectual of his day. Two recent biographies, one by Robert B. Westbrook (*John Dewey and American Democracy,* 1991) and one by Alan Ryan (*John Dewey and the High Tide of American Liberalism,* 1995), are both worth studying for insights into this remarkable public philosopher—why his views fell from grace, and why they are returning to vogue once more.

Even discounting for Dewey's prose style, shouldn't the integration of service and academic study have started expanding in the 1930s instead of languishing for a half century? A partial answer is that it did start then in many applied and professional disciplines. In schools for social workers, nurses, teachers, and other professionals, the ruling guilds insisted on practical as well as theoretical training, and in many situations, that training was what we would now call service-learning. As the undergraduate curriculum of most colleges and universities has increasingly become dominated by fields of preprofessional education such as urban studies, community service has been linked to academic study through techniques such as internships and cooperative education.

Yet, until recently the arena of a liberal undergraduate education seemed largely immune to service-learning. In that arena, abstract reasoning is the highest order of inquiry. The education that dominated American liberal arts colleges was—and still largely is—an education in what Alan Ryan calls "the passive virtues: receptivity to existing truth and existing achievement" (1995, p. 281). These are the virtues that Hutchins extolled. The academy teaches them because they are intellectually interesting to teach, because the results can be readily assessed, and because there is something comforting about the notion that almost anyone who has read Virgil can rule the British Empire.

The collapse of that empire was one of a number of forces that brought into question the whole idea of a liberal education divorced from the social problems that surround us. Dewey wrote that education should be the primary means of social progress, not just a means to develop the intellect for its own sake. And this approach found increasing receptivity in the America of the 1960s, when a generation of young people responded to President Kennedy's call to "ask what you can do for your country." The Peace Corps and VISTA were programs of national service, as is AmeriCorps, the Corporation for National Service program established under the leadership of President Clinton. A key component of the corporation is the Learn and Serve America program that helps more than 500,000 students in primary, secondary, and higher education engage in service-learning.

With these changes on the national scene has come a rapid growth of service-learning courses in the arts and sciences, as well as in professional and preprofessional fields. In a 1991 speech to Campus Compact, Lee Shulman of Stanford University suggested that service-learning may become the "clinical practice of the liberal arts." We are a long way from that goal in American higher education, but we are well down the road.

Part of the blame for the languishing of service-learning must certainly be laid at the feet of those of us active in the field. Some do not want to join the academic mainstream; they find the margins more comfortable. Some practitioners resist the idea that faculty members who are skeptical about service-learning deserve a theoretical framework that fits service-learning within the larger learning aims of higher education, as well as evidence that service-learning actually furthers those aims. Too often the skeptics seem to be told that if they do not understand service-learning, then the true believers are not about to explain it.

Barbara Jacoby and the contributors to this book have gone a long way toward meeting the challenges of the skeptics. Readers will not find it argued that service-learning ought to be part of every course or the pedagogy of every faculty member. But taken together, these excellent chapters explain the theoretical framework for service-learning, the advantages of the various techniques that together constitute service-learning, and the practical means of realizing those advantages at institutions of higher education— large and small, public and private.

July 1996   Thomas Ehrlich
                                      Distinguished University Scholar
                                      California State University
                                      President Emeritus, Indiana University

                                      Former Chair of Campus Compact
                                      and the Commission on National and
                                      Community Service

                                      Vice Chair, Board of Directors,
                                      Corporation for National Service

References

Barber, B. *An Aristocracy of Everyone.* New York: Oxford University Press, 1992.

Coles, R. *The Call of Service.* Boston: Houghton Mifflin, 1993.

Ryan, A. *John Dewey and the High Tide of American Liberalism.* New York: Norton, 1995.

Westbrook, R. B. *John Dewey and American Democracy.* Ithaca, N.Y.: Cornell University Press, 1991.

Preface

This book is about the practice of service-learning in today's higher education. Service-learning has tremendous potential as a vehicle through which colleges and universities can meet their goals for student learning and development while making unique contributions to addressing unmet community, national, and global needs.

Both college students and the communities they serve stand to reap substantial benefits from engaging in service-learning. Among frequently cited benefits to student participants in service-learning are developing the habit of critical reflection; deepening their comprehension of course content; integrating theory with practice; increasing their understanding of the issues underlying social problems; strengthening their sense of social responsibility; enhancing their cognitive, personal, and spiritual development; heightening their understanding of human difference and commonality; and sharpening their abilities to solve problems creatively and to work collaboratively.

Community benefits include new energy and assistance to broaden delivery of existing services or to begin new ones; fresh approaches to solving problems; access to resources; and opportunities to participate in the teaching and learning process. Through improved town-gown relationships, colleges and universities also gain additional experiential learning settings for students, and new opportunities for faculty to orient research and teaching to meet human and community needs.

Higher education experts, government and business leaders, and society at large are more loudly and more frequently calling on higher education to sustain and increase its commitment to resolving social problems and meeting human needs and, at the same time, to focus more sharply on student learning and development.

Service-learning has the potential to advance both of these agendas. Despite this great potential, neither student learning and development nor community enhancement simply happens as a result of good intentions and hard work.

It is for these reasons that this book on service-learning is crucial and timely. What distinguishes service-learning from other community service or volunteer experiences is the *intentional* integration of service and learning and the reciprocal nature of both the service and the learning among all parties in the relationship: students, the community, and the academy. This book is based on the premise that opportunities to create high-quality service-learning experiences exist in both the curriculum and the rich array of programs in which student affairs professionals engage students.

While service-learning that is embedded in the curriculum provides opportunities for faculty to enhance students' learning by integrating course content with practical experience in a structured manner intended to meet course objectives, powerful opportunities for student learning and development also occur outside the classroom. Student affairs professionals can and do involve students in cocurricular service-learning programs that contribute to their learning and development. And while service-learning that is connected to faculty research and community involvement can lead to more broad-based and long-term community enhancement, shorter-term service projects also make considerable contributions to communities in both direct and indirect ways. In fact, even one-time experiences that are designed to achieve specific student learning and development outcomes and to address community needs as defined by the community can be appropriately called service-learning.

Audiences

Service-Learning in Higher Education: Concepts and Practices was written for several audiences. It is intended to help presidents and senior officers for academic affairs, student affairs, administration, and development discover the value of service-learning to students, institutions, and communities. They will learn why and how it deserves and needs support from each of their perspectives. The book will introduce academic deans, department chairs, and faculty to how service-learning contributes to teaching, learning, and research.

It is not a primary purpose of this book to provide specific guidance to faculty in developing service-learning experiences to meet course objectives in a particular discipline. Nevertheless, they will find here many examples of how service-learning can be integrated into courses, and the pros and cons of the various approaches. They also will encounter thoughtful discussion of the issues to consider in deciding whether service-learning is an appropriate methodology for meeting the objectives of a course.

The ideas and program examples presented will assist student affairs professionals and campus ministers in designing a range of service-learning activities that promote many facets of student development. Student leaders will also find the book useful in several ways. It will enable them to incorporate the essential service-learning elements of reflection and reciprocity into the design and implementation of programs and activities organized by individual students and student groups. *Service-Learning in Higher Education* provides information and rationales that students can use in advocating the development of service-learning in both the curriculum and the cocurriculum at their colleges and universities.

Since service-learning involves both institutions of higher education and communities, community leaders and nonprofit agency staff will find the book full of information that can lead to the development of mutually beneficial partnerships. The book also contains numerous implications for public policymakers, foundation and corporate executives, and religious leaders. Their understanding and support of service-learning is necessary if it is to be sustained over time and successful in meeting human and community needs.

Overview of the Contents

Service-Learning in Higher Education is organized into three parts. In Part One, I begin in Chapter One by defining service-learning and placing it in the context of today's higher education. In Chapter Two, Suzanné D. Mintz and Garry W. Hesser discuss the principles on which solid, viable service-learning programs should be based and the interactions of principles and practice. Marylu K. McEwen, in Chapter Three, presents theories of student learning and development useful for understanding the potential outcomes of student involvement in service-learning and for designing programs to encourage desired outcomes. Chapter Four, by Catherine R. Gugerty and Erin D. Swezey, discusses the development of campus-community relationships.

Part Two cites numerous examples of and approaches to service-learning from a wide range of institutions across the United States. It is important that colleges and universities offer a spectrum of curricular and cocurricular service-learning opportunities intentionally designed for students at different points in their education and at various stages of development. In Chapter Five, Mark D. McCarthy explains how one-time or short-term experiences are important first steps into service-learning for many students. Chapter Six, by Cesie Delve Scheuermann, covers ongoing cocurricular service-learning. Sandra L. Enos and Marie L. Troppe focus in Chapter Seven on service-learning in the curriculum. In Chapter Eight, Gail Albert describes intensive service-learning experiences, including alternative breaks, summer experiences, and national and international service. Irene S. Fisher addresses in Chapter Nine how to assist students in making career and lifestyle choices based on the values they acquire through service-learning.

Organizational, administrative, and policy issues that affect service-learning are the focus of Part Three. Diana A. Bucco and Julie A. Busch, in Chapter Ten, provide important information and steps for starting a service-learning program. In Chapter Eleven, Penny Rue addresses the successful administration of service-learning, both curricular and cocurricular. Keith Morton in Chapter Twelve examines issues for faculty and academic administrators to consider regarding the integration of service-learning into the curriculum. Sharon Rubin, in Chapter Thirteen, explains how service-learning can be institutionalized to ensure that it is sustainable over time. In the final chapter, I outline a mandate for action to secure the future of service-learning in higher education.

The two appendixes list national organizations that support service-learning, as well as programs and resources useful to service-learning educators in helping students make postcollege service and career choices.

Acknowledgments

Many people contributed to the development of this book, and I am indebted to them all. First, I acknowledge and thank the chapter authors for their wisdom and hard work. I am proud to have had the opportunity to work with such outstanding educators.

The consultation and assistance of several individuals were invaluable: Allen Wutzdorff, Sally Migliore, Gita Gulati-Partee, and Nancy Bailey of the National Society for Experiential Education; Nancy Rhodes, Marie Troppe, Sandra Enos, and other members of the staff of Campus Compact; and Bob Sigmon, Tom Ehrlich, Susan Komives, Peggy Barr, Jeanne Likins, Sylvia Stewart, Penny Rue, Suzanné Mintz, and Kathleen Rice. I am also grateful for the many useful thoughts and suggestions from the members of the Service-Learning Listserv Discussion Group organized by Robin Crews at the University of Colorado at Boulder.

I thank the staff of the Office of Commuter Affairs and Community Service Programs at the University of Maryland at College Park for their unfailing support. As always, Anita K. Ahalt and her staff did terrific work in preparing the manuscript.

Gale Erlandson at Jossey-Bass is responsible for giving this book considerably greater depth and focus. She is truly outstanding at what she does for authors and their work. The fine book *Realizing the Educational Potential of Residence Halls,* edited by my colleagues Charles Schroeder and Phyllis Mable and published by Jossey-Bass in 1994, served as an inspiration and guide to me and several of my associates throughout the writing and editing process. Rachel Livsey's editorial assistance was consistently helpful.

With deepest appreciation, I acknowledge my wonderful husband and partner of twenty-five years, Steve Jacoby. His endless enthusiasm for this project served as continual and much-needed motivation for me. This preface, as well as the first and last chapters, benefited significantly as a result of his thoughtful and meticulous readings. On more than one occasion he helped me turn chaos into order.

Finally, as I always try to take the time to do, I thank those who went before. In this case, it is the many creative, talented, and hard-working individuals whose labors in the vineyards of service-learning have provided a solid foundation for our current endeavors.

Silver Spring, Maryland   Barbara Jacoby
July 1996

The Authors

Barbara Jacoby is director of the Office of Commuter Affairs and Community Service Programs at the University of Maryland at College Park. She also serves as director of the National Clearinghouse for Commuter Programs, the only national organization that exists solely to provide information and assistance to professionals in designing programs and services for commuter students. She is affiliate assistant professor of college student personnel and lecturer in French at the University of Maryland at College Park. She earned her B.A. (1971), M.A. (1972), and Ph.D. (1978) degrees in French language and literature at the University of Maryland at College Park.

Jacoby is the author of *The Student as Commuter: Developing a Comprehensive Institutional Response* (1989) and has written more than twenty-five articles and book chapters on topics that include service-learning in higher education, enhancing the educational experience of college students, and change in student affairs. She has been featured on two national teleconferences on commuter students and adult learners. Jacoby has consulted extensively at colleges and universities across the country and has made numerous keynote speeches and presentations. She is active in promoting service-learning nationally, in the state of Maryland, and on her campus.

Over the years she has held many leadership positions in the American College Personnel Association and the National Association of Student Personnel Administrators. She has also been on the board of directors of the Council for the Advancement of Standards in Higher Education for fifteen years. Her Services, Programs, Advocacy, and Research (SPAR) model—a comprehensive approach to meeting the needs of diverse student populations—

has been adopted for use by a number of institutions. Jacoby's institution and professional associations have recognized her outstanding contributions on several occasions.

Gail Albert is a service-learning educator with the Vermont Commission on National and Community Service. Prior to that appointment she served for eight years in various capacities, including interim director and assistant director of the University of Vermont Center for Service-Learning. She edited *The Service-Learning Reader: Reflections and Perspectives on Service,* published in 1995 by the National Society for Experiential Education (NSEE). Albert is a member of the board of directors of NSEE, and from 1993 through 1995 served as cochair of NSEE's Service-Learning Special Interest Group. She received her B.A. degree (1965) in Russian from Vassar College and her M.S. degree (1978) in communication science and disorders from the University of Vermont.

Diana A. Bucco is executive director of One to One Allegheny County. Before that, she was the executive director for Pennsylvania Campus Compact. She has coedited three Campus Compact publications: *Students Trained in Advocacy and Community Service Manual; Building Sustainable Programs: A Guide to Developing and Maintaining Service-Learning at Community Colleges;* and *Service-Learning: Linking Academics and the Community.* In 1995 she was selected by *Who Cares* magazine as one of ten Pennsylvania leaders of the twenty-something generation. Bucco received her B.A. degree (1988) in communications and political science from the University of Pittsburgh.

Julie A. Busch is an independent consultant working with organizations including Campus Compact, the Corporation for National Service, and the American Youth Foundation. Previously she served as executive director of Michigan Campus Compact, and she has been in administrative positions at Albion College, Bowling Green State University, and the University of South Carolina. She received her B.A. degree (1980) in communications from Albion College and her M.A. degree (1982) in college student personnel from Bowling Green State University.

Sandra L. Enos is project director for Campus Compact's Project on Integrating Service with Academic Study. She served as a VISTA volunteer in rural Alabama in the early 1970s. She earned her B.A. degree (1971) in sociology from Rhode Island College and her M.A. degree (1974) from Brown University in sociology and inter-disciplinary urban affairs. She is adjunct professor of sociology at Rhode Island College and a doctoral candidate at the University of Connecticut in sociology, with special interests in organizational responses to community crises and families in stress. Enos is the author of a chapter on qualitative research in a forthcoming book on research methodology, and an organizer of several activities dealing with service-learning in the discipline of sociology.

Irene S. Fisher is director of the Lowell Bennion Community Service Center at the University of Utah, where she is also an adjunct faculty member in the School of Social Work and the Department of Family and Consumer Studies. She formerly directed the Utah Issues Information Program. She currently chairs the Coalition for Utah's Future, and she is past president of the League of Women Voters of Salt Lake and founder of Utah Children. She received her B.A. degree (1959) in speech communication and elementary education from Northern State College.

Catherine R. Gugerty is a member of the religious community of the School Sisters of Notre Dame. She is director of Urban Immersion Programs at Loyola College in Maryland, as well as a staff member of the Beans and Bread Meal Program and Homeless Outreach. She has fifteen years of experience working with people who are homeless in Baltimore. Gugerty earned her B.A. degree (1981) in sociology from the College of Notre Dame of Maryland, completed course work in theology and philosophy at St. Louis University in 1985–86, and earned a certificate in nonprofit management (1992) from Loyola College. Currently, she is working on her M.S. degree in pastoral counseling at Loyola College. She has written about spiritual ministry with persons who are poor and homeless.

Garry W. Hesser is professor of sociology and urban studies and director of experiential education at Augsburg College. He earned his B.A. degree (1961) in history and religion from Phillips University, his M.Div. (1964) in social ethics and biblical studies from Union Theological Seminary, a certificate in international relations (1964) from Columbia University, and his M.A. (1970) and Ph.D. (1972) degrees in sociology at the University of Notre Dame. Hesser teaches three service-learning courses, and supervises internships in a wide range of public and community service placements. He is past president of the National Society for Experiential Education and of the Higher Education Consortium for Urban Affairs, and has led workshops on experiential education and service-learning on many campuses and at professional meetings. He is the author of numerous articles and papers on experiential education, housing, neighborhood revitalization, and liturgy.

Mark D. McCarthy is dean of student development and director of the Center for Student Development and Community Service at Marquette University. He received his B.A. degree (1976) in liberal studies from Pennsylvania State University, his M.A. degree (1979) in college student personnel administration from the University of Maryland at College Park, and his Ph.D. degree (1993) in educational administration from Marquette University. He is the Midwest regional vice president of the Jesuit Association of Student Personnel Administrators, and a volunteer with several churches, schools, and community organizations.

Marylu K. McEwen is associate professor and director of the College Student Personnel program, Department of Counseling and Personnel Services, University of Maryland at College Park. Previously she was affiliated with Auburn University and Purdue University. She received her B.S. degree (1968) in mathematics from Purdue University, her M.S.Ed. degree (1970) in college student personnel administration from Indiana University, and her Ph.D. degree (1974) in counseling and personnel services from Purdue University. She is associate editor of the *Journal of College Student Development,* and has published widely on student development theory, multiculturalism, and the profession of student affairs.

Suzanné D. Mintz is coordinator of service-learning initiatives at the University of Maryland at College Park. She earned her B.S.

degree (1981) in sociology from the University of Florida and her
M.S. degree (1985) in higher education and student affairs from
Indiana University. She has been engaged in experiential education and community service for more than ten years, formerly in
positions at the Catholic University of America, the University of
Maryland at College Park, and the American Council on Education. Most recently Mintz oversaw training and technical assistance
for the Learn and Serve America: Higher Education program, and
also served as a program officer of the Corporation for National
Service. She is coeditor of *Community Service as Values Education*
(1990). She has published and presented on service-learning,
women's issues, and diversity issues, and has been active in repro-
ductive rights issues and with an inner-city day-care center.

Keith Morton is assistant professor of English and associate director of the Feinstein Institute for Public Service at Providence College. His B.A. degree (1979) is in English and history from the
University of Massachusetts at Amherst; his M.A. (1982) and Ph.D.
(1986) degrees are in American studies from the University of
Minnesota. He has worked in the areas of community development, community service, and community theory for the past fifteen years. Prior to joining Providence College in 1994, he was
program director and then executive director of the University of
Minnesota YMCA, and director of Campus Compact's Project on
Integrating Service with Academic Study. Morton serves on the
boards of several local and national organizations dedicated to
improving the quality of life for people in their communities and
is particularly interested in youth development. He also serves
regularly as a workshop leader and trainer for educational and
community-based organizations.

Sharon Rubin is vice president for academic affairs at Ramapo College of New Jersey and a frequent writer and speaker on service-
learning and other forms of experiential learning. Previously
president of the National Society for Experiential Education, she
also served on the Maryland Governor's Advisory Board on Service
and Citizenship. She received her B.A. (1965) and M.A. (1966)
degrees in English literature from the University of Chicago, and
her Ph.D. degree (1972) in American studies from the University

of Minnesota. Rubin was one of the first recipients of a W. K. Kellogg Foundation National Fellowship, and she participated in the Fulbright International Educational Administrators Program in Japan and Korea.

Penny Rue is associate dean of students at Georgetown University. Prior to serving in this position, she served for seven years as Georgetown's director of student programs. Before coming to Georgetown, she held posts at the University of Maryland at College Park and the University of North Carolina at Chapel Hill. Rue has taught Contemporary Issues in Leadership for Women in the Georgetown M.B.A. program and has chaired the National Conference for College Women Student Leaders. She received her B.A. degree (1975) from Duke University in English and religion, her M.A. degree (1977) in student personnel work from Ohio State University, and her Ph.D. degree (1988) in counseling and personnel services from the University of Maryland at College Park.

Cesie Delve Scheuermann is a consultant in Salem, Oregon. She is former director of student activities at the University Center at Willamette University, and served as director of the Volunteer and Public Service Center at Georgetown University. She is coeditor of *Community Service as Values Education* (1990). Scheuermann received her B.A. degree (1980) in English from Westmont College and her M.A. degree (1985) in college student personnel from the University of Maryland at College Park.

Erin D. Swezey is director of community service and codirector of the Center for Values and Service at Loyola College in Maryland. She received her B.S. degree (1980) in human development from the University of California, Davis; her M.A. degree (1982) in college student personnel administration from Michigan State University; and her master of pastoral ministry degree (1989) from Seattle University. She was a panelist of a national teleconference, "Partnerships in Community Service and Learning," sponsored by the National Association for Student Personnel Administrators. Swezey wrote a chapter on service-learning from a faith perspective for *Community Service as Values Education* (1990). She also authored a paper, "Creating a Foundation of Support," for the Campus Compact publication *Service Counts: Lessons from the Field of Service and Higher Education* (1995).

Marie L. Troppe is project associate for Campus Compact's Project on Integrating Service with Academic Study. She earned a B.A. degree (1987) in English literature from the Catholic University of America and an M.A. degree (1992) in English from Georgetown University, where she was assistant director of the Volunteer and Public Service Center. She has written a number of articles on service-learning, including "Participatory Action Research: Merging the Community and Scholarly Agendas," published by Campus Compact in 1994, and "From the Margin to the Mainstream: Campus Compact's Project on Integrating Service with Academic Study" (1995). Her current professional interests focus on action research and the epistemology of service-learning.

To Pearl and Herb Gendler,
my beloved parents—the world's best

Service-Learning
in Higher Education

Foundations and Principles of Service-Learning

Although the concept and practice of service-learning are still relatively new to higher education, considerable foundations and principles exist. Part One examines the theoretical and practical perspectives that serve as a firm base for the development of service-learning in all types of institutions of higher education—large and small, public and private, commuter and residential, two year and four year. The foundations and principles are applicable to the design of service-learning to achieve a wide range of educational and community outcomes.

Part One provides educators with a thorough grounding in the broad issues that underlie successful service-learning, whether it is based in the curriculum or the cocurriculum, so that they can develop programs truly beneficial to students, communities, and institutions. Service-learning is different from many other educational endeavors in that it cannot happen within the confines of a classroom, a discipline, or a campus. By necessity, service-learning involves partnerships between the institution and communities, and affects students in multiple ways. The chapters in Part One establish the foundation for realizing the potentials and understanding the implications of service-learning.

Chapter One

Service-Learning in Today's Higher Education

Barbara Jacoby

Higher education is being called on to renew its historic commitment to service. Its foremost experts are urging colleges and universities to assume a leadership role in addressing society's increasing problems and in meeting growing human needs. Indeed, their calls to action serve as a collective mandate for higher education to become actively engaged in responding to these problems and needs (Bok, 1982, 1986; Boyer, 1990, 1994; Ehrlich, 1995; Hackney, 1994; Kerr, 1963; Newman, 1985; Wingspread Group on Higher Education, 1993). Ernest Boyer (1994) urges colleges and universities to "respond to the challenges that confront our children, our schools, and our cities, just as the land-grant colleges responded to the needs of agriculture and industry a century ago" (p. 48). Derek Bok (1982) agrees: "There is no reason for universities to feel uncomfortable in taking account of society's needs; in fact, they have a clear obligation to do so" (p. 301). A renewed commitment to service will go a long way in responding to higher education's critics who bemoan its "fortress mentality" in isolating itself from the encroaching problems of both its local communities and the rest of the nation (Harkavy, 1993, p. 45).

At the same time, higher education is questioning its effectiveness at achieving its most fundamental goal: student learning.

Numerous articles and reports have criticized indifferent undergraduate teaching, overemphasis on esoteric research, failure to promote moral character and civic consciousness, and narrow focus on preparing graduates for the job market (Ehrlich, 1995; Hackney, 1994; Pew Higher Education Roundtable, 1994; Wingspread Group on Higher Education, 1993).

Today's college students, however, feeling compelled to confront society's problems, are participating in community service in record numbers. In Alexander Astin's research on a sample of students who entered college in the fall of 1994, more than 70 percent reported that they had performed volunteer work in high school (Astin, Korn, and Sax, 1994). As more and more elementary and secondary schools are requiring community service, this percentage will only increase.

Indeed, Arthur Levine's (1994, p. 4) 1993 survey of nine thousand undergraduates reveals that 64 percent were involved in volunteer activities. This involvement occurs at all types of institutions of higher education: community colleges (59 percent), four-year colleges (67 percent), and universities (68 percent). Both men (62 percent) and women (66 percent) are involved, as are both older (63 percent) and younger (65 percent) students. The percentages are high for white students (65 percent), as well as for students of color (62 percent). And the trend is established in all regions of the country: the Northeast (61 percent), the Midwest (65 percent), then South (64 percent), and the West (67 percent). Students participate in a wide range of community service activities, working with children, teenagers, people with physical and mental disabilities, people who are elderly, battered women, and people with AIDS. Their work addresses issues of hunger, homelessness, illiteracy, health care, educational disadvantage, the environment, and numerous others. Robert Coles (1993), the well-respected Harvard service-learning educator, points out that in contrast to the young people of the 1960s, "today's students are likely to express their lofty political and social impulses and practical desires to change the world through community service" (p. 40).

As colleges and universities across the country are developing programs to enable their students to serve their communities, the nation, and the world—and at the same time to enrich undergraduate education—it is critical that these programs embrace the concept of service-learning. This chapter defines service-learning and elucidates the differences between service-learning and traditional community service. It provides a historical overview and a context for understanding the essential linkage of service and learning; it describes the current state of practice; and it highlights the relationship between service-learning and institutional educational goals.

Service-Learning Defined

Robert Sigmon (1994) notes that "many definitions and approaches have been used within the general framework of linking service with learning" (p. 1). In the introduction to *Combining Service and Learning* (1990), Jane Kendall states that she participated in hundreds of debates about the language used in combining service and learning, "debates that will probably rage forever" (p. 18). She adds that she encountered 147 terms in the literature she reviewed; even more are in use today.

For the purposes of this book, service-learning is defined as follows:

> Service-learning is a form of experiential education in which students engage in activities that address human and community needs together with structured opportunities intentionally designed to promote student learning and development. Reflection and reciprocity are key concepts of service-learning.

The hyphen in *service-learning* is critical in that it symbolizes the symbiotic relationship between service and learning (S. Migliore, personal communication, April 1995). The term *community* in the definition of service-learning refers to local neighborhoods, the state, the nation, and the global community. The human and community needs that service-learning addresses are those needs that are *defined by the community*.

Sigmon (1994) proposes a useful service and learning typology with four variations found at colleges and universities: "service-LEARNING," which implies that learning goals are primary and service outcomes secondary; "SERVICE-learning," in which the service agenda is central and the learning secondary; "service learning," in which the absence of the hyphen indicates that the two are viewed as completely separate from each other; and "SERVICE-LEARNING," in which service and learning goals are of equal weight and "the hyphen is essential" (p. 2). This last relationship, which Sigmon prefers, is advocated in this book.

This book takes the firm stance that service-learning is both curricular and cocurricular, because all learning does not occur in the classroom. Although some current definitions of service-learning insist that it must be integrated into the curriculum, student learning is indeed structured and facilitated by student affairs professionals, campus ministers, trained student leaders, and community members in addition to faculty. Although the structure afforded by the curriculum (class meetings, syllabi, assignments, grading, and credit) makes it easier to hold students accountable for achieving the desired outcomes of service-learning, skillfully designed and implemented cocurricular experiences can yield rich results. And learning and developmental outcomes are not necessarily related to a discipline or to particular course content. These potential outcomes are discussed in Chapter Three.

Discussion also continues about whether one-time or short-term experiences, such as serving in a soup kitchen or participating in an environmental cleanup project, can be called service-learning. This book posits that they can if they include the fundamental concepts of reflection and reciprocity, which distinguish service-learning from other community service and volunteer programs. Some of these programs include some elements of these concepts, but many do not. The use of the term *service-learning* implies the centrality of reflection and reciprocity to both conception and practice.

Reflection

As a form of experiential education, service-learning is based on the pedagogical principle that learning and development do not necessarily occur as a result of experience itself but as a result of a reflective component explicitly designed to foster learning and development. The work of theorists and researchers on learning—from Jean Piaget to William Perry, from James Coleman to David Kolb, from John Dewey to Donald Schon—indicates that we learn through combinations of thought and action, reflection and practice, theory and application (Kendall, 1988). Different service-learning programs emphasize different types of learning goals: intellectual, civic, ethical, moral, cross-cultural, career, or personal (Kendall, 1990). Programs also highlight different combinations of these goals.

Service-learning programs are also explicitly structured to promote learning about the larger social issues behind the needs to which their service is responding. This learning includes a deeper understanding of the historical, sociological, cultural, economic, and political contexts of the needs or issues being addressed (Kendall, 1990). Reflection could be designed, for example, to encourage students working in a homeless shelter to ask such questions as Why are there homeless people? What national and state policies affect homelessness? Why do we create homeless shelters rather than identify and solve the root causes of the problem? If homelessness is a global problem, how do other countries deal with it? Reflection can take many forms: individual and group, oral and written, directly related to discipline-based course material or not. Reflection should include opportunities for participants to receive feedback from those persons being served, as well as from peers and program leaders (Porter Honnet and Poulsen, 1989).

Reciprocity

The other essential concept of service-learning is reciprocity between the server and the person or group being served. "All parties in service-learning are learners and help determine what is to be learned. Both the server and those served teach, and both learn" (Kendall, 1990, p. 22). In service-learning, those being served control the service provided. The needs of the community, as determined by its members, define what the service tasks will be. Service-learning avoids placing students into community settings based solely on desired student learning outcomes and providing services that do not meet actual needs or perpetuate a state of need rather than seeking and addressing the causes of need.

Through reciprocity, students develop a greater sense of belonging and responsibility as members of a larger community.

Community members being served learn how to take responsibility for their own needs and become empowered to develop mechanisms and relationships to address them. Thus, reciprocity creates "a sense of mutual responsibility and respect between individuals in the service-learning exchange" (Kendall, 1990, p. 22). Service-learning thus stands in contrast to the traditional, paternalistic, one-way approach to service, where one person or group has resources that they share with a person or group that they assume lacks resources. Reciprocity also eschews the traditional concept of volunteerism, which is based on the idea that a more competent person comes to the aid of a less competent person. In the old paradigm, volunteers often attempt to solve other people's problems before fully understanding the situation or its causes. Service-learning encourages students to do things *with* others rather than *for* them. Everyone should expect to change in the process (Karasik, 1993).

Some authors have legitimately challenged the use of the word *service* in service-learning (Cruz, 1994; Kendall, 1990; Seidel, 1994). They point out that it suggests inequality among the participants in service-learning, with an individual or group doing something to another individual or group. It goes against the "parity of esteem," as Howard Berry (1988, p. 3)) terms the mutuality of the service-learning exchange. For many African Americans and other people who have experienced oppression, *service* still connotes involuntary servitude. *Service* is also used in a self-righteous sense to mean well-endowed persons "doing things" for those who are less fortunate than themselves. Nevertheless, I agree with Kendall (1990) and Berry (1994) that although the word *service* is problematic, it is the most common and accessible word to use.

Service-Learning as Program, Philosophy, and Pedagogy

In this book, and in numerous other contexts, service-learning is often referred to as a program. Although it is convenient to speak of service-learning programs in higher education, it is important to note here that service-learning is also a philosophy and a pedagogy; unfortunately, it is sometimes construed as a political stance. As a program, service-learning emphasizes the accomplishment of tasks to meet human and community needs in combination with "intentional learning goals and with conscious reflection and critical analysis" (Kendall, 1990, p. 20). Tasks in which participants engage are often direct services, such as tutoring, work in soup kitchens and homeless shelters, assistance in hospitals and other health settings, environmental cleanups, and renovation and construction of homes and community facilities. Tasks also include advocacy and policy-level work on such issues as housing, economic development, the environment, education, and human services. Service-learning programs have different goals and different approaches. For example, curricular programs can view service-learning as discipline-based or as part of general education. Cocurricular programs can have goals of leadership, citizenship, or spiritual development. Reflection components are thus designed to focus on different learning outcomes and to use a wide range of methodologies. As a program type, service-learning encompasses evaluation of its effects on students, as well as on individuals and communities served.

Service-learning is also a philosophy of "human growth and purpose, a social vision, an approach to community, and a way of knowing" (Kendall, 1990, p. 23). It is the element of reciprocity that elevates it to the level of philosophy, "an expression of values— service to others, community development and empowerment, reciprocal learning—which determines the purpose, nature and process of *social and educational exchange* between learners (students) and the people they serve" (Stanton, 1990, p. 67). Service-learning is therefore a philosophy of reciprocity, which implies a concerted effort to move from charity to justice, from service to the elimination of need.

As a pedagogy, service-learning is education that is grounded in experience as a basis for learning and on the centrality and intentionality of reflection designed to enable learning to occur. Based on the work of Dewey, Piaget, and Kurt Lewin, Kolb's concept of the experiential learning cycle (1984) is useful in elucidating the role of service-learning as pedagogy. His model outlines the learning experience as a constantly revisited four-step cycle: concrete experience, reflection on the experience, synthesis and abstract conceptualization, and active experimentation—that is, testing the concepts in new situations. Although one may enter the cycle at any point, a person engaged in service-learning often begins with concrete service experience and then embarks on a period of reflection on that experience, analyzing what actually occurred and what implications arise from those observations. In the next step, reflection stimulates the learner to integrate observations and implications with existing knowledge and to formulate concepts and questions to deepen the learner's understanding of the world and the root causes of the need for service. In the fourth step of the model, the learner tests these concepts in different situations. This experimentation leads the learner to begin the cycle again and again. Chapter Three elaborates on Kolb's model and its relevance to service-learning.

Recent discussions in which I have been involved have focused on service-learning as a political stance. With its commitment to social justice, service-learning is clearly not value free. Nevertheless, I believe firmly that proponents and practitioners of service-learning must strenuously avoid directly or indirectly influencing participants toward specific political parties or toward their personally held political views. This type of influence is inappropriate and exclusionary and can adversely affect an institution's willingness to integrate service-learning into its mission and practices.

Higher Education's Tradition of Service

It is important to ground today's concept and practice of service-learning in higher education's long tradition of service. In his preeminent history of higher education, Frederick Rudolph (1962) reminds us: "From the beginning, the American college was cloaked with a public purpose, with a responsibility to the past and the present and the future" (p. 177). Since the founding of Harvard College in 1636, the goals of American higher education have included the preparation of citizens for active involvement in community life (Smith, 1994, p. 55).

Following the Revolutionary War, the purposes of higher education slowly began to shift from the focus on individual students to the building of a new nation (Boyer, 1994). Rudolph (1962) notes that the founding of institutions such as Rensselaer Polytechnic Institute in 1824 responded to the need for builders of railroads, bridges, and other physical and social structures.

In 1862 the passage of the Land-Grant Act inextricably linked higher education and the concept of service, specifically related to agriculture and industry. This linkage led Woodrow Wilson, who would become president of Princeton University in 1902, to state: "It is not learning but the spirit of service that will give a college a place in the annals of the nation" (cited by Boyer, 1994, p. 48). In 1903 David Starr Jordan, president of Stanford University, declared that "the entire university movement, in this country was progressing towards 'reality' and 'practicality'" (cited by Boyer, 1994, p. 48).

In "Creating the New American College," Boyer (1994) contends that this vision of service has been reaffirmed over and over again. When the economy collapsed, causing the Great Depression, President Franklin D. Roosevelt recruited outstanding scholars to serve as his consultants. During World War II research universities joined with the government to create solutions to new problems. Two important government–higher education partnerships were founded in the war's wake: the National Science Foundation and the GI Bill. Once the Soviet Union launched *Sputnik* in 1957, higher education joined yet another partnership with government, seeking to improve education in primary and secondary schools. And as Boyer (1994) points out, "the very title of the National Defense Education Act of 1958 clearly linked higher education to the security of our country" (p. 48).

The Emergence of Service-Learning

College student community service has a long history that includes the YMCA, 4-H, the Scouting movement, Greek-letter organizations, and many campus ministry initiatives. It grew dramatically in both numbers and in public attention in the 1960s, inspired by President John F. Kennedy's launching of the Peace Corps in 1961. Volunteers in Service to America (VISTA) followed in 1965, engaging young people, mostly college students or recent graduates, to tackle problems within the United States. The civil rights movement of the 1960s challenged both institutions of higher education and students to participate in the burgeoning demand for social justice.

As a form of experiential education, service-learning has its roots in Dewey's theory of experience, which "has become the philosophical touchstone of the experiential movement" (Smythe, 1990, p. 296). Along with internships, cooperative education, and other forms of experiential learning, service-learning established itself and flourished on many college campuses in the late 1960s and the 1970s.

The term *service-learning* first emerged in the work of Sigmon and William Ramsey at the Southern Regional Education Board in 1967 (Giles and Eyler, 1994). In 1969 the Office of Economic Opportunity established the National Student Volunteer Program, which shortly became the National Center for Service-Learning. Two years later, this program, along with VISTA and the Peace Corps, combined to form the federal agency ACTION. As a national center for student service, ACTION published a magazine, *Synergist;* developed a network; and distributed seed money. One of its projects, the University Year for ACTION, involved more than ten thousand students from over one hundred colleges and universities in the 1970s. Many campus-based service programs were started during this period. Some have vanished, but others still exist. In addition, regional and consortium programs emerged in the 1960s and 1970s, such as the Southern Regional Education Board's resource development internships, the Philadelphia Urban Semester (Great Lakes Colleges of the Midwest), Chicago Urban Semester (Associated Colleges of the Midwest), and the Twin Cities Metropolitan Urban Studies Term and City Arts (Higher Education Consortium for Urban Affairs, HECUA).

Although the National Center for Service-Learning was relatively short-lived, colleges and universities interested in service-learning continued to network through organizations that developed outside the federal agency. In 1978 the National Society for Internships and Experiential Education (NSIEE; as of 1994, the National Society for Experiential Education, NSEE) was formed by fusing separate groups for field experience education and service internships. NSIEE became the repository and distributor for the considerable written resources on service-learning of the National Center for Service-Learning. Along a parallel track, the Council for Adult and Experiential Learning did much work to lay the foundation for the acceptance of experiential education in colleges and universities (G. Hesser, personal communication, 1995).

Lessons Learned from the 1960s and 1970s

The service-learning movement that had acquired a foothold on college campuses in the 1960s and 1970s did not last. Kendall identifies three pitfalls that brought about the demise of many programs that involved college students in service:

1. Most of the programs were not integrated into the central mission and goals of the schools and agencies where they were based. . . .
2. Those in the community service movement learned several important programmatic lessons about the balance of power and the pitfalls of "helping others" or "doing good." . . . Paternalism, unequal relationships between the parties involved, and a tendency to focus only on charity—"doing for" or "helping" others—rather than on supporting others to meet their own needs all become gaping pitfalls for program after well-intentioned program. . . .
3. We learned that while it sounds great to help young people learn through service experiences in the community, the service experience does not ensure that either significant learning or effective service will occur [1990, pp. 8–10].

Kendall (1990) reports that a number of educators, community leaders, and students who believed in the potential of service-learning continued through the "me generation" of the late 1970s and the 1980s to identify the elements that need to be incorporated into successful, sustainable programs. Their work has served to encourage the recent great surge of interest in service-learning by institutions of higher education, students, communities, and the federal government.

Service-Learning Today

In 1985 college student community service gained new momentum. The Education Commission of the States began Campus

Compact: The Project for Public and Community Service. Campus Compact, an organization of college and university presidents who have pledged to encourage and support academically based community service at their institutions, now has over five hundred members. While the presidents were establishing Campus Compact, a group of recent college graduates formed the Campus Outreach Opportunity League (COOL) to encourage students to serve their communities. As a result, many student-initiated service projects were born, and COOL has an ever-expanding national network. COOL works with approximately one thousand colleges and universities, and more than two thousand students attend COOL's annual conferences. COOL's Critical Elements of Thoughtful Community Service have served as guides for the development of hundreds of high-quality community service projects (Campus Outreach Opportunity League, 1993).

From 1983 to 1989 consultants trained by NSEE, with support from the Fund for the Improvement of Postsecondary Education, worked with more than five hundred colleges and universities to develop and strengthen experiential education. The consultations were based on the premises that service-learning (and all other experiential education) must be firmly rooted in the mission of the institution, involve faculty, be integrated into the curriculum, and be grounded in sound theory and pedagogical practice (Kendall, 1990).

In response to the burgeoning growth of community service and service-learning programs and the increasing awareness that effective service and learning do not necessarily happen automatically, NSEE began a process of articulating and refining a set of principles of good practice in 1987 (Kendall, 1990). The intense and thorough process culminated in a 1989 Wingspread conference hosted by the Johnson Foundation at which the *Principles of Good Practice in Combining Service and Learning* (Porter Honnet and Poulsen, 1989) were hammered out. Although there are numerous definitions of service-learning in wide use today recorded in articles, books, laws, and scholarly and institutional documents, all recent definitions are based on the key statement in the preamble to the Wingspread principles: "Service, combined with learning, adds value to each and transforms both" (Porter Honnet and Poulsen, 1989).

On the heels of the Wingspread principles, Kendall and associates published the seminal three-volume set, *Combining Service and Learning*, in 1990, under the auspices of NSEE, in collaboration with ninety-one national and regional associations. It brought together a wide range of resources on service-learning in K–12 settings, as well as higher education, including many previously published and new historical, theoretical, policy-related, practical, and programmatic pieces, plus an annotated bibliography of the service-learning literature. In the same year, Jossey-Bass became the first mainstream educational publisher to produce a volume on service-learning, *Community Service as Values Education*, edited by Cecilia I. Delve, Suzanné D. Mintz, and Greig M. Stewart.

The 1990s have seen a veritable explosion of literature and conferences on service-learning. In 1991 NSEE sponsored another Wingspread conference, which spawned the *Research Agenda for Combining Service and Learning in the 1990s* (Giles, Porter Honnet, and Migliore, 1991). With the support of the Kellogg Foundation, the Office of Community Service Learning at the University of Michigan brought out *Praxis I: A Faculty Casebook on Community Service* (Howard, 1993); *Praxis II: Service Learning Resources for University Students, Staff, and Faculty* (Galura and others, 1994); and *Praxis III: Voices in Dialogue* (Galura and others, 1995). These volumes focus on curricular service-learning and are valuable for faculty in designing service-learning courses. In response to the call for published research on the effects of service-learning, the *Michigan Journal of Community Service Learning* was launched in fall 1994. In the same year, NSEE published the *Service-Learning Reader: Reflections and Perspectives on Service* (Albert, 1994), a textbook designed to facilitate students' thoughtful reflection on their service experiences. Campus Compact continues to produce important resources, such as *Rethinking Tradition: Integrating Service with Academic Study* (Kupiec, 1993), *Redesigning Curricula: Models of Service Learning Syllabi* (Jackson, 1994), *Service Matters: A Sourcebook for Community Service in Higher Education* (Cha and Rothman, 1994), and *Service Counts: Lessons from the Field of Service and Higher Education* (Smith, 1995).

The national conferences and regular publications of many higher education associations whose primary focus is not service-learning or experiential education have featured large numbers of speakers and articles on service-learning. Among these organizations are the American Association of Higher Education, the Council of Independent Colleges, the United Negro College Fund, the American Association of Community Colleges, the National Association of Student Personnel Administrators, the American College Personnel Association, the National Association of Student Employment Administrators, the National Association of Campus Activities, and the Association of College Unions–International.

The federal government's interest in and support of service-learning increased substantially in the 1990s with the passage of the National and Community Service Trust Act of 1990. This act represented the culmination of George Bush's 1988 presidential campaign recognition of "a thousand points of light," which inspired the creation of the first White House Office of National Service and the Points of Light Foundation. After the excitement created by Bill Clinton's presidential campaign for a large-scale national service program, a long and heated congressional debate finally culminated in the passage of the National and Community Service Trust Act of 1993. As a result, the Commission on National and Community Service, ACTION, and the newly established National Civilian Community Corps merged to form the Corporation for National and Community Service, generally referred to as the Corporation for National Service.

In its first year, the corporation funded the creation of twenty thousand positions in the AmeriCorps national service program, as well as service-learning programs in both K–12 and higher education settings through Learn and Serve America. The corporation's programs have given tremendous impetus to service-learning in colleges and universities. Many institutions of higher education have entered into partnerships with community agencies and schools to engage college students in addressing a wide range of needs. AmeriCorps participants receive living subsidies plus a substantial postservice educational stipend to be used to pay off acquired educational debts or to finance future education and training. In addition, the Higher Education Amendments of 1992 regarding student financial aid stipulated that beginning in July 1994, 5 percent of the federal work-study program funds allocated to each institution must be used to compensate students engaged in community service.

On September 8, 1994, President Clinton wrote a letter to all college and university presidents—the first time any president has ever done so for any reason—asking for their help in "inspiring an ethic of service across our nation." In response to the president's call to service, the American Association of Higher Education and Campus Compact convened the Colloquium on National and Community Service in January 1995. The colloquium has already spawned many additional meetings, workshops, and materials that deal with service-learning in higher education.

Institutional Traditions, Approaches, and Models

Different types of institutions have distinctly different missions, traditions, and approaches regarding service and service-learning. Some embrace service-learning as a philosophy and have developed programs that encompass the critical elements of reflection and reciprocity. Others support student involvement in community service to varying extents and may or may not include the fundamental concepts of service-learning.

At church-related colleges and universities like Notre Dame, Azusa Pacific, Messiah College, and Loyola College in Maryland, service-learning is firmly grounded in the institution's spiritual mission and in the quest for social justice. Other institutions, such as Rutgers, Baylor, and Providence College, have chosen to found their programs primarily on the relationship of service to citizenship, civic responsibility, and participatory democracy. At both private institutions like Stanford, Brown, and Bentley and public ones like Portland State, University of Washington, and Brevard Community College, a center for service-learning links service to academic study. The University of Richmond uses the connection of service and leadership as the basis of its program. The University of Minnesota, the University of Pennsylvania, Miami-Dade Community College, and Gettysburg College, as well as many historically black institutions (Clark Atlanta University, Chicago State University, and Southern University and A&M College), ground their service-learning programs in community partnerships and public problem solving. Some institutions whose service-learning programs are based on community collaboration are members of consortiums with other colleges and universities, including the

Shriver Center Consortium in Baltimore, the Urban Community Service Program in California, and the Regional Action Team in Colorado.

More and more institutions, among them Franklin and Marshall, Portland State, Alverno College, Waynesburg College, and Chandler-Gilbert Community College, have integrated service-learning into the core undergraduate curriculum. Many others envision service-learning as a way to achieve greater depth in a particular field of knowledge. Programs based in student affairs generally emphasize psychosocial, moral, leadership, and citizenship development, together with honing practical skills and deepening students' appreciation of individual differences and commonalities.

Service-learning programs exist at a wide range of levels of institutional commitment. At institutions where service-learning is central, it is a prominent and highlighted aspect of the mission; institutional funding is secure; policies explicitly support service; student, faculty, and staff involvement in service-learning is recognized and rewarded; and a strong commitment to service-learning is shared among all constituents. At the other end of the continuum are many colleges and universities where those who promote and attempt to coordinate service-learning remain on the periphery of their institutions' policies and practices, where funding is scarce and constantly in question, and where those who engage in service-learning feel isolated from the institutional mainstream.

Community service and service-learning programs are housed in various locations on campus. Student organizations were among the first coordinators of service programs, and many continue to be the institution's focal point for service. According to Campus Compact's 1994 survey of its members, offices such as student affairs and student activities are the most common home (45 percent) for service programs (Cha and Rothman, 1994). Religious institutions often house their service programs within the campus ministry, and many programs originated with campus ministers in public institutions as well. While some programs are based in career centers and internship offices, an increasing number each year are under the purview of an academic department or dean. And at some colleges and universities, service-learning reports jointly to academic and student affairs, while at others, it reports directly to the president's office (Cha and Rothman, 1994).

Programs primarily associated with academic affairs tend to reflect a high institutional commitment; result in a more centralized, coordinated program; and risk overemphasizing learning and underemphasizing service. Programs housed in student affairs tend to be more flexible in responding to student needs and more open to student initiatives; respond more effectively to community needs; risk overemphasizing service and underemphasizing learning; are often of a lower priority to the institution and less stable financially; and are linked with only one academic department, if any (National Center for Service-Learning, 1980). Regardless of where service-learning is administratively located, it is the premise of this book that if service-learning is to be central rather than marginal, it must be integrated into both academic and cocurricular practice.

Moving from Community Service to Service-Learning

Observers of higher education and contemporary society strongly believe that higher education has a rich array of resources and tremendous potential to make a significant positive difference in meeting growing human needs and in addressing increasingly complex social and economic problems. However, although the public, together with many federal and state officials, may believe that colleges and universities are blessed with underworked faculty, fat operating budgets, and abundant staff, the reality is to the contrary. In what is actually a time of reduced public support, soaring costs, decaying infrastructures, and ever-diversifying student bodies with greater needs for services, institutions of higher education are thinking strategically about what they can and cannot do. More and more are harkening back to their fundamental missions and focusing more sharply on their primary purposes.

This is why this book is about service-learning rather than student volunteer or community service. If higher education is to sustain its historical commitment to service in this time of great societal needs and increased competition among its own priorities, it is essential that developing opportunities for students to engage in service-learning must also enable colleges and universities to meet their own educational goals for students. Although community service has generally been perceived as a good thing, all good things cannot be the province of higher education. Service-learning, with its intentional goals for student learning and development, fits far more clearly into higher education's mission and priorities than volunteer or community service programs, which lack its reflection component and intentional learning goals.

The higher education community has turned much attention to the need to strengthen the quality of undergraduate education (Association of American Colleges, 1988; Boyer, 1988; Chickering and Gamson, 1987; Study Group on the Conditions of Excellence in American Higher Education, 1984; Wingspread Group on Higher Education, 1993). There are concerns about fragmented and incoherent curricula, lack of clarity about purposes and goals, absence of values, the need to integrate out-of-class experiences with education, and the need to prepare students better for the world of work. The Wingspread Group on Higher Education (1993) identifies at least three fundamental issues common to all U.S. colleges and universities: "taking values seriously; putting student learning first; and creating a nation of learners" (p. 7). As a means of addressing these issues, the group recommends that colleges and universities organize and sustain community service programs for large numbers of students and "wholeheartedly commit themselves to providing students with opportunities to experience and reflect on the world beyond the campus" (p. 10). Boyer proposes judging the quality of a college education by asking if "students see the connection between what they learn and how they live, looking for the deeper significance, for the moral dilemmas and the ethical responses" (1988, p. 296). He goes on to say that "the college succeeds as its graduates are inspired by a larger vision, using the knowledge they have acquired to form values and advance the common good" (p. 296). Chickering and Gamson (1987, p. 1) articulate seven principles for the improvement of undergraduate education, which point clearly toward service-learning:

Good practice in undergraduate education:

1. Encourages student-faculty contact.
2. Encourages cooperation among students.

3. Encourages active learning.
4. Gives prompt feedback.
5. Emphasizes time on task.
6. Communicates high expectations.
7. Respects diverse talents and ways of learning.

Another goal that service-learning effectively addresses is citizenship education and preparation for participation in a democracy. According to Frank Newman (1985), "If there is a crisis in education in the United States today, it is less that test scores have declined than it is that we have failed to provide the education for citizenship that is still the most significant responsibility of the nation's schools and colleges" (p. 31). It is virtually impossible to "teach" students what it means to be a citizen or to participate in democracy (Barber, 1993; Astin, 1994). "People cannot be told how to be responsible, knowledgeable, or caring citizens. They must be involved in the process" (Cirone, 1989, p. 5). Astin (1994) cites service-learning as the most effective means of accomplishing higher education's "stated mission: to produce educated citizens who understand and appreciate not only how democracy is supposed to work but also their own responsibility to become active and informed participants in it" (p. 24).

Besides preparing students for citizenship and democratic participation, higher education's goals include preparing them for the world of work (Boyer, 1988; Pew Higher Education Roundtable, 1994). Academic knowledge cannot be successfully applied without well-developed cognitive and social skills. In addition, students must acquire a set of transferable skills rather than prepare for a single lifelong career. Service-learning affords students opportunities to develop such skills as the ability to synthesize information, creative problem solving, constructive teamwork, effective communication, well-reasoned decision making, and negotiation and compromise. Other qualities that can be developed through service-learning include initiative, flexibility and adaptability, openness, and empathy. Service-learning in professional education leads to an increased sense of social responsibility on the part of physicians, lawyers, business leaders, government officials, and other key practitioners and decision makers.

Another shared goal among institutions of higher education is to develop students' appreciation of human differences and commonalities and to teach individuals to live peacefully and productively in communities that value persons of different races, genders, physical and mental abilities, religions, class backgrounds, and sexual orientations. Service-learning, which has as basic tenets reciprocity among those who are servers and those who are served and a reflective component with intentional learning goals, helps participants develop a deeper understanding of these issues, as well as how values and norms are socially constructed and the causes of social injustice.

It is unwise and inexpedient to propose a blueprint or model for institutional programs that involve college students in service to the local, national, and global communities. However, it is clearly in the best interest of students, communities, and institutions alike if higher education commits itself to service-learning rather than to community service and volunteer programs lacking service-learning's principles, which so clearly enable colleges and universities to meet their already established educational goals.

Conclusion

This chapter began by defining service-learning and clarifying its distinctions from volunteerism and community service. It has discussed higher education's tradition of service, the emergence of service-learning, and an overview of service-learning at today's colleges and universities. This introduction has also affirmed that service-learning is both curricular and cocurricular and can be designed to yield a wide range of outcomes for student learning and development, as well as for community enhancement. Service-learning is in fact a significant means through which higher education can achieve its overarching goals. Service-learning activities, be they course based or not, one-time or intensive, merit such designation if they include the basic elements of structured reflection and reciprocity. The remaining chapters of this book examine how educators can engage in the practice of service-learning to promote student learning, strengthen teaching and research, and bring human and other resources to bear on addressing society's problems and meeting its greatest needs.

References

Albert, G. (ed.). *Service-Learning Reader: Reflections and Perspectives on Service.* Raleigh, N.C.: National Society for Experiential Education, 1994.

Association of American Colleges. *A New Vitality in General Education.* Washington, D.C.: Association of American Colleges, 1988.

Astin, A. W. "Higher Education and the Future of Democracy." Inaugural lecture as Allan Murray Cartter chairholder, University of California, Los Angeles, Oct. 1994.

Astin, A. W., Korn, W. S., and Sax, L. J. *The American Freshman: National Norms for Fall 1994.* Los Angeles: Higher Education Research Institute, University of California, 1994.

Barber, B. R. "A Mandate for Liberty." In S. Sagawa and S. Halperin (eds.), *Visions of Service: The Future of the National and Community Service Act.* Washington, D.C.: National Women's Law Center and American Youth Policy Forum, 1993.

Berry, H. A. "Service-Learning in International/Intercultural Settings." *Experiential Education,* 1988, *13*(3), 3.

Berry, H. A. "Reexamining Service-Learning in an International Context." Paper presented at the International Experiential Learning Conference, Washington, D.C., Nov. 1994.

Bok, D. *Beyond the Ivory Tower: Social Responsibilities of the Modern University.* Cambridge, Mass.: Harvard University Press, 1982.

Bok, D. *Higher Learning.* Cambridge, Mass.: Harvard University Press, 1986.

Boyer, E. L. *College: The Undergraduate Experience in America.* New York: HarperCollins, 1988.

Boyer, E. L. *Scholarship Reconsidered: Priorities of the Professoriate.* Princeton, N.J.: Carnegie Foundation for the Advancement of Teaching, 1990.

Boyer, E. L. "Creating the New American College." *Chronicle of Higher Education,* Mar. 9, 1994, p. 48.

Campus Outreach Opportunity League. *Into the Streets: Organizing Manual, 1993–94 Edition.* St. Paul, Minn.: COOL Press, 1993.

Cha, S., and Rothman, M. *Service Matters: A Sourcebook for Community Service in Higher Education.* Providence, R.I.: Campus Compact, 1994.

Chickering, A. W., and Gamson, Z. F. *Seven Principles for Good Practice in Undergraduate Education.* Racine, Wisc.: Johnson Foundation, 1987.

Cirone, W. J. "Linkages Between Civic Literacy and the State History/Social Science Framework." Address to Constitutional Rights Foundation Area VI, Santa Barbara, Calif., May 1989.

Coles, R. *The Call of Service: A Witness to Idealism.* Boston: Houghton Mifflin, 1993.

Cruz, N. "Reexamining Service-Learning in an International Context."
    Paper presented at the International Experiential Learning Con-
    ference, Washington, D.C., Nov. 1994.
Delve, C. I., Mintz, S. D., and Stewart, G. M. (eds.). *Community Service as*
    Values Education. New Directions for Student Services, no. 50. San
    Francisco: Jossey-Bass, 1990.
Ehrlich, T. "Taking Service Seriously." *American Association of Higher Edu-*
    cation Bulletin, 1995, *47*(7), 8–10.
Galura, J., and others. *Praxis II: Service Learning Resources for University Stu-*
    dents, Staff, and Faculty. Ann Arbor: OCSL Press, 1994.
Galura, J., and others. *Praxis III: Voices in Dialogue.* Ann Arbor: OCSL Press,
    1995.
Giles, D. E., and Eyler, J. "The Theoretical Roots of Service-Learning in
    John Dewey: Toward a Theory of Service-Learning." *Michigan Jour-*
    nal of Community Service Learning, 1994, *1*(1), 77–85.
Giles, D., Porter Honnet, E., and Migliore, S. *Research Agenda for Combining*
    Service and Learning in the 1990s. Raleigh, N.C.: National Society for
    Experiential Education, 1991.
Hackney, S. "The Roles and Responsibilities of Urban Universities in
    Their Communities: Five University Presidents Call for Action."
    Universities and Community Schools, 1994, *1–2,* 9–11.
Harkavy, I. "Community Service and the Transformation of the American
    University." In S. Sagawa and S. Halperin (eds.), *Visions of Service:*
    The Future of the National and Community Service Act. Washington,
    D.C.: National Women's Law Center and American Youth Policy
    Forum, 1993.
Howard, J. (ed.). *Praxis I: A Faculty Casebook on Community Service Learning.*
    Ann Arbor: OCSL Press, 1993.
Jackson, K. (ed.). *Redesigning Curricula: Models of Service Learning Syllabi.*
    Providence, R. I.: Campus Compact, 1994.
Karasik, J. "Not Only Bowls of Delicious Soup: Youth Service Today." In
    S. Sagawa and S. Halperin (eds.), *Visions of Service: The Future of the*
    National and Community Service Act. Washington, D.C.: National
    Women's Law Center and American Youth Policy Forum, 1993.
Kendall, J. C. "From Youth Service to Service-Learning." In A. C. Lewis,
    Facts and Faith: A Status Report on Youth Service. Washington, D.C.:
    Youth and America's Future: William T. Grant Foundation Com-
    mission on Work, Family, and Citizenship, 1988.
Kendall, J. C. "Combining Service and Learning: An Introduction." In J.
    C. Kendall (ed.), *Combining Service and Learning: A Resource Book for*
    Community and Public Service, Vol. 1. Raleigh, N.C.: National Society
    for Experiential Education, 1990.

Kerr, C. *The Uses of the University.* Cambridge, Mass.: Harvard University Press, 1963.

Kolb, D. *Experiential Learning: Experience as the Source of Learning and Development.* Englewood Cliffs, N.J.: Prentice Hall, 1984.

Kupiec, T. Y. (ed.). *Rethinking Tradition: Integrating Service with Academic Study on College Campuses.* Providence, R.I.: Campus Compact, 1993.

Levine, A. "Service on Campus." *Change,* July/Aug. 1994, pp. 4–5.

National Center for Service-Learning. *The Service-Learning Educator: A Guide to Program Management.* No. J302–513. Washington, D.C.: U.S. Government Printing Office, 1980.

Newman, F. *Higher Education and the American Resurgence.* Princeton, N.J.: Carnegie Foundation for the Advancement of Teaching, 1985.

Pew Higher Education Roundtable. "To Dance with Change." *Policy Perspectives,* 1994, *5*(3), 1–12.

Porter Honnet, E., and Poulsen, S. J. *Principles of Good Practice for Combining Service and Learning.* Racine, Wisc.: Johnson Foundation, 1989.

Rudolph, F. *The American College and University: A History.* Athens: University of Georgia Press, 1962.

Seidel, R. "Reexamining Service-Learning in an International Context." Paper presented at the International Experiential Learning Conference, Washington, D.C., Nov. 1994.

Sigmon, R. *Linking Service with Learning.* Washington, D.C.: Council of Independent Colleges, 1994.

Smith, M. *Service Counts: Lessons from the Field of Service and Higher Education.* Providence, R.I.: Campus Compact, 1995.

Smith, M. W. "Issues in Integrating Service-Learning into the Higher Education Curriculum." In *Effective Learning, Effective Teaching, Effective Service.* Washington, D.C.: Youth Service America, 1994.

Smythe, O. "Practical Experience and the Liberal Arts: A Philosophical Perspective." In J. C. Kendall (ed.), *Combining Service and Learning: A Resource Book for Community and Public Service,* Vol. 1. Raleigh, N.C.: National Society for Experiential Education, 1990.

Stanton, T. "Service-Learning: Groping Toward a Definition." In J. C. Kendall (ed.), *Combining Service and Learning: A Resource Book for Community and Public Service,* Vol. 1. Raleigh, N.C.: National Society for Experiential Education, 1990.

Study Group on the Conditions of Excellence in American Higher Education. *Involvement in Learning.* Washington, D.C.: U.S. Department of Education, 1984.

Wingspread Group on Higher Education. *An American Imperative: Higher Expectations for Higher Education.* Racine, Wisc.: Johnson Foundation, 1993.

Chapter Two

Principles of Good Practice in Service-Learning

Suzanné D. Mintz, Garry W. Hesser

Did you ever gaze through a kaleidoscope, marveling at what you saw, then being amazed by the changing patterns that developed when you rotated the cylinder in either direction? Derived from the Greek words meaning "beauty," "form," and "to look at," the kaleidoscope becomes a dynamic metaphor for assessing principles of good practice in service-learning. Consider the multiple partners—students, community residents, faculty, student affairs professionals, government officials, and community-based agency staff—who engage with one another in the service-learning venture. Like the varying hues and facets of the pieces of glass in a kaleidoscopic configuration, these partners bring different assets, needs, perspectives, and values to the service-learning enterprise. Together they strive to achieve a balance within the working relationship, the kind of balance one might liken to the symmetry viewed through the kaleidoscope when, with each turn of the instrument, the pieces of glass fall together in a beautiful pattern.

The goal of this chapter is to create a dynamic framework that service-learning partners can use to create principles and practices that acknowledge the changing contexts and challenges faced at almost every turn in the journey of combining service and learning. The chapter focuses on five sets of principles that seem most relevant to good practice in service-learning and examines them using the metaphor of the kaleidoscope. Like any other social construction of knowledge and practice, each set of principles was developed in particular contexts and in response to challenges and opportunities that existed at the time of their development. Our thesis is that service-learning principles grow out of lessons learned through practice, and that these practice-driven principles, in turn, inform practice if they are viewed through the three meta-principles, or lenses, of the service-learning kaleidoscope: collaboration, reciprocity, and diversity. Thus, the kaleidoscope brings into focus both insights and ongoing dilemmas, highlighting the constantly changing, usually nonlinear patterns and paradoxes that come from the combination of service and learning.

Practice to Principle to Practice

Stephen Covey (1992) describes the value of principles:

> If our planning is centered on an overall purpose or vision and on a commitment to a set of principles, then the people who are closest to the action in the wilderness can use that compass and their own expertise and judgment to make decisions and take action. . . . Principles are not practices. Practices are specific activities or actions that work in one circumstance but not necessarily in another. . . . If you focus on principles, you empower everyone who understands those principles to act without constant monitoring, evaluating, correcting, or controlling. Principles have universal application. And when these are internalized into habits, they empower people to create a wide variety of practices to deal with different situations [p. 98].

Covey's thoughts on the uses of principles and the distinction between principles and practices are insightful, but they are also challenged in the context of service-learning. Covey seems to assume that practitioners can share a common understanding of the principles that underlie their practice and be in universal agreement on them. Yet, in service-learning there is much that remains contested.

We continue to grapple with and learn about service-learning's diverse and sometimes divergent aspects, and consensus is far from being reached. The debate about the definition of service-learning continues; some still question whether service-learning can be both cocurricular and curricular; classification of who and what compose "the community" is often diffuse and unclear; and the distinctions among internships, practicums, cooperative education, and service-learning remain blurred.

Moreover, Covey does not address the intersection between practice and principles and how each influences the other, particularly with regard to the influence of practice on principles. We assert, however, that both the principles and practices of service-learning are interdependent and must be continually reassessed. Principles provide essential benchmarks for developing practices; practice, in turn, serves to inform and refine principles.

In their Practice-to-Theory-to-Practice (PTP) model, Wells and Knefelkamp (1984) reinforce the notion that theory is developed out of hands-on experiences, and in the process of evaluation and assessment, practice-based theory is translated into better, more appropriate practice. Borrowing from the thesis of the PTP model, we propose a practice-to-principles-to-practice model for service-learning programs. We believe it affirms the significance of the field's work and ongoing efforts and encourages commitments to improve on current practice.

The Principles of Service-Learning

The 1960s witnessed the emergence of experiential learning programs that combined service and learning: state-government internship programs, rural and urban studies semester or summer programs, and the Urban Corps. Educators and community members affirmed the synergy that occurs when service informs learning and learning improves the quality of service.

Sigmon's Three Principles

In 1979, Robert Sigmon, one of the early leaders in these endeavors, drafted three principles that underlie most subsequent sets of service-learning principles:

1. Those being served control the service(s) provided;
2. Those being served become better able to serve and be served by their own actions; and

3. Those who serve also are learners and have significant control over what is expected to be learned [p. 10].

These principles grew out of the early service-learning efforts, which were more often grounded in the community than in colleges and universities. For example, the Southern Regional Education Board, using federal dollars, created a service-learning internship model. Similarly the Urban Corps programs drew on federal work-study funds to place students in the community, with agencies and governmental units taking the lead to identify positions and opportunities. This integration of "public task with conscious educational growth" (Sigmon, 1979, p. 9) was closely connected to the issues of community and student empowerment. Thus, these early principles grew out of and influenced the issues and practices of the 1960s and 1970s.

Wingspread Principles of Good Practice for Combining Service and Learning

The subsequent decade was marked by a revitalized interest in experiential education. As a result of this growing interest in active modes of learning, and in service-learning in particular, the National Society for Experiential Education (NSEE), initiated and coordinated a process of consulting with more than seventy organizations, creating nine drafts, and assisting the Johnson Foundation in convening a working group at Wingspread in Racine, Wisconsin, in 1989. This effort culminated in the publication of the *Principles of Good Practice for Combining Service and Learning* (Porter Honnet and Poulsen, 1989). The Wingspread principles, as they are generally known, built on earlier efforts and addressed the issue of service-learning's marginal status within educational institutions. They emphasize program development and sustainability, partly in response to the tenuous status of earlier service-learning initiatives, such as the University Year for ACTION and the National Center for Service-Learning, which were marginalized or phased out when their funding ended. Hence, the Wingspread principles reflect a major concern for creating sound educational programs that could succeed in being institutionalized within the academy.

An effective and sustained program that combines service and learning:

1. Engages people in responsible and challenging actions for the common good.
2. Provides structured opportunities for people to reflect critically on their service experience.
3. Articulates clear service and learning goals for everyone involved.
4. Allows for those with needs to define those needs.
5. Clarifies the responsibilities of each person and organization involved.
6. Matches service providers and service needs through a process that recognizes changing circumstances.
7. Expects genuine, active, and sustained organizational commitment.
8. Includes training, supervision, monitoring, support, recognition, and evaluation to meet service and learning goals.
9. Insures that the time commitment for service and learning is flexible, appropriate, and in the best interests of all involved.
10. Is committed to program participation by and with diverse populations [Porter Honnet and Poulsen, 1989].

Critical Elements of Thoughtful Community Service

Representing students engaged in community service and based on lessons its organizers learned from several years in the field, the Campus Outreach Opportunity League (COOL) developed the Critical Elements of Thoughtful Community Service:

Community Voice

Community voice is essential if we are to build bridges, make change, and solve problems. Any community service organization should make sure that the voice and needs of the community are included in the development of the community service program.

Orientation and Training

Orientation and training are important first steps for any community service experience. Information should be provided for student volunteers about the community, the issue, and the agency or community group.

Meaningful Action

Meaningful action means that the service being done is necessary and valuable to the community itself. Meaningful action makes people feel like what they did made a difference in a measurable way and that their time was utilized well. Without this, people will not want to continue their service no matter how well we do with the other four elements.

Reflection

Reflection is a crucial component of the community service learning experience. Reflection should happen immediately after the experience to discuss it—reactions, stories, feelings, and facts about the issues which may dispel any stereotypes or an individual's alienation from service—and reflection should place the experience into a broader context.

Evaluation

Evaluation measures the impact of the student's learning experience and the effectiveness of the service in the community. Students should evaluate their learning experience and agencies should evaluate the effectiveness of the student's service. Evaluation gives direction for improvement, growth and change [Campus Outreach Opportunity League, 1993].

These five elements have guided hundreds of institutions across the country in developing community service programs. And yet, a chasm exists between the development of principles and the success achieved in their application through practice. COOL estimates that 60 percent of its members can recite the critical elements, 40 percent are trying to implement them, and 20 percent are implementing them well (J. Bastress, personal communication, 1995).

Principles of Good Practice in Community Service-Learning Pedagogy

Just as each of the preceding sets of principles grew out of a historical context and focused on the then-current challenges and opportunities in service-learning practice, so did these principles, proposed by Jeffrey Howard in *Praxis I* (1993). The subtitle of the book, *A Faculty Casebook on Community Service Learning,* reveals the major thrusts of the early 1990s—increasing faculty involvement in course-embedded service-learning, concern for academic integrity, and emphasis on the assessment of learning outcomes:

1. Academic credit is for learning, not for service.
2. Do not compromise academic rigor.
3. Set learning goals for students.
4. Establish criteria for the selection of community service placements.
5. Provide educationally-sound mechanisms to harvest the community learning.
6. Provide supports for students to learn how to harvest the community learning.
7. Minimize the distinction between the student's community learning role and the classroom learning role.
8. Re-think the faculty instructional role.
9. Be prepared for uncertainty and variation in student learning outcomes.
10. Maximize the community responsibility orientation of the course [Howard, 1993, pp. 5–9].

Principles of Continuous Improvement

The resurgent participation of the federal government in the service-learning arena through the Corporation for National Service has resulted in a set of principles designed to guide the development of a wide range of national service programs, with specific attention to programs addressing education, human needs, the environment, and public safety. Acknowledging the evolving nature of program development and the dynamic character of collaborations, the corporation's *Handbook for Continuous Improvement* (1995) provides eight principles for improving organizations and programs engaged in national service:

1. Our "customers" are the reason we exist. We must stay attuned to their needs and strive always to exceed their expectations.
2. Volunteers, participants and staff are customers too. They must be motivated, trained and satisfied if they are to serve our customers well.

3. It is not enough to talk about customer satisfaction. We must set measurable goals, communicate them throughout our organization, regularly and systematically gauge our progress against these goals, and take action to continuously improve our performance.

4. Anytime we learn we are falling short, we have an opportunity to improve. Anytime we learn we are meeting or exceeding standards, we have an opportunity to set higher standards.

5. Continuous improvement is the responsibility of everyone in our organization. It starts with a willingness to learn from people within and outside our organization.

6. Effective communication within our organization is essential to continuous improvement. To help improve the organization, staff must understand what customers value and how well customers think the program is doing.

7. Constructive criticism is a positive step toward a solution, not a negative spotlight on a mistake. We learn from our failures as well as from our successes.

8. Creating energized, empowered teams is the best catalyst for improving an organization. Motivated teams can produce extraordinary results—results that exceed those achieved by individuals or less cohesive groups [Office of Evaluation, Corporation for National Service, 1995, p. I].

These principles cover a broad range of public and community service, and they are relevant to service-learning in higher education as well. They arise out of a renewed commitment to program accountability and to assessment of the impacts of service efforts on the community. Many national service programs, those housed in institutions of higher education and in community-based organizations, incorporate service-learning. These principles are currently undergoing the challenge of being translated into practice.

Each of the five sets of principles that has been highlighted is indeed a social construction of practice and knowledge, created in a specific context to respond to challenges and opportunities that prevailed at the time. Similarly, the three meta-principles we have identified—collaboration, reciprocity, and diversity—have emerged from our participation in service-learning and our learning from the practice-to-principles-to-practice dialogue of the past three decades. We propose them as lenses of the service-learning kaleidoscope through which to assess the ongoing interactions of principles and practice.

The Kaleidoscope

Service-learning involves working in a creative tension marked by collaboration, reciprocity, and diversity. This tension is generated within the context of the interrelationships among three domains or partners in service-learning: the academy (college and university faculty, staff, senior officials, and boards of control), the students (part-time and full-time, graduate and undergraduate, residential and commuter), and the community (community members, community leaders, nonprofit and community-based organizations, and government and public agencies). Each of these domains comes to the service-learning partnership with particular experiences, expectations, and attitudes. How each views the principles laid out and the practices implemented is shaped largely by its perception of the genuineness of the collaboration, the degree of reciprocity in the relationship, and the extent to which its inherent differences are acknowledged and incorporated in the process.

The kaleidoscope's lenses of collaboration, reciprocity, and diversity enhance the possibility of viewing both service-learning principles and practices from the perspectives of all of the partners. Turning the kaleidoscope permits the examination of the principles and practices from multiple vantage points. The relationship among the lenses shifts with every turn of the instrument. It is incumbent on the viewers (academy, students, community) to capture the intersection of the three lenses so that the most comprehensive assessment of the principles is attained. Whenever one examines the existing principles through the lenses of collaboration, reciprocity, and diversity, it is always in the context of the everchanging and unique relationships among the three partners, which gives the entire enterprise its life and energy.

Collaboration

Chrislip and Larson (1994) define collaboration as "a mutually beneficial relationship between two or more parties who work toward a common goal by sharing responsibility, authority, and accountability for achieving results. . . . The purpose of collaboration is to create a shared vision and joint strategies to address concerns that go beyond the purview of any particular party" (p. 5). They view collaborative leadership as the key to how citizens and civic leaders can make a difference. In service-learning, the parties Chrislip and Larson refer to are the academy, students, and the community. Each party comes to the table with its own set of interests, concerns, and expectations, and each must be heard, acknowledged, and addressed. Even more important, each partner brings to the enterprise certain skills, knowledge, and assets. Balancing interests, concerns, and expectations with skills, knowledge, and assets to achieve mutually beneficial outcomes demands that levels of control be distributed equally to ensure that power is not abused and that there is a common belief that the whole is greater than the sum of its parts.

As we stress in the discussion of the third lens of diversity, collaboration involves reacculturation or renegotiating memberships in groups or cultures we already belong to and becoming members of other groups or cultures as well. It involves modifying or renegotiating our participation in the language, values, knowledge, and mores of the communities we come from, as well as becoming fluent in those same elements of the partners and communities with whom we collaborate. Reacculturation is one of the hardest tasks we ever undertake. It is complex and in most cases forever incomplete (Bruffee, 1995, p. 14).

Looking at service-learning through the lens of collaboration requires that the stakeholders engage in the challenging and time-consuming strategies of regularly exchanging information, altering activities, sharing resources, and enhancing each other's capacities (Himmelman, 1994). Genuine collaboration challenges the partners to develop a trusting environment, secure a common goal or purpose, and share responsibility and authority (Gabelnick, 1993). As difficult and demanding as it is, collaboration is a necessary part of service-learning, laying the groundwork for trust and community building that is inclusive and reciprocal.

Reciprocity

If there is a fundamental or comprehensive concept that has driven efforts to achieve high quality in the combining of service and learning, it is reciprocity. Reciprocity suggests that every individual, organization, and entity involved in service-learning functions as both a teacher and a learner. Participants are perceived as colleagues, not as servers and clients. At the center of virtually every set of core principles (Sigmon, 1979; Porter Honnet and Poulsen, 1989; Howard, 1993) is a call for a reciprocity among those engaged in service-learning such that all participants are learning from and serving each other. Practice has shown us over and over again that, for example, the tutored child or the homeless adult serves college students by allowing them to come into their lives and their communities, providing them with a larger view of the world as articulated through their own voices and insights.

When service-learning emphasizes student learning and the academy's agenda without stressing reciprocal learning and service, there is a real risk of exploiting or coercing both the community and the student. Service-learning invites, even requires, the partners to reassess the realities of power and control over the learning and service goals. A tension will always exist between the impact on the student and the impact on the community. The degree to which we enter the service-learning endeavor committed to reciprocal relationships will determine whether we move the academy away from seeing the community as a learning laboratory and toward viewing it as a partner in an effort to increase each other's capacities and power.

These criteria and the concept of community that they represent can be employed to hold us accountable to reciprocity, with those serving and those being served indistinguishable in principle, if not in practice. Reciprocity suggests that as students learn from faculty, the community, and one another, faculty should also learn from the students, the community, and one another, and so on. This expansion of the community of learners and servers substantially enriches the outcomes.

Reciprocity is clearly illustrated in the examples of the early rural and urban semester programs that used community members and activists as teachers and facilitators in courses. Today Augsburg College and Georgetown University engage students in side-by-side learning with maximum-security prisoners through courses taught in prisons. At Providence College, all of the gateway courses to the major and minor in public service include community members as coteachers in the classroom. Among many outcomes cited in the Providence program, the community partners have been more fully engaged in the students' learning processes, thus increasing their commitment to service-learning and revitalizing their own thinking about issues raised by the students; the students have benefited from the community voice in the classroom, thus fostering a community consciousness not normally found on college campuses. And Providence faculty coteaching the courses are challenged not to consider the classroom their private domain, an outcome that has fostered an appreciation of the power of service-learning on both the students and the community (R. Battistoni, personal communication, October 1995).

Diversity

Ronald Takaki (1995) identifies two primary reasons for the imperative and the value of viewing higher education through the lens of diversity—arguments for weaving multiculturalism into the curriculum that apply equally well to its infusion into service-learning:

- Multiculturalism allows us to gain a more accurate and inclusive understanding of who we are as U.S. Americans and of U.S. American history.

- There is a need to connect intellectual reason with moral reason and multiculturalism aims to make that connection [p. 13].

While racial, ethnic, and gender differences are often the focus of diversity initiatives, service-learning involves other differences as well: socioeconomic status, ages, geographic affinities, sexual orientations, and physical and mental abilities. Such a broad range of perspectives, multiple contexts, and life situations affords all the partners in service-learning the opportunity to grow as caring, thoughtful citizens of a very diverse world. As such, the diversity lens provides a way of viewing culture so that all forms of human difference are appropriately highlighted.

Service-learning is a venue for gaining a more comprehensive understanding of human diversity and challenges us to connect the critical thinking goals of the academy with our personal value systems. When service-learning is viewed through the lens of diversity, opportunities (in addition to those that emerge when service-learning is viewed through the lenses of collaboration and reciprocity) to discover the gifts and capacities of all of the partners are increased. Diversity is an asset that brings to the process varied resources, talents, knowledge, and skills. Yet, an appreciation for and an understanding of diversity does not necessarily happen by chance. Working within a diverse context requires deliberate attention to cultural differences and commonalities, as well as to the links among power, privilege, prejudice, and oppression. Programmatic design that engages all partners in ongoing discussions and in agreement that issues related to diversity will be continually raised and addressed is essential.

Maurianne Adams's (1992) principles for creating a multicultural classroom apply well to service-learning: "In recognizing (1) cultural differences, not deficits, among students, (2) we must create learning environments for all, not some, students, (3) based on multicultural, not ethnocentric, principles of teaching and learning that are inclusive rather than exclusive, responsible and flexible rather than fixed or predetermined, and derived from (4) cross-cultural or multicultural models of cultural reciprocity and interaction that ultimately benefit all students" (p. 14). Janelle Waldock's (1995) research, conducted in collaboration with Minnesota Campus Compact, supports speculation that service-learning educators need to place diverse students side by side in their service-learning experiences to foster cross-cultural understanding. Waldock encourages written institutional policies or goals that bring together teams of diverse students to serve and learn together. For such experiences to be successful, preparation and reflection must integrate multicultural perspectives.

Takaki (1995) and Bruffee (1995) remind us that an emphasis on diversity and reacculturation is critical to educated citizenship. The prejudices and misunderstandings that are deeply rooted in our society make the task both essential and difficult. Our approach to service-learning should ensure that human differences are viewed in their context, not in isolation or by the standards of one's own perspective, background, and experiences. When this happens, potentially divisive differences can become the source for affirming our own capacities and those of others.

When we strive for collaboration, reciprocity, and an affirmation of diversity, we come closer to what Kretzmann and McKnight (1993) suggest should be the goal of building communities. They urge us to stop seeing communities (and one another) primarily in terms of deficiencies and needs. They depict the proverbial glass as half full rather than half empty and issue a clarion call for community building that stresses the capacities and assets of all the partners in the service-learning enterprise. Further, the ability of each partner to view the process from his or her own vantage point as well as that of each of the other's increases the likelihood of high-quality service-learning programs. The synergy that develops through the shifts in levels of collaboration, reciprocity, and diversity in service-learning creates a tension that can be positive and growth producing. And when these lenses of the kaleidoscope frame and focus our practice-to-principles-to-practice approach, they facilitate the catalytic synergy that serves to develop both stronger service-learning principles and practices.

Using the Kaleidoscope to Examine Service-Learning Principles

The sets of service-learning principles that provide the foundation for the development of service-learning programs were themselves derived from practical experience. As the practice of service-learning continues to evolve, so must practice continue to translate into principles.

The kaleidoscope with its lenses of collaboration, reciprocity, and diversity enables the service-learning partners—the academy, students, and the community—to assess the principles through the three different lenses: collaboration, which engages the partners to work together by sharing authority and resources to enhance each other's capacities to reach goals; reciprocity, which underscores that the partners are both teachers and learners, servers and those served; and diversity, which means that all three partners see differences as assets and that they employ those assets in service-learning endeavors.

Although considering service-learning principles through only one of the lenses is incomplete and insufficient, the service-learning kaleidoscope makes it possible and desirable to focus on a principle or set of principles using one lens at a time. Of course, the viewer must always remember that each lens is but one of three and that the combination of the lenses is never constant. Each time a viewer looks through the kaleidoscope, the lenses of collaboration, reciprocity, and diversity come together to form a new pattern, and the pattern is influenced by the direction or backdrop (principles) toward which the kaleidoscope is pointed.

Because of the nature of its lenses, the kaleidoscope enables, even forces, viewers to look at the principles from their partners' perspectives. It is important that viewers come to the service-learning enterprise with their own perspectives yet with the capacity and willingness to take their partners' perspectives into account, to see things their way. Using the kaleidoscope constantly reminds all partners that the relationships among academy, students, and community are shifting, unpredictable, and delicate, requiring regular and ongoing communication. Further, the kaleidoscope underscores the fact that, in service-learning, the whole is indeed greater than the sum of the parts.

Looking through each of the lenses from the perspective of each partner provides structure for asking critical questions about a set of principles. One of these questions concerns partners who appear less central in the context of the principles. For example, Sigmon's three principles of service-learning focus primarily on the community and students; the academy is less central. Although it is important to ask critical questions from all of the partners' perspectives, the kaleidoscope might first be used to examine Sigmon's principles from the perspective of the academy.

Viewing Sigmon's principles from the academy's perspective and through the collaboration lens raises a number of questions: What should be the faculty member's role in service-learning? How are institutional controls such as grading and academic credit best exercised? What needs to happen if most of the power and resources seem to reside in the academy? Continuing on with the reciprocity lens from the academy's perspective, examination of Sigmon's principles leads to more questions: What can the academy learn from students and from the community? How can students and the community serve the academy? Similar use of the lens of diversity brings to the fore such questions as: How can the culture of the academy be an asset to the community? How can the diverse assets of the community and the academy complement one another in service-learning? How can limited and short-term exposure to diversity avoid the tendency to confirm stereotypes?

In addition to reviewing sets of principles in their entirety through the three lenses, a principle-by-principle approach is appropriate. Like the process used to view principles in their entirety, we may also ask critical questions principle by principle. We use the Wingspread principles to illustrate this process. Keeping in mind that the Wingspread principles focus on the academy and the institutionalization of service-learning programs suggests that questions be asked from the perspectives of the community and the student, as well as of the academy. As an example, we offer an abbreviated step-by-step assessment, viewing principles 1, 2, and 3 through the collaboration lens; principles 4, 5, 6, and 7 through the reciprocity lens; and principles 8, 9, and 10 through the diversity lens. The questions that follow are intended as an example for beginning one's own engagement in the practice-to-principles-to-practice dialogue.

Through the collaboration lens:

1. An effective program engages people in responsible and challenging actions for the common good.

   Sample questions: Are students and community members involved in defining the common good? Does the definition of the common good include empowerment of individuals and communities and the sharing of power and resources? Do the actions taken enhance the capacities of students and communities to be active agents in shaping their own futures? How do we avoid doing harm to one another?

2. An effective program provides structured opportunities for people to reflect critically on their service experience.

   Sample questions: Are faculty and community members as well as students involved in critical reflection? Does reflection address the unequal distribution of power and resources among the partners, as well as the root causes of this inequality? Are there opportunities for shared reflection among the partners?

3. An effective program articulates clear service and learning goals for everyone involved.
   Sample questions: Are students and community members, along with service-learning educators, equal partners in setting the goals? Do the learning and service goals encourage the enhancement of the capacities of all involved? Do the goals include providing community access to the resources of the college or university?

Through the reciprocity lens:

4. An effective program allows for those with needs to define those needs.
   Sample questions: Do all partners—the academy, students, and the community—have the opportunity to define their needs? How can the process of defining needs become a learning opportunity for all involved? How does attention to reciprocity shift the focus from needs and deficiencies to needs and capacities?

5. An effective program clarifies the responsibilities of each person and organization involved.
   Sample questions: Do the assigned responsibilities draw from and enhance the strengths and capacities of each partner? How do we ensure that the community's responsibilities involve engagement in the students' learning and development? What structures have been established for the initial and ongoing clarification of both learning and service goals for all partners?

6. An effective program matches service providers and service needs through a process that recognizes changing circumstances.
   Sample questions: What can the tracking of changing circumstances teach all partners about the large societal issues that affect the need for service? How can the academy, students, and the community work together continually to assess service needs and how well they are being met? How do we build in a system of checks and balances in which everyone has the right to say no and yes to changes in original plans?

7. An effective program expects genuine, active, and sustained organizational commitment.
   Sample questions: Are the partners effectively using all the means at their disposal to ensure the sustainability of the partnership? Are the partners giving each other access to appropriate resources that augment their capacities to learn and serve one another well into the future? Where should the locus of sustenance reside, both within the three partners' domains and across domains? How does the outcome result in long-term, sustained community building?

Through the diversity lens:

8. An effective program includes training, supervision, monitoring, support, recognition, and evaluation to meet service and learning goals.
   Sample questions: Are training, supervision, monitoring, support, recognition, and evaluation designed to accommodate diverse backgrounds, orientations, and styles? Are these differences considered assets rather than problems?

9. An effective program ensures that the time commitment for service and learning is flexible, appropriate, and in the best interests of all involved.
   Sample questions: Does the program encourage participation of individuals with a variety of schedules? Do program organizers view participants' varied schedules as an asset and not a liability? Does the program address the differences between the academic calendar and the community's calendar?

10. An effective program is committed to program participation by and with diverse populations.
    Sample questions: Does program diversity extend to persons of various ages, socioeconomic levels, sexual orientation, and physical and mental abilities, as well as race and gender? How effectively does the program employ the assets of its diverse participants to meet its service and learning goals? Is participants' involvement in various components of the program limited by which domain they represent or by the viewpoints they express? In what ways does the program

actively promote and ensure participation by and with diverse populations in all three domains?

The method we have demonstrated—asking critical questions of each principle through the lenses of collaboration, reciprocity, and diversity—enables the service-learning partners to modify existing principles or formulate new ones to fit the context of their joint endeavors. Nadinne Cruz (1995) took this approach a step further, reassessing the Wingspread principles from the perspective of diversity and then formulating a set of alternative or corollary principles:

A program committed to diversity . . .

1. Engages people to notice, reflect on, and participate in dialogues about differences in defining, interpreting and expressing concepts of "responsibility," "action," and "common good."
2. Encourages a variety of ways to "do" and express "reflection," including nondirective discussion, story-telling, varieties of artistic expression in various media . . . in addition to analytic modes more commonly regarded as "legitimate" especially in the academy.
3. Respects and acknowledges different cultural practices that shape how people define "goals," develop them, and feel a comfort level with precise definitions or lack thereof. In addition, a program committed to diversity provides time and structure for participants to experience together a process of struggling across differences in coming to consensus and/or principled disagreement in defining what is to be accomplished and what is to be learned.
4. Recognizes that some people may not view themselves primarily in terms of "need," and that the concept of "need" may be contested by those who view themselves as having borne the costs of historical legacies of colonialism, slavery, patriarchy, and other forms of subjugation or oppression.
5. Honors varying organizational cultures, some of which may define responsibilities more formally and explicitly according to a more rational-legal model, while others may be organized in more fluid, informal ways.
6. Respects the different cultural approaches that inform different participants about who is to be "matched," by whom, with whom, and how.

7. Respects varying ways by which "commitment" is culturally defined and expressed, and accounts for the possibility that failure to honor commitments may unequally and negatively affect different people involved in the program.
8. Respects culturally different ways by which training, supervision, monitoring, support, recognition, and evaluation are defined and expressed.
9. Makes possible the effective participation of low-income working people, single parents, and others who experience constraints defined by different economic and cultural realities.
10. Commits the necessary resources to encourage expression of voices of diverse participants who hold to competing interpretations of the "Principles of Good Practice in Service-Learning" and to competing assumptions that underlie them.

The service-learning kaleidoscope and Cruz's approaches are examples of ways to examine principles of good practice critically. We invite our readers to join us in using this kaleidoscope, with its meta-principles or lenses of collaboration, reciprocity, and diversity, in the ongoing process of assessing and improving the principles upon which we base service-learning.

Using the Kaleidoscope to Assess the Practice of Service-Learning

Wells and Knefelkamp (1984) remind us that the ability to translate a set of principles into practice serves to improve our service-learning efforts. Across the country, colleges and universities are employing service-learning principles in ways that have ensured program success and growth. The following three examples of service-learning practice exemplify the challenge and value of shaping our work in terms of collaboration, reciprocity, and diversity.

Minnesota Campus-Community Collaboration

Minnesota Campus Compact, involving forty-five college and university presidents, the Minnesota state legislature and the governor, in concert with the Corporation for National Service, has obtained funding to support the development of campus-community collaborations that address significant long-term community problems and contribute to students' academic and civic development.

Campus-community collaborations developed as a result of this program will be used as models for other institutions and communities throughout the nation.

Funding is being allocated directly to local campus-community projects, with additional statewide funding to provide training, coordination, technical assistance, evaluation, and dissemination. The entire process is particularly illustrative of the collaboration meta-principle. Significant grants will go to campus-community collaborations that include institutions representing diversity in size, institution type, and geographic location, and to collaborations that demonstrate the development of long-term commitment to a specific local community program that the community has played the central role in defining. Both higher education institutions and community-based organizations in Minnesota are eligible to receive funding, although "in the spirit of true collaboration, applicants are encouraged to consider sharing both responsibilities and resources in order to ensure that project outcomes are achieved" (Minnesota Campus Compact, 1995, p. 2).

Successful collaborations must demonstrate exceptional institutional commitment through involvement of top-level officials in program planning and through a strong commitment of resources before, during, and beyond the grant period. The collaborations must incorporate both direct community service activities and more long-term community mobilization and development activities. And finally, the successful collaborations will develop intensive training and ongoing educational experiences for students that will assist them in understanding the larger social and political issues connected to their service, develop their understanding of and skills in citizen participation, and connect their experiences to academic content and career development.

The centrality of collaboration, reciprocity, and diversity was underscored by bringing Nadinne Cruz and John McKnight to Minnesota to conduct planning workshops for campus-community teams who are developing their partnerships and proposals. Kretzmann and McKnight's book, *Building Communities from the Inside Out* (1993), which focuses on community assets rather than needs, is being used as a model for community development strategies. The collaborations that are emerging will embrace the full range of experiential education options and action research, with a strong commitment to building sustained institutional commitments and student involvement. In every instance, the collaborations will go well beyond the institutions' current programmatic approach to service-learning to embrace the three meta-principles of collaboration, reciprocity, and diversity more fully.

Colorado State University

The Service Integration Project at Colorado State began in 1993 with the intention of engaging faculty more fully in the process of integrating service and study. The project's small staff conducted consultations with individual faculty, focusing primarily on meeting the needs of faculty seeking to integrate service into their courses. This one-on-one faculty consultation approach resulted in variations in the quality of service-learning courses and was quickly wearing out the talented, high-achieving staff. Moreover, students were unclear about the connection between service expectations and the course learning objectives, and the community agencies simply took whatever assistance they could get. With a genuine commitment to developing a high-quality service-learning initiative, the Service Integration Project staff embarked on a year of intentional reflection on the service-learning courses that had been developed. They spoke with community agencies and faculty, listened intently to student voices through both meetings and course evaluations, and surveyed peer institutions. They came to the conclusion that more structure and more concrete expectations were necessary to strengthen the service-learning initiative. The flexibility with which they initially entered the process had served to dilute their energies, and it also created vague understandings and weakened outcomes.

They then began working with a faculty steering committee to develop a set of guidelines to be used by the staff in working with faculty interested in integrating service into their courses. The result is a set of *Essential Characteristics for Course Inclusion in the Service Integration Project* (1994):

1. The syllabus is developed or revised to incorporate the service experience into the teaching and learning objectives of the course.
2. Involve students in at least 5 hours of service in the community for each hour of credit they are receiving for the course.

3. Students do not receive credit for the time spent performing service, but for their knowledge in connecting their service experience with course content.
4. The service experience must be connected to the course through readings and presentations in class.
5. Reflection on the service experience includes dialogue about social, psychological, political and ethical considerations involved in the service and the need for the service.
6. The faculty member is willing to become acquainted with each community agency (understands the agency mission, clientele, location and student role) that students are placed with. This knowledge could be obtained through the Service Integration Project or through direct contact with the agency.
7. The course will provide students with information about the agency and the clients and/or issue area that it serves before the service begins.
8. Students, faculty and community agencies participate in an evaluation process provided by the Service Integration Project.

Through the application of these guidelines to service-learning courses, the meta-principles of collaboration and reciprocity were put into practice at Colorado State. An early assessment of the impact of these characteristics in the development of new service-learning courses shows that about twenty of the approximately fifty-two service-learning courses that have traveled through the Service Integration Project are or are in the process of, reaching high quality. In addition, the burden on program staff has lessened as the faculty, community, and students have become more fully involved. It is clear to the staff that a revisit of the essential characteristics is due. Preliminary discussions indicate that the numbers of service hours required might increase and the meta-principle of diversity might be woven through the elements (V. Keller, personal communication, October 1995).

University of Maryland at College Park
The You Can Make a Difference Program (YCMAD) is a student-led, cocurricular service-learning program sponsored by the office of Community Service Programs and designed specifically for commuter students at the University of Maryland. YCMAD engages up

to ten students in a one-year commitment to working with home-less, runaway, and abused youth. In this train-the-trainer model, paid student coordinators undergo intensive, ongoing training in reflection, leadership skill development, and issues related to diversity. They then provide similar training to a corps of volun-teers. YCMAD intentionally connects service-learning with issues of diversity, while applying the Wingspread principles and COOL's five critical elements.

One of the critical starting points for the program—recruit-ment of a diverse corps of student volunteers—has been achieved, especially with respect to racial and age diversity. Preparation and training in the first semester focus on understanding the commu-nity and the service site. The relationships of homelessness, power, privilege, and oppression are the primary topics. In each reflection session, students discuss both what they have learned from the young people they work with and how they have applied the insights acquired through reflection to their service. During the second semester, reflection sessions center around the "isms" (racism, classism, sexism, heterosexism, antisemitism) and how they are part of the root causes and perpetuation of homelessness.

Student coordinators meet regularly with the agency volunteer coordinator to secure feedback on impacts, processes, and addi-tional needs of the agency, and they work directly with the young people. This ensures a consistent feedback loop and allows student coordinators to engage in meaningful action. Ongoing evaluations of the program from student participants, agency staff, and com-munity participants have served to strengthen the program's impacts on students and the community and to improve the diversity-focused content of the training and reflection sessions.

Student participants and agency personnel note that the diver-sity training and reflection sessions have had a positive effect on the participants' interactions with the young people. For example, when the youth make sexist comments, the University of Maryland volunteers know how to respond effectively.

While it achieves its objectives for student learning, YCMAD, like most other service-learning programs, faces the ongoing challenge of measuring its outcomes for the community. The program con-sciously seeks to achieve true reciprocity and collaboration, while maintaining its strong commitment to diversity, as it continues to develop (K. Rice and L. Tenley, personal communication, November 1995).

Conclusion

How will we know that we have principle-centered service-learning programs? We suggest that the partners in service-learning can and should examine their practices through the meta-principles, or lenses, of collaboration, reciprocity, and diversity and ask the larger questions as well: Is the service-learning partnership truly collaborative? Does reciprocity guide all aspects of the program's service and learning? Is diversity valued and embraced to the fullest possible extent? The creative tension that the kaleidoscope provides is not for those who want formulas or program blueprints. It is doubtful that such prescriptions and static models work well with any programs, but they are certainly antithetical to service-learning.

Principles offer vision and guidance as we struggle with the difficult issues and daily details in the complicated synergy of service and learning. The kaleidoscope and the meta-principles that we propose have grown out of the practice-to-principle-to-practice journey of the past four decades, and it is our hope that this organic process will continue to sharpen both the principles and practice of service-learning.

Margaret Wheatley's (1994) ideas about the application of quantum theory to today's practice in many fields are particularly relevant to service-learning: "In our past explorations, the tradition was to discover something and then formulate it into answers and solutions that could be widely transferred. But now we are on a journey of mutual and simultaneous exploration. . . . We cannot expect answers. Solutions, as quantum reality teaches, are a temporary event, specific to a context, developed through the relationship of persons and circumstances. . . . Reality changes shape and meaning because of our activity. And it is constantly new. We are required to be there, as active participants. It can't happen without us and nobody can do it for us" (pp. 150–151). The kaleidoscope can serve as a guide on our journey of mutual exploration into the world of service-learning.

References

Adams, M. "Cultural Inclusion in the American College Classroom." In L.L.B. Border and N.V.N. Chism (eds.), *Teaching for Diversity*. New Directions for Teaching and Learning, no. 49. San Francisco: Jossey-Bass, 1992.

Bruffee, K. "Sharing Our Toys: Cooperative Learning Versus Collaborative Learning." *Change*, Jan.–Feb. 1995, pp. 12–18.

Campus Outreach Opportunity League. *Into the Streets: Organizing Manual, 1993–94 Edition*. St. Paul, Minn.: COOL Press, 1993.

Chrislip, D. D., and Larson, C. E. *Collaborative Leadership: How Citizens and Civic Leaders Can Make a Difference*. San Francisco: Jossey-Bass, 1994.

Covey, S. *Principle-Centered Leadership*. New York: Simon & Schuster, 1992.

Cruz, N. "Multicultural Politics of Difference in Service-Learning." Paper presented at the Council of Independent Colleges's National Institute on Learning and Service, St. Charles, Ill., May–June 1995.

Essential Characteristics for Course Inclusion in the Service Integration Project. Fort Collins: Colorado State University, 1994.

Gabelnick, F. "Collaboration." Paper presented at the Bush Regional Collaboration Conference, Minneapolis, Minn., Nov. 1993.

Himmelman, A. *Communities Working Collaboratively for a Change*. Unpublished working paper, 1994.

Howard, J. (ed.). *Praxis I: A Faculty Casebook on Community Service Learning*. Ann Arbor: OCSL Press, 1993.

Kretzmann, J. P., and McKnight, J. L. *Building Communities from the Inside Out: A Path Toward Finding and Mobilizing a Community's Assets*. Evanston, Ill.: Center for Urban Affairs and Policy Research, Northwestern University, 1993.

Minnesota Campus Compact. *Campus-Community Collaborations Program*. Minneapolis: Minnesota Campus Compact, 1995.

Office of Evaluation, Corporation for National Service. *Handbook for Continuous Improvement*. Washington, D.C.: Corporation for National Service, 1995.

Porter Honnet, E., and Poulsen, S. J. *Principles of Good Practice for Combining Service and Learning*. Racine, Wisc.: Johnson Foundation, 1989.

Sigmon, R. "Service-Learning: Three Principles." *Synergist*, 1979, *8*(1).

Sigmon, R. *Linking Service with Learning*. Washington, D.C.: Council of Independent Colleges, 1994.

Takaki, R. "Diversity in Higher Education." *AAHE Bulletin*, 1995, *47*(10), 13.

Waldock, J. M. *Achieving Cross-Cultural Understanding Through Service-Learning in Higher Education*. Unpublished report. Mankato, Minn.: Mankato State University, 1995.

Wells, E. A., and Knefelkamp, L. L. *The Practice-to-Theory-to-Practice Model.* Washington, D.C.: American College Personnel Association, 1984. (Companion to PTP videotape.)

Wheatley, M. *Leadership and the New Science: Learning About Organization from an Orderly Universe.* San Francisco: Berrett-Koehler, 1994.

Chapter Three

Enhancing Student Learning and Development Through Service-Learning

Marylu K. McEwen

Carefully designed service-learning experiences can lead to profound learning and developmental outcomes for students, the primary reason that institutions of higher education engage in service-learning. Understanding the potential learning and development outcomes of service-learning enables service-learning educators—be they faculty, student affairs professionals, campus ministers, or community-based volunteer coordinators—to shape desired outcomes and design service and reflection experiences to achieve them. Learning and personal development naturally complement each other in service-learning as well as in other experiential and classroom activities, and this natural complementarity can be enhanced through intentional planning and course or program design. For example, service and reflection experiences can be shaped to increase students' knowledge of course content while encouraging them to think in a more critical and complex manner. Similarly, students can deepen their understanding of pressing social issues while exploring their own racial identity and how it affects their thoughts and actions. In fact, some faculty, in determining course objectives, include desired developmental outcomes, such as moral or ethical development, along with discipline-related content knowledge. (Chapter Twelve addresses issues related to setting objectives for courses that involve service-learning.)

This chapter examines several theoretical domains of learning and development and relates them to service-learning. Theories provide valuable perspectives for understanding students as they enter service-learning experiences, how students experience the process of their involvement in service-learning, and what their learning and developmental outcomes might be. Because theories of learning and development inform service-learning educators about students as both learners and service providers, they offer critical insights into designing and evaluating service-learning experiences.

To put theory into a more practical context, consider three hypothetical college students who might be involved in service-learning.

Amanda, a junior, is a twenty-five-year-old African American woman who lives in a predominantly African American urban neighborhood. She completed two years at a community college, then lived at home for several years working full-time and also caring for her elderly grandfather. As far back as she can remember, Amanda has been informally involved in service to her community.

Janice is a senior, twenty-two years old, a white woman who grew up in the rural Midwest. She is a biology major who wants to become a veterinarian, perhaps practicing in an economically depressed area of West Virginia or New Mexico. Besides attending classes and studying, Janice spends most of the remainder of her time with her church. She regularly attends two different Bible study groups, serves as a leader for a Christian youth group, and participates in a variety of church social activities.

George is Chinese American, a first-year student who is a member of a fraternity. He is nineteen years old and came to college from a West Coast city where community service was a requirement for high school graduation.

Let us suppose that each of these students is enrolled in a course in which service-learning is a component. Several questions are raised by these three examples: What, in general, is known about Amanda, Janice, and George? Are there any expected differences in how each of these students enters a service-learning experience? How will they experience service-learning, both similarly as well as differently? How will they reflect on the service they have provided? What will they learn? How will service-learning affect their development? How will they experience the reciprocity of service-learning? What will they bring to the classroom? What will they have achieved as a result of their involvement in service-learning?

To enable service-learning educators to understand more fully the rich possibilities of both curricular and cocurricular service-learning for student learning and development, this chapter begins with a general description of the nature of development and of different families of developmental models. It then highlights specific theories and models of student learning and development regarding different ways in which students think and learn, how they develop in terms of their moral reasoning, and how they develop spiritually. It examines the personal and psychological developmental issues students face during college and how they are likely to relate to their experiences in service-learning, and concludes with some thoughts about the relationship of service-learning and career development.

Developmental Models

Theories about how students learn and develop provide important information about both the nature of college students who are participating in service-learning and about the learning and developmental outcomes that can be expected from their participation. Before examining individual theories, it is important to define what is meant by development, to consider conditions that are necessary for development to occur, and to present a brief overview of families of theories of student learning and development.

Development Defined

Defining the term *development* offers a backdrop and a foundation from which to understand the theories, most of which describe developmental processes of college students. According to Nevitt Sanford (1967), development is the "organization of increasing complexity" (p. 47) or, stated another way, increasing differentiation and integration (Sanford, 1962, p. 257). Development represents a redefining of the self in more complex and more distinct ways, yet at the same time putting all the parts together in an integrated fashion. For instance, development for Amanda might mean exposure to and increased tolerance for Latino persons, a new understanding of the different nationalities and ethnic groups that make up the Latino population, and putting these two together to see that involvement in service in an urban, predominantly African American community may be significantly different from working with Chicanos in rural California.

Conditions for Development

Two conditions must exist for development to occur: a readiness for development within the person and stimuli to challenge the individual, to upset an existing psychological equilibrium within the person (Sanford, 1962, 1967). Knefelkamp (1974) elegantly summarizes Sanford's thoughts about the nature of challenge in relation to development, and notes that a delicate balance of challenge and support must exist for development to occur: "If the challenge or disequilibrium is too great, the individual will retreat; if the support system [is too great and] impedes challenge, the individual will stagnate" (p. 38). Development is promoted by offering the challenges to the individual that require new responses while simultaneously offering sufficient support for the student to confront the challenge. Note that there is no prescribed amount of challenge or support. Rather the critical components are the complementarity of the challenge and support and the appropriateness of the balance for the individual.

Families of Theories of Student Learning and Development

Some theories about the development of college students pertain specifically to college students; others come from the broader area of human development. Following is one means to organize the various theories and models useful in considering potential outcomes of service-learning:

Cognitive developmental theories describe how students think and the process of students' thinking, but not the content of their thinking (Knefelkamp, Widick, and Parker, 1978b). These theories describe qualitatively different ways of thinking, from simple to complex, from concrete to abstract.

Learning styles models describe some of the persistent and consistent differences among individuals (Knefelkamp, Widick, and Parker, 1978b) regarding how they deal with the world and predictable ways in which individuals encounter and react to their environments.

Theories of psychosocial development describe the "what" or content of college students' development (Knefelkamp, Widick, and Parker, 1978b). They represent the kinds of issues or developmental tasks students face.

Dimensions of identity development concern characteristics attributed to individuals, such as race, gender, sexual orientation, and disability. Other relevant dimensions are culture, ethnicity, national origin, age, geographical region, parental education levels, religious identity, and social class. The overriding issue is how one perceives these characteristics about oneself.

Theories and models of career development focus on how individuals make career choices.

Cognitive Development

Cognitive developmental theories describe how students think, the structural ways in which they reason, and the process they use for thinking. Cognitive developmental models are based on the work of Jean Piaget (Wadsworth, 1971). Cognitive development, according to Knefelkamp, Widick, and Parker (1978b), is conceptualized "as a sequence of irreversible stages involving shifts in the process by which individuals perceive and reason about their world" (p. xii). Each stage is qualitatively different from the preceding stages, "transcends the earlier ones" (Perry, 1981, p. 78), and subsumes all preceding stages. Although one develops a more complex way of thinking, one continues to have access to all previous ways of thinking; thus, at times, one may think in less complex and abstract ways (King, 1978).

The three models of cognitive development particularly salient to college students and to service-learning are William Perry's

(1970, 1981) scheme of intellectual and ethical development; Mary Belenky, Blythe Clinchy, Nancy Goldberger, and Jill Tarule's (1986) women's ways of knowing; and Marcia Baxter Magolda's (1992) gender-related patterns in students' intellectual development. Two implications of these models for service-learning are that students will develop as more complex thinkers and that they will understand their service-learning experiences in different ways, depending on their own level of cognitive development.

We will also examine two specific kinds of cognitive development: moral development and, more briefly, spiritual development.

Perry's Scheme of Intellectual and Ethical Development

Perry's (1970, 1981) scheme represents the developmental progression from concrete and simple ways of thinking to more abstract and complex ways. This more complex form of thinking leads to implications for an individual's personal meaning-making in the world, which represents the ethical component of Perry's model.

Perry's scheme comprises nine positions, arranged in four groupings, that represent qualitatively different ways in the structure or process of students' thinking:

Dualism (positions 1–2). In position 1, the student experiences no diversity of opinion. The student in position 2 experiences diversity of opinion as either right or wrong and looks to authorities for the right answers. Authorities may be teachers, peers, parents, or books.

Multiplicity (positions 3–4). In position 3, the student experiences diversity of opinion as right, wrong, and yet to be known. Focus is on the right process to acquire knowledge. The student is concerned with fairness and perceives that quantity equals quality. The student is beginning to become comfortable with multiple perspectives. In position 4, the student accepts that not all knowledge is known and thus believes that some knowledge is known, some is yet to be learned, and some may never be known. Emphasis is on either the right way to think or the belief that all knowledge is equally valid and that everyone has a right to his or her own opinion.

Contextual Relativism (positions 5–6). The student in position 5 comes to see that some opinions and some knowledge are better than others, that knowledge is developed and known within a context, and that "good" knowledge exists with proper evidence, justification, and a given context. The student is comfortable with "knowing" within a variety of contexts. In position 6, the student begins to apprehend the need to make commitments.

Commitment in Relativism (positions 7–9). The student makes an initial commitment in an aspect related to self (career, life partner, lifestyle) or in a belief or attitude (social justice, politics, religion). The student then experiences the implications of the initial commitment (what it is like to be a journalist or to live in a city, for example) and of multiple commitments he or she is making. The student continues to make commitments and experiences implications of ongoing commitments.

Perry's (1981, p. 97) scheme should be thought of as a helix in that individuals revisit each of the positions continually in their lives, often in increasingly more complex ways. Research suggests that traditional-age students generally enter college in position 2 or 3 and leave college in position 4 or 5. Cornfeld and Knefelkamp (1979) discuss several differences among these positions: how students view knowledge, the role of the instructor, the role of the student, students' views of peers in the learning process, evaluation issues, primary intellectual tasks, sources of challenge, and sources of support.

Perry's scheme examines the complex, personal, and delicate nature of development and is particularly applicable to service-learning. First, Perry (1978) says that learning is an ego-threatening task. He describes the affective component of learning. For example, when a student enters a classroom or participates in a service-learning activity, there is an affective challenge, as well as a cognitive one, of being faced with new knowledge and new experiences.

Second, Perry reminds us that people are not positions. Thus, students should not be defined by the samples of their thinking; rather, the samples of students' thinking provide significant clues about the cognitive structures they are using.

Third, Perry (1981) believes that true development in an individual occurs *between* positions, with the positions merely representing the moments, the plateaus of development. For example, a student's slow, almost imperceptible move away from Dualism into slightly increasing comfort with multiples (early Multiplicity) represents the extraordinary moments of development rather than what is revealed in samples of students' thinking at various positions.

Finally, Perry (1978) eloquently points out the losses, the grieving, and the costs of growth. These costs are especially evident in the movement from position 6 to 7, as the student makes an initial commitment and realizes the closing of other possibilities, often before seeing the opening up of the new choice. Perry (1981) underscores "the educator's responsibility to hear and honor, by simple acknowledgment, the students' losses" (p. 108).

The examples of the hypothetical students put Perry's scheme to use in the context of service-learning. George, a first-year student, is likely to be at an early position of cognitive development, perhaps position 2 or 3. He is taking a sociology course, Contemporary Social Issues, which includes a community service component, and is participating in short-term service projects through his fraternity. Because George is thinking in generally simple and concrete ways, it may be difficult for him to differentiate the benefits to him and to the community of the semester-long versus short-term community service activities. In the sociology course, George is expected to engage in multiple kinds of reflection: a personal journal, reflective discussion with his peers facilitated by a teaching assistant, and two meetings during the semester with the coordinator of service-learning. George views these activities as redundant; he sees no value of discussions with his peers and rarely has much to write in his journal. Because his cognitive development is at an early position, George does not understand the roles of his peers or himself as agents in his learning. He sometimes feels duped in the classroom when the instructor presents multiple models of delivery of social services, wishing the instructor would just present the model that she really wants students to use and believes is most effective. George is a reasonably compliant student but confused by the complex relationships of social issues and community service.

Janice, also enrolled in Contemporary Social Issues, sees her service-learning experiences in a different light. Although she thinks very complexly (position 5) in her biology and science courses, her cognitive development in other areas such as the social sciences is not as advanced. Janice's cognitive development in her sociology class is generally at position 4 (late Multiplicity); she is comfortable with many ways of knowing but is not able to support and justify her beliefs and knowledge in Contextual Relativism (position 5). Janice enjoys all the different opportunities for reflection offered in the class and is intrigued with some of the ideas presented, but she has her own ideas about delivering social services and does not understand why the teaching assistant and the instructor continue to challenge her about her thinking.

Thus, two students participating in essentially the same activities engage with them and understand them in very different ways.

Belenky, Clinchy, Goldberger, and Tarule's Women's Ways of Knowing

Belenky and her colleagues (1986) drew on their extensive interviews with 135 women to propose five qualitatively different ways of knowing used by the women in their sample: silence, received knowledge, subjective knowledge, procedural knowledge, and constructed knowledge. The researchers suggest that these ways of knowing represent "different perspectives from which women view reality and draw conclusions about truth, knowledge, and authority" (p. 3).

For the purposes of service-learning, the two patterns of separate and connected knowing are especially relevant. Separate knowing, according to Belenky and others, means coming to know through doubting, through questioning, and through the knower's separating the self from that to be known. Separate knowing is a common way of knowing in the traditional academic community. Connected knowing, on the other hand, is coming to know through believing, through the knower's connecting with, having empathy with, the subject matter. Connected knowing is a highly relational way of knowing and is often not practiced within traditional societal or academic structures. Connected knowing in the Belenky and others' study was the preferred way of knowing of most women, and thus was termed a gender-related pattern of knowing. Belenky and her colleagues believe that people need to develop both kinds of knowing and that using both separate and connected knowing is needed for constructed knowledge, the fifth way of knowing.

The structured reflection of a service-learning experience can help students acquire, or affirm for them, an empathic way of knowing and thus develop as connected knowers (Belenky and others, 1986). Through structured reflection students are asked to think about themselves and to connect both affectively and cognitively with their service experiences. Additional implications for service-learning of the Belenky and others' model are that many women students (and perhaps other subgroups of students, such as students of color) will learn primarily through connection with the subject matter, through believing their and others' experiences, rather than through questioning or doubting, and that they will be more comfortable with connected knowing than with separate knowing. Male students are more likely to be separate knowers; they might tend to question more strongly their involvement in service-learning experiences and to distance themselves from knowing and understanding the life situations and experiences of community members, as well as from the relationship of service-learning to social justice.

Baxter Magolda's Gender-Related Patterns in Intellectual Development

Baxter Magolda (1992), in a five-year longitudinal study of 101 students at Miami University of Ohio, found four qualitatively different kinds of knowing and gender-related patterns within three of the four ways. Her book, *Knowing and Reasoning in College* (1992), contains five excellent chapters offering implications for teaching and learning. For each gender-related pattern of knowing, she also describes how students with that particular pattern view the teaching-learning process and their learning preferences. Baxter Magolda draws on three concepts important in students' learning: confirmation, contradiction, and continuity. Confirmation serves to affirm or support students in their learning, contradiction to offer challenges, and continuity to provide connections with or a familiar base from which students can engage in their learning.

The implications of Baxter Magolda's work for service-learning are best summarized through her three principles of "validating the student as a knower, situating learning in the students' own experience, and defining learning as jointly constructing meaning" (1992, p. 270). Service-learning provides excellent opportunities for the practice of all three principles. Through structured reflection, service-learning educators, together with other students, can affirm students for what they have learned and for what they "know" from their experiences and reflections. Because of its very nature, service-learning situates learning in the context of the students' own experiences. Skillfully constructed and conducted reflection can lead students to understand their learning as meaning jointly constructed by themselves, fellow students, faculty, community members, and community-based organization staff.

Moral Development

Moral development is a specific kind of cognitive development. One's level or complexity of moral development can be no greater than one's general cognitive development. Moral development concerns itself with the process and structures of moral reasoning, not with the moral action itself or with the content of moral judgment (Kohlberg, 1975, p. 671). One might ask how moral issues could be considered without attention to moral action. Moral action represents a behavior, an outcome of moral reasoning. Although higher forms of moral development do not necessarily lead to higher forms of moral action, Kohlberg believed that most people prefer action that corresponds to their levels of moral development. Further, a specific moral action could come about from varied ways of moral reasoning. Thus, higher levels of moral reasoning do not imply certain kinds of moral action, nor does moral action imply specific kinds of moral reasoning.

Recognizing the relationship of moral development to service-learning is important because moral dilemmas are likely to arise from students' involvement in service and during the reflection process. Knowledge of moral development can help service-learning educators understand how students think about the moral dilemmas that service-learning introduces and how reflection about these dilemmas can lead to more complex moral reasoning.

Lawrence Kohlberg's Theory of Moral Development Kohlberg, one of the major theorists of moral development, built on the work of Piaget and Dewey. Kohlberg (1975) posits three levels of moral reasoning, each comprising two stages, to describe the developmental process of moral reasoning, with each stage representing increasingly more complex and more abstract moral reasoning:

1. *Preconventional level.* The first stage is the punishment-and-obedience orientation, in which "avoidance of punishment and unquestioning deference to power are valued in their own right" (Kohlberg, 1975, p. 671). Stage 2 is the instrumental-relativist orientation, in which "right action consists of that which instrumentally satisfies one's own needs and occasionally the needs of others" (p. 671).
2. *Conventional level.* The moral imperative at this level concerns what will maintain the expectations of others, including one's family, one's peers, or one's society. Stage 3 is the interpersonal concordance or "good boy–nice girl" orientation: "good behavior is that which pleases or helps others and is approved by them" (Kohlberg, 1975, p. 671). Stage 4 is the law-and-order orientation, in which what is right involves maintaining the social order.
3. *Postconventional level.* Stage 5 is the social-contract, legalistic orientation, in which "right action tends to be defined in terms of general individual rights, and standards which have been critically examined and agreed upon by the whole society" (Kohlberg, 1975, p. 671). In stage 6, the universal ethical principle orientation, "right is defined by the decision of conscience in accord with self-chosen *ethical principles* appealing to logical comprehensiveness, universality, and consistency" (p. 671).

According to Kohlberg (1975), the stage 4 law-and-order orientation is the normative moral development stage in U.S. society. The stage 5 social-contract, legalistic orientation represents the official morality of the U.S. government and Constitution. The stage 6 universal ethical principle orientation, the highest-order stage, is one that less than 1 percent of the population reaches. Examples of persons reasoning at stage 6, according to Kohlberg, were Gandhi and Martin Luther King, Jr. Kohlberg found that most students entering college reason at stage 4, but about 20 percent regress during their first year to stage 3 interpersonal concordance reasoning. Based on his extensive research, Kohlberg found that individuals can understand reasoning *only one stage beyond their own.* In his research on just communities, Kohlberg (1975) found that moral discussion meeting three conditions can enhance and raise one's level of moral development: "exposure to the next higher stage of reasoning; exposure to situations posing problems and contradictions for the child's [person's] current moral structure, leading to dissatisfaction with his [or her] current level; and an atmosphere of interchange and dialogue combining the first two conditions, in which conflicting moral views are compared in an open manner" (p. 675).

Kohlberg's theory of moral development uses justice and rights as the context for moral reasoning. Thus, moral reasoning and moral dilemmas are evaluated within this context. In his research, Kohlberg frequently used "Heinz and the Drug Dilemma," in which participants discuss what Heinz should do when he is faced with a dying wife and an inordinately expensive drug. In Kohlberg's theory, the issues ultimately are those of which is the greater right, life or property.

Kohlberg's theory casts light on Amanda's and Janice's experiences as students in a philosophy course on ethics in which community service is a significant course component. In reflection and discussion about the ethics of providing soup kitchens for persons who are homeless, Amanda feels that individuals have a certain right to food, shelter, and the opportunity to lead a productive life. And although she believes strongly that soup kitchens and shelters are necessary, they are not sufficient; special training and employment opportunities should also be made available to those individuals who do not wish to be homeless. Janice, however, thinks that homeless persons are fortunate to have free food and shelter. She believes that people should work for what they get, and if they do not choose to work (after all, there are jobs available; they just might be hard to find), then they should be grateful for the gifts from those who have more. From these brief snapshots of moral reasoning, Amanda seems to be speaking out for general individual rights, which go beyond the one-for-one exchange of work for goods; this may represent stage 5, a form of principled, postconventional reasoning. The structures underlying Janice's reasoning seem to be stage 4 law and order, a social exchange of food and shelter for work and a given social agreement of charity toward the less privileged.

Kohlberg's theory suggests three key implications for service-learning educators. First, it is the complexity of students' moral reasoning that is the focus of moral development, not their specific moral judgments or decisions. Thus, service-learning educators should intentionally structure reflection to help students reflect on and clearly articulate their reasoning behind their moral judgments. Second, because moral development is promoted through dialogue and interchange, service-learning educators should design interactive opportunities such as group discussions to enable students to examine thoughtfully the moral dilemmas raised in their service experiences. Interchange that includes exposure to higher levels of moral development promotes more complex thinking and more advanced moral development. Finally, service-learning educators should design reflection based on the premise that students process moral issues and discussions through their individual cognitive structures and are able to understand complexity of reasoning only one level beyond their own level of moral development.

Carol Gilligan's Ethic of Care   Carol Gilligan (1982), in her own research using the Heinz dilemma, found that young girls often focused on issues concerning the relationship between Heinz and his wife. Gilligan proposes that girls employ a "different voice," another context of moral reasoning—one of care and responsibility—that contrasts with Kohlberg's (1975) justice and rights context. Gilligan believes that these contexts are gender *related,* not gender *based,* such that women typically but not necessarily use the context of care and responsibility, men the moral context of justice and rights. According to Gilligan, these represent truly different voices of moral reasoning; she believes that individuals need to be able to consider and use both contexts in their moral reasoning and moral decisions.

In Gilligan's three-stage model, "women's moral judgments proceed from an initial focus on the self at the *first level* to the discovery, in the transition to the *second level,* of the concept of responsibility as the basis for a new equilibrium between self and others"

(p. 492). In the second level, the concept of responsibility is further developed as "good is equated with caring for others" (p. 492). However, with only others as the recipients of moral care, eventually the woman experiences a disequilibrium or absence of caring for self, which marks the transition to the *third level,* where she negotiates a new equilibrium between selfishness and responsibility. According to Gilligan (1982), "The self becomes the arbiter of an independent judgment that now subsumes both conventions and individual needs under the moral principle of nonviolence" (p. 492).

Implications for service-learning concern the balance or equilibrium, or lack thereof, in students', particularly women's, care for others and care for self. In a service-learning course, care for others may be expressed through community service, and care for self through diligence in work for the course or engagement in regular reflection. Gilligan's theory also illuminates how, for students involved in service-learning, the underlying moral imperative of care and nonviolence ("do no harm") frequently competes with the moral imperative of rights and justice. With this understanding, service-learning educators can design reflection to lead students to grapple with these competing moral imperatives and thus encourage moral development. It is important for service-learning educators to know that students may use at least two different contexts, one of care and responsibility and the other of rights and justice, as they think about and discuss moral issues in their service experiences. The salient issue is not which of the contexts is right but how both contexts inform students' thinking about the many moral and social dilemmas raised in service-learning.

Including George in Amanda's and Janice's discussion about the ethics of soup kitchens in the Kohlberg example adds another dimension. George argues that what is most important is caring for others and, more than anything else, to be sure not to do any harm. Therefore he believes that the overriding issue with soup kitchens is whether they really are helpful to the persons who are being served (the principle of doing no harm). The competing issues, in a discussion among these three students, might be ones of care and responsibility for persons who are homeless versus justice and rights for those without food and shelter.

Spiritual Development

James Fowler (1981) and Sharon Parks (1986) provide models about the development of faith or spirituality. Fowler's model is a cognitive one, in which faith develops from a simple to a more complex form, following the pattern of other cognitive-developmental theories.

Parks (1986) "focuses on the search for faith by students and details the unique contributions that higher education makes in that developmental process" (Rutledge, 1989, p. 17). Parks (1986) speaks about the importance of community for young adults, between ages eighteen and thirty. Parks's work underscores the potential of learning communities, community service, and structured reflection in addressing community needs and promoting the development of faith and spirituality in college students. Drawing on Parks's (1986) writings, Mark Rutledge (1989) notes that "students are vulnerable and need to be held in communities that confirm and challenge their new insights and affirm that their journey is worthwhile" (p. 27). The connections between service and learning provide an important link in fostering students' journeys of faith and meaning making. (For further discussion of spiritual development, see Fowler, 1981, 1987; Parks, 1986; Rutledge, 1989; Swezey, 1990; Worthington, 1989.)

Kolb's Model of Experiential Learning and Learning Styles

Because service-learning is a form of experiential education, David Kolb's experiential learning model (1981, 1984) is particularly useful for service-learning educators. Drawing significantly on the works of John Dewey, Kurt Lewin, and Jean Piaget, it portrays the "important role that experience plays in the learning process" (1981, p. 235).

Experiential Learning

The core of Kolb's experiential learning model "is a simple description of the learning cycle—of how experience is translated into concepts, which, in turn, are used as guides in the choice of new experiences" (1981, p. 235). A person can enter this cycle at any of the four points in the process but must complete the entire cycle in order for effective learning to occur. Kolb summarizes the learning cycle as follows: "Immediate concrete [affective] experience is the basis for observations and reflection. An individual uses these observations to build an idea, generalization or 'theory' from which new implications for action can be deduced. These implications or hypotheses then serve as guides in acting to create new experiences" (p. 235).

Effective learning requires four different kinds of learning abilities, corresponding to the four points in the learning cycle: Concrete Experience (CE) abilities, Reflective Observation (RO) abilities, Abstract Conceptualization (AC) abilities, and Active Experimentation (AE) abilities. Describing the learning cycle and these four abilities, Kolb states that learners "must be able to involve themselves fully, openly, and without bias in new experiences (CE); they must be able to observe and reflect on these experiences from many perspectives (RO); they must be able to create concepts that integrate their observations into logically sound theories (AC); and they must be able to use these theories to make decisions and solve problems (AE)" (p. 236). Kolb (1985) also presents the learning cycle as "learning from feeling" (CE), "learning by watching and listening" (RO), "learning by thinking" (AC), and "learning by doing" (AE) (p. 5). It is important to note that Concrete Experience might be more effectively described as the affective component of learning.

Three implications of the experiential learning model are central to service-learning. First, a course or other experience should be structured to present multiple opportunities continually to enable students to move completely and frequently through the learning cycle. Second, Kolb's model underscores how central and important reflection is to the entire process of learning. Third, in Kolb's model, reflection *follows* direct and concrete experience and *precedes* abstract conceptualization and generalization. Placing reflection at another point in the learning process is likely to create a less effective learning experience for students because they will not have the most direct and immediate link to the affective (concrete) experience of learning.

Let us consider an example of how the faculty member teaching the Contemporary Social Issues course might apply Kolb's experiential learning model. A student might enter the course, and the learning cycle, by being introduced through readings and lecture to a new theory about the root causes of social problems. Then written assignments and class discussions can be designed to assist students to apply these abstract concepts to the issue of homelessness and to draw implications about its root causes. These assignments and discussions serve as a springboard for students' engagement in a concrete service experience related to homelessness. The faculty member would lead students to reflect, individually or as a group, on their concrete experiences and to make observations about them. These reflections and observations can then be structured to provide a connection for the students back to the original theory, encouraging new questions or hypotheses about it.

Learning Styles

Kolb describes four different learning styles, based on one's preferences for two of the four learning abilities. The two learning abilities represent adjacent points of the learning cycle and each of the two dimensions of concrete versus abstract and active versus passive. The four learning styles are labeled Converger, Accommodator, Diverger, and Assimilator.

"*Convergers'* dominant learning abilities are Abstract Conceptualization and Active Experimentation. Their greatest strength lies in the practical application of ideas" (Kolb, 1981, p. 238). They organize knowledge using hypothetical-deductive reasoning to focus on specific problems. They prefer to deal with things rather than people and tend to have narrow interests.

Accommodators' dominant learning abilities are Active Experimentation and Concrete Experience. Their greatest strength is in doing things, carrying out plans, and becoming involved in new experiences. They tend to be risk takers, and they "tend to excel in situations that call for adaption to specific immediate circumstances. . . . They tend to solve problems in an intuitive trial-and-error manner" (Kolb, 1981, p. 238), relying on people rather than analytical ability. "Accommodators are at ease with people but are sometimes seen as impatient and 'pushy'" (p. 238).

Divergers' dominant learning abilities are Concrete Experience and Reflective Observation. Their greatest strength is in their imaginative ability. "They excel in the ability to view concrete situations from many perspectives and to organize many relationships into a meaningful 'gestalt'" (Kolb, 1981, p. 238). They are good at generating ideas, interested in people, imaginative and emotional, and have broad cultural interests.

Assimilators' dominant learning abilities are Reflective Observation and Abstract Conceptualization. "Their greatest strength lies in their ability to create theoretical models. They excel in inductive reasoning, in assimilating disparate observations into an integrated explanation. . . . They . . . are less interested in people and more concerned with abstract concepts, but less concerned with the practical use of theories" (Kolb, 1981, p. 238).

Divergers and Convergers have opposite learning strengths, as do Assimilators and Accommodators. Extensive research by Kolb (1981, 1984) and others provides evidence of varying dominant learning styles among people in different disciplines. Further, individuals' cognitive development varies as a function of the area or content focused on, known as cognitive domain. Thus, one may think complexly about things but not about people, or vice versa. Or, in the context of service-learning, one may think concretely about socioeconomic issues but not about social justice.

Kolb's work on learning styles has several implications for service-learning. Teachers and facilitators tend to teach to their own learning styles and thus may need to stretch themselves or consult with others regarding ways in which to design both service and reflection experiences for students with learning styles different from their own. In addition, the design of a course and the service-learning experiences may be a better fit, and thus more conducive to learning, for some students than for others. Depending on their learning abilities, some students may not fully enter or engage in the learning cycle until they are able to use one of the abilities with which they are comfortable and skilled. Ultimately, if teachers and facilitators intend to enable all students to complete the learning cycle, they will need to provide opportunities appropriate for all learning styles. (For a more comprehensive discussion of learning styles and service-learning, refer to Stewart, 1990.)

Let us suppose that Amanda is a Diverger and George a Converger. Because Divergers' strengths are concrete (affective) experience and reflective observation, Amanda is very comfortable with service-learning. She likes the practical service experience and enjoys the opportunities to reflect on her experiences. She also has many ideas about different methods of providing service and about ways in which agencies might be more effectively organized in working with service acquirers. Amanda, however, has difficulty in trying to apply some of the principles she is learning in her Contemporary Social Issues course to her service experiences. George, on the other hand, has strengths and challenges as a Converger opposite those of Amanda. He is very interested in trying to apply the principles and theories to his service-learning experiences. When service-learning educators observe him at his service experience, they note that he focuses primarily on activities that provide indirect service and prefers to work with some of the administrative systems rather than directly with people.

Theories of Psychosocial Development

Psychosocial development focuses on the issues and preoccupations relating to college students' development. Psychosocial development theories portray a specific developmental progression that results from the interaction of the individual with his or her environment. Most theorists describe the pattern with which developmental issues emerge as typical but not invariant. The relatively successful or unsuccessful resolution of previous psychosocial issues provides the building blocks for the negotiation of future developmental issues.

Psychosocial theories are based on the work of Erik Erikson's (1980) theory of human development over the life span. Here we examine Arthur Chickering's model of psychosocial development (Chickering, 1969; Chickering and Reisser, 1993) because it is the most comprehensive and most current of the perspectives on the psychosocial development of college students. His vectors, an expansion of the stage of identity versus role diffusion in Erikson's theory of development over the life span, have also been applied to work with adult students (Schlossberg, Lynch, and Chickering, 1989). In addition to offering a useful framework for understanding the development of students while in college, Chickering and Reisser propose key elements of a collegiate environment that foster student development, some of them especially relevant to service-learning. (For information on other models and theories that address the psychosocial development of college students, refer to Knefelkamp, Widick, and Parker 1978a; Moore, 1990; Rodgers, 1990; Chickering and Reisser 1993; and Evans, 1996.)

Chickering, through his research in the 1960s on students at thirteen small colleges in the Northeast and the subsequent modifications of his theory with Linda Reisser, describes college student development through seven vectors (a term implying both magnitude and direction):

Vector 1: Developing competence: Encompassing intellectual competence, physical and manual skills, interpersonal competence, and an overall sense of competence.

Vector 2: Managing emotions: Developing an increasing awareness of both positive and more difficult emotions and learning how to handle and integrate these emotions in appropriate ways.

Vector 3: Moving through autonomy toward interdependence: Developing emotional and instrumental independence, which lead to a recognition and acceptance of interdependence.

Vector 4: Developing mature interpersonal relationships: Developing tolerance and appreciation of differences and a capacity for true and healthy intimacy.

Vector 5: Establishing identity: Developing a solid and comprehensive sense of one's own being.

Vector 6: Developing purpose: Clarifying goals and making plans in regard to one's vocation, avocational interests, and lifestyle.

Vector 7: Developing integrity: Clarifying a personally valid set of beliefs that have some internal consistency and that provide at least a tentative guide for behavior (Chickering and Reisser, 1993, pp. 43–52).

According to Chickering and Reisser (1993), the first four vectors are prominent in the earlier part of a student's college career. These four vectors must be minimally resolved to serve as a foundation for the development of a student's identity, vector 5, which is a foundation for the remaining two vectors. Further, all of these issues may occur throughout a student's college career, and many may recur throughout the life span. What is reflected in Chickering and Reisser's model, however, is the prominence of certain vectors at certain points in a student's development.

Chickering's vectors are important to service-learning in that educators should be aware of the kinds of psychosocial issues students may be facing as they engage in service-learning. A first- or second-year student, for example, may be struggling with issues of competence or a sense of confidence, or perhaps with becoming less dependent on others. George, as an example, is trying to become more comfortable and skilled in working with other people; his joining a fraternity and living in the fraternity house is one way that he is focusing on his interpersonal development. He also is very dependent on his siblings, who still live at home, so his challenges as a first-year student are to become less dependent and more autonomous and interdependent.

A senior student, on the other hand, may be facing prominent issues of life purpose or congruency within his or her life. Psychosocial issues prominent with Janice may be developing purpose and developing integrity. She is putting much energy into considering and applying to colleges of veterinary medicine and attempting to integrate her career goal with a college that will support a veterinary internship in an economically depressed location. Her involvement in service-learning and the quality of her reflections about service may relate to whether these prominent psychosocial issues complement or conflict with her service-learning experiences. Service-learning, depending on how it is designed, may facilitate development in one or more vectors, but which vectors are facilitated is likely a function of the interaction of the experience with the issues a student is facing developmentally.

Chickering and Reisser (1993) also identify seven key influences on student development: institutional objectives, institutional size, student-faculty relationships, curriculum, teaching, friendships and student communities, and student development programs and services. Of these, the influences that follow seem most relevant to service-learning. According to Chickering and Reisser (1993), development is fostered when the following conditions exist:

1. "(Impact increases as) institutional objectives are clear and taken seriously and as the diverse elements of the institution and its programs are internally consistent in the service of the objectives" (p. 266).

2. "When student-faculty interaction is frequent and friendly and when it occurs in diverse situations calling for varied roles and relationships" (p. 269).
3. "An educationally powerful curriculum" exists (p. 270).
4. "When teaching calls for active learning, encourages student-faculty contact and cooperation among students, gives prompt feedback, emphasizes time on task and high expectations, and respects diverse talents and ways of knowing" (p. 272).

These influences suggest that the effectiveness of service-learning is affected by the institution's support (or lack thereof) of it, as well as by the nature of the contact and interactions among students, faculty, and community service providers. Chickering and Reisser's work also encourages faculty to strive constantly for an "educationally powerful curriculum" and supports service-learning as a significant means of creating opportunities for active learning. Two of the influences serve as reminders of the importance of respecting diverse learning styles and providing a variety of situations for student learning and development.

Dimensions of Identity Development

An emerging set of perspectives about identity development concerns those particular characteristics that are critical for individuals personally as well as within social environments. For instance, how an individual views and understands his or her own race, not the essential nature of race, represents an important part of that person's identity. Racial identity is the primary emphasis of this section because of its salience in U.S. society and the availability of theories about the development of individual attitudes and perspectives about one's racial self. Identity dimensions of social class, sexual orientation, and ability and disability are also addressed.

People have multiple identities. Although individuals may view their identities in isolated and separate ways, it is the intersection of these identities that defines the uniqueness of each individual. Identity development serves as one of the major filters through which students experience service-learning. In other words, how students view themselves in regard to their own race and their social class, for instance, becomes the lens through which they interact with both community members and peers in the service setting. Students' identity development also provides one of the structures through which they think about course material, reflect on their service experience, and make the connections between community service and class readings and discussions.

To the degree that any of these identity dimensions is relevant in the service-learning experience, particularly race and social class, how one thinks about one's self in regard to the particular identity dimension is likely to shape the service-learning experience. For instance, how salient race is to Amanda, to Janice, and to George may affect what kind of community service experience they select and how they function in that setting. Or the degree to which Amanda, George, or Janice has considered his or her social class will be a factor in how he or she reflects on work in the community service setting. Students' identities related to the particular characteristics they hold (race, gender, and so on) are externally defined by society and also internally developed. Thus the specific experiences students have in their community service settings may both trigger and be affected by their development in these identity dimensions. (For a more comprehensive discussion of identity development, see McEwen, 1996.)

Racial Identity Development

Racial identity "refers to a sense of group or collective identity based on one's perception that he or she shares a common racial heritage with a particular racial group" (Helms, 1990a, p. 3). Although racial identity development has generally been conceived as relevant to persons of color—individuals of Asian, African, Latino, and American Indian descent—it is also necessary to consider the racial identity of white persons as well as the racial identity of persons of mixed or "blended" races. Each of us has a race, to paraphrase Janet Helms (1992); thus, a part of each person's identity is the development of his or her racial identity.

White Racial Identity Development The racial identity of white persons in the United States has historically been ignored, essentially because, as the dominant racial group in the United States, white people have not had to face or name their own race and the various characteristics, attributes, and privileges associated with being white.

Helms (1990b, 1992) provides the most extensive theoretical and research work on white racial identity. Central to the construct of white racial identity is racism, its presence in the United States, and white people's role in perpetuating racism. According to Helms (1990b, 1992), it is impossible to develop a healthy white identity without acknowledging, understanding, and working to rid oneself of deep and internalized racism. Helms (1990b, 1992) posits a six-status model of white racial identity development, with two phases.

Phase 1 is *abandoning a racist identity*. In the Contact status, one is cognitively aware, for the first time, of the actuality of black people and other persons of color. As the white person becomes aware of how persons of color in the United States are treated, the person may enter the next status, Disintegration. Now this person faces the moral dilemmas of being white: the conflicts between seeing the racism experienced by persons of color and wanting to believe that racism is not the fault of whites. A desire to reduce the discomfort in this status and to be accepted by other white persons characterizes the transition into Reintegration. Here a white person begins to see herself or himself as white and believes that race-related inequities are the fault of persons of color and are the earned rights of whites. According to Helms (1990b), it is easy for many whites to hold Reintegration attitudes. In the transition to the next phase and status, through a "personally jarring event," the white person "begins to question her or his previous definition of Whiteness and the justifiability of racism in any of its forms" (Helms, 1990b, p. 61).

Phase 2 is *developing a nonracist white identity*. In Pseudo-Independence, a white person increasingly questions the assumption that persons of color are inferior, acknowledges responsibility of whites for racism, and becomes aware of the privileges of being white, but behaviorally works to make persons of color more like whites. This status represents an intellectualization of being white and often describes the "white liberal." If personal rewards are great enough to encourage one to continue to pursue a positive white identity, then a white person may move to the Immersion/Emersion status and seek to understand what it means to be white in the United States. The person turns to other whites, to autobiographical and biographical accounts of being white, and to self-reflection about being white. The focus is on changing white people rather than on changing others. With increased security in one's white identity, one may move to the Autonomy status, which represents a racially transcendent worldview. In Autonomy, a white person has internalized a positive, nonracist white identity and continually seeks to acknowledge and abolish racial oppression. This process is ongoing and is never completed.

Helms's (1990b, 1992) model is especially useful in looking at oneself as a white person, as well as at other white persons, to understand what racial attitudes one holds and thus how one is viewing and acting on racial matters and racial interactions, and in considering how a traditionally white institution of higher education or a predominantly white environment may be perceiving and handling racial issues. Helms's model also provides a blueprint for how white persons can help themselves to develop as healthy racial beings and about how educators can assist white students in developing healthy racial attitudes and behaviors.

Consider Janice, the senior biology major, who, as a white woman growing up in a rural area in the Midwest, attended public schools with a few students of color but never truly confronted the presence of persons of color until she came to college. Through her classes and other campus activities, she observed some of the different ways in which students of color were treated and their relative lack of presence in certain campus roles. After making a number of these observations, she raised some questions about racial inequities with members in her Bible study groups. One day she even discussed the issue with her academic adviser. Yet, after each attempt to discuss racial issues Janice felt alienated from her white friends and even from her adviser, because neither her white friends nor her adviser conveyed to her that they understood her concern about the inequities she had been observing. Observing inequities not usually observed by other white people becomes very uncomfortable for a white person with Disintegration attitudes. However, as Janice looked more closely at racial issues on campus, and listened to comments from her friends and adviser, she realized that perhaps her friends' and adviser's attitudes were right and the attitudes she had been holding were wrong. It became apparent to her that students of color should work harder and participate in the activities open to them. Thus far, Janice has experienced the Contact status, then Disintegration, and then Reintegration.

When Janice learns through reading and lectures in the Contemporary Social Issues course what racism really is, observes social racism through her community service work, and then has the opportunity to reflect on and discuss her observations in the weekly group meeting with her teaching assistant, she begins to see herself as white and develops an intellectualized understanding of racism. She talks with members of her two Bible study groups about inviting some black, Asian, and Latino students to join them. Janice wants to change her community service involvement from the soup kitchen to a day-care center in the African American community. Yet, with all her energy and genuineness she has little awareness of changing herself and other white people. This is characteristic of Pseudo-Independence.

Minority Identity Development Racial identity development for persons of color has received increasing attention in the literature over the past twenty-five years. This chapter focuses on the minority identity development (MID) model of Atkinson, Morten, and Sue (1993) with its broad applicability to persons of color. Because all racial-ethnic groups comprising persons of color are subjected to various kinds and forms of discrimination and racism, Atkinson, Morten, and Sue believe that these groups share a common experience in regard to their racial and ethnic identity development. (The term *minority* is used here to represent persons of color in the context of the MID model. It is used cautiously and with some misgivings, as *minority* often implies "less than" or "not equal to"; such is not the intent here. Also, in some parts of the United States, persons of color are not a numerical minority but rather the majority.)

The MID model comprises five stages. The developmental process evolves from an implicit acceptance of the socially prescribed status as part of an oppressed group (Conformity) to a questioning of one's beliefs about one's self as a "minority" person (Dissonance). Developmentally the individual then rejects dominant society and moves toward an acceptance of and immersion in one's own racial or ethnic group (Resistance and Immersion). In the fourth stage, an individual begins to evaluate the strengths and the weaknesses of his or her own group, of other oppressed groups, and of the dominant group (Introspection). In stage 5 (Synergistic), one experiences a sense of pride and identification with one's own culture and a strong sense of individual self-worth. The person also has deeper understanding and a greater sense of support of other oppressed groups and an openness to constructive aspects and persons of the dominant group. Although each stage is distinct and qualitatively different, Atkinson, Morten, and Sue suggest that "the MID is more accurately conceptualized as a continuous process in which one stage blends with another and boundaries between stages are not clear" (1993, p. 28).

The MID model is appropriate to apply to both Amanda and George. Amanda, in the sociology course, requests a community service assignment in an African American community. George, however, indicates he would like to do something with just "regular" people, like persons who are disabled or in job training programs. His instructor has encouraged him, as an Asian American, to work with Laotian immigrants who are learning the English language. This assignment does not quite fit with what George had in mind, but he agrees to do it. George appears to have accepted the socially prescribed status quo, in which it is expected that he will want to work with other Asians (although he is Chinese and they are Laotian). He does not challenge the way in which he was channeled into what might be a stereotypical service activity, yet he also expressed no preference for working with Asian Americans. George is probably at Conformity (stage 1), especially since there is no evidence of engagement with other Chinese Americans or with others of Asian descent and George does not seem to resist the assignment.

Everything Amanda does seems to be with other African Americans—her church, her community service, her friends, her involvement in the Black Student Union. For the class, Amanda indeed takes on a project in an African American community involving parent education. By the end of the semester, however, she begins expressing concern about issues with AIDS (from her work with mothers who are HIV positive) and with some of the Latino women who also came to the parent education classes. These brief examples suggest that Amanda may have been initially in Resistance and Immersion (stage 3), but by the end of the semester may have been moving into Introspection (stage 4).

Social Class

Social class is an important element of identity that interacts with other dimensions of identity, such as race, ethnicity, and gender. Bonnie Thornton Dill (1994) points out that much of the literature about race and gender tends to omit consideration of social class, just as the class and gender literature tends to ignore race.

Donna Langston (1995) addresses the myth of the classless society—that one can pull oneself up by one's bootstraps, that "ambition and intelligence alone are responsible for success"—and discusses the effects of power in relation to social class (p. 101). Social class involves economic security, choices perceived and those available, and cultural background, including education, language, and behavior (Langston, 1995). The chain or cycle of maintaining the social classes is described by Langston, as follows:

> [The myth] perpetuates the false hope among the working-class and poor that they can have different opportunities in life. The hope that they can escape the fate that awaits them due to the class position that they were born into. Another way the rags-to-riches myth is perpetuated is by creating enough visible tokens so that oppressed persons believe that they, too, can get ahead. The creation of hope through tokenism keeps a hierarchical structure in place and lays the blame for not succeeding on those who don't. This keeps us from resisting and changing the class-based system. Instead, we accept it as inevitable. . . . The myth also keeps the middle class and upper class entrenched in the privileges awarded in a class-based system. It reinforces middle- and upper-class beliefs in their own superiority [1995, p. 101].

In service-learning, issues of social class apply to both the students themselves and their interactions with others. Students' understanding and identity about their own social class may influence the way they conceptualize service and their manner and style of interacting with others, especially when social class issues are salient. Social class for students is evidenced in how they think about economic security, the choices they perceive for themselves and others and the choices available, and some of the components of their cultural background, such as education, language, and behavior (Langston, 1995). (Although there are no developmental models about social class, two excellent sources for further reading about social class are Rubin, 1976, and Weis and Fine, 1993.)

Using Amanda, Janice, and George as examples helps to illustrate how social class may interact with service-learning experience. Suppose that both Amanda and Janice are from socioeconomically middle-class families and that George is from a lower-middle-class family. In their community service settings, Janice and Amanda work with community members who have fewer material advantages. How aware they are of being part of the middle class and their own privileges will affect how they comprehend social issues and interact with community members of a different social class from themselves. Although George's family has struggled economically, George may have difficulty understanding both the cultural and social class challenges of the Laotian immigrants without reflecting on his own social class and that of others.

Sexual Orientation

The developmental literature on sexual identity focuses on how people come to terms with their own sexual orientation, particularly that of being gay or lesbian (Levine and Evans, 1991). Many models of sexual identity development describe sequential and chronological stages or positions that evolve from a period of questioning and confusion about one's sexual identity to certainty and pride as a lesbian or gay man. There is some literature on development of a bisexual identity, in which bisexuality represents a unique identity, not an identity representing sexual confusion or ambiguity. There are no models of heterosexual identity development in the literature.

Service-learning activities, such as work with persons with HIV-AIDS, are likely to trigger social, political, or personal issues of sexual orientation with students. These issues may challenge students to reflect on their own sexual orientation and their attitudes about it. This may be especially painful and difficult for students questioning or struggling with their own sexuality and for those with highly homophobic attitudes. (For further discussions about sexual orientation, refer to Evans and Wall, 1991; Fassinger, 1991; Atkinson and Hackett, 1995; and McEwen, 1996.)

Ability and Disability

Focusing on issues of ability and disability should serve as a reminder that all persons have different physical and mental abilities. According to Atkinson and Hackett (1995), "We all have varying levels of mental and physical ability given the environmental conditions in which we happen to be (in the case of a blind and a sighted person in an unlighted room, being sightless may actually be an asset)" (p. 8).

A guide for college and university faculty and staff (President's Commission on Disability Issues, 1990) describes three kinds of disabilities: visible disabilities (easily recognizable physical impairments), hidden disabilities (learning disabilities, hearing impairment, and psychiatric or seizure disorders, for example), and multiple disabilities. Disabilities may be congenital, such as blindness, the absence of an arm, a seizure disorder, or a learning disability; or they may be acquired, for example, AIDS, multiple sclerosis, or paralysis or deafness resulting from an accident. For acquired disabilities, the age of onset is an important dimension of how the person views and is affected by the disability.

Abilities and disabilities should be understood as socially constructed experiences (Harris and Wideman, 1988; Jones, in press; Scheer, 1994). "A disability has a social meaning and it is that indisputable fact that constitutes the major difficulty" (Harris and Wideman, 1988, p. 116) for persons with disabilities. Jones (in press) suggests that "understanding disability as socially constructed is to celebrate the uniqueness of individual difference while directing one's attention toward social change and transformation of oppressive structures. It is to distinguish between the biological fact of disability and the handicapping social environment in which the person with disabilities exists."

Through service-learning, students frequently encounter persons who view themselves as having disabilities or individuals whom *students believe* have disabilities. There are two interrelated implications. First, it is important to learn how an individual understands and conceptualizes his or her disability, in contrast to relying on the ways in which the particular disability has been socially constructed in society. Second, one should understand oneself in terms of how one views disability. Harlan Hahn's research (cited by Asch and Fine, 1988) indicates that disabilities in another "often elicit . . . powerful existential anxieties" (p. 17) about ourselves— our own helplessness, our needs, and our dependencies. In working with an individual with a disability, one may act on one's own insecurities and needs rather than on those of the other person.

One of the persons with whom Janice works in the soup kitchen lost an arm at an early age in an accident. Janice behaves in a patronizing way toward this man and frequently offers to help him do his work; yet Janice's on-site supervisor told her that this individual volunteers there frequently and is one of the soup kitchen's most consistent and effective workers. When Janice expressed to her coworker how terrible she felt that he had no arm, he replied that he had learned to deal with this disability very comfortably and does not need or want Janice to feel sorry for him. Later, when the supervisor speaks with Janice, she learns that Janice is preoccupied with how such a potential loss of one of her own limbs might affect her in her veterinary practice. In other words, Janice's response to her coworker seems to relate more to her own concerns than to how he views his own disability. (Sources for further information about disabilities and identity development are Atkinson and Hackett, 1995, and Fine and Asch, 1988.)

The scenarios involving Amanda, Janice, and George illustrate how identity development is a student's perspective about self that he or she brings to bear on many components of the service-learning experience. They also offer numerous examples of how service-learning educators can use their knowledge about identity development to work with students in selecting service sites, minimizing students' potential to "do harm" in the service setting or to reinforce stereotypes, and tailoring reflection to facilitate a particular facet of identity development.

Career Choice

The social-learning approach to career decision making (Krumboltz, Mitchell, and Jones, 1976) suggests that four kinds of factors influence career decision making: genetic endowment and special abilities, environmental conditions and events, learning experiences, and task approach skills. The last two relate directly to potential outcomes of service-learning. In service-learning, students are likely to have many opportunities to engage directly in a variety of learning experiences, to receive feedback from others, and to have many cognitive and affective responses to the set of experiences. Students also have opportunities to observe others in the setting—peers, other volunteers, agency staff, and community members, as well as faculty members and college or university administrators. In addition, students can test out and reflect on task approach skills that they bring to the service-learning experience, including "performance standards and values, work habits, perceptual and cognitive process, . . . mental sets, and emotional responses" (Krumboltz, Mitchell, and Jones, 1976, p. 73).

The following examples of Janice and George show how their involvement in service-learning and their career development are intertwined. Janice views her Contemporary Social Issues course and its service-learning component as directly linked to her career goals to work as a veterinarian in an economically depressed area. She believes that it is important to understand issues related to social class and to have a deep involvement in the community in order to be responsive to her future clients. As a first-year student, George has given little thought to his career, except that he realizes he is not well suited to scientific and technological fields. The service-learning experience enables him to receive direct feedback about his interpersonal skills and his potential for work in a social-service setting. He has had little work experience, so the expectations of the community service agency, together with structured reflection, permit him to develop appropriate work habits, attitudes, and values.

There are a number of theories and models of the process of career development and how people make career choices. Osipow (1983) describes five kinds of career theories: (1) *trait-factor theories,* which involve a direct matching of an individual's abilities and interests with those required for various vocations and careers; (2) *vocational choice and personality theories,* in which a variety of "particular personality factors [are] involved in career choice and career satisfaction" (p. 10); (3) *accidental theory of career choice,* in which "societal circumstances beyond the control of the individual contribute significantly to career choices" (p. 10); (4) *developmental theories,* or *self-theories,* which portray the process by which individuals seek to implement their beings in their career choices; and (5) *behavioral theories,* in which career choices are a complex function of the individual and his or her environmental experiences. These theories may be of interest to service-learning educators, particularly in working with colleagues in career development to create opportunities for students to relate their service-learning experiences to their career choices. Chapter Nine offers specific examples of such opportunities. (Two good sources for additional information on theories of career development are Brown, Brooks, and Associates, 1990 and Osipow, 1983.)

Conclusion

Service-learning is an educationally and socially powerful intervention that holds great potential for enhancing the learning and development of college students. Knowledge about students' learning and development provides an important and valuable foundation for the intentional design of service-learning experiences.

Students are at different levels in a variety of spheres of development: cognitive, moral, and spiritual development; psychosocial development; identity development; and career development. All of these aspects, but especially cognitive development, affect how students conceptualize course material, reflect on their community service, and make connections among the formal classroom experience, their community service, and their own lives. Further, prominent developmental issues or current preoccupations (psychosocial and identity development) in the lives of students serve as powerful filters that influence how they experience service-learning and interact with those they encounter. These developmental issues may or may not vary depending on whether a student is toward the beginning or the latter part of undergraduate work.

In addition, students have different ways of knowing and different learning styles. Implications of learning style for service-learning include the reality that some service experiences will be a better fit for students with particular learning styles than for other students. Similarly, students with certain learning styles will enjoy reflection, while others will find it more difficult. Service-learning presents opportunities for educators to challenge students to use and to develop their nonpreferred ways of knowing.

Students develop through a balance of challenge and support. Examining this balance in a service-learning experience may be helpful in working with students who seem to struggle. Service-learning may be more developmentally challenging for some students, who will require additional supports. On the other hand, those who have more service-learning experience may need more challenge or less support for development to occur.

Service-learning can have a variety of anticipated learning and developmental outcomes. In the area of learning and cognitive development, students who engage in service-learning may develop greater complexity in their thinking; ethical commitments regarding themselves, their lifestyles, and what they know and believe; movement toward higher levels of moral reasoning; and development and clarity about their faith and spirituality. Potential outcomes related to psychosocial and identity development include greater competence and sense of competence; increased awareness and integration of their emotions; more autonomy and interdependence; greater awareness of themselves as a racial being and of their own racial, ethnic, and cultural heritage; greater sense of their place in U.S. and global society; increased tolerance and empathy; greater clarity about themselves and their life purposes; and development and maturity of their values.

These potential outcomes of service-learning suggest several implications for course and program design. Service-learning educators should consider and be intentional in identifying desired student learning and development outcomes, and then design the course or program so that it promotes specific goals and identified outcomes. Finally, in designing service-learning experiences, educators should draw on relevant theoretical perspectives about the development of college students from the cognitive, psychosocial, identity, and career development domains.

References

Asch, A., and Fine, M. "Introduction: Beyond Pedestals." In M. Fine and A. Asch (eds.), *Women with Disabilities: Essays in Psychology, Culture, and Politics*. Philadelphia: Temple University Press, 1988.

Atkinson, D. R., and Hackett, G. *Counseling Diverse Populations.* Dubuque, Iowa: W. C. Brown and Benchmark, 1995.

Atkinson, D. R., Morten, G., and Sue, D. W. *Counseling American Minorities: A Cross-Cultural Perspective.* (4th ed.) Dubuque, Iowa: W. C. Brown and Benchmark, 1993.

Baxter Magolda, M. B. *Knowing and Reasoning in College: Gender-Related Patterns in Students' Intellectual Development.* San Francisco: Jossey-Bass, 1992.

Belenky, M., Clinchy, B., Goldberger, N., and Tarule, J. *Women's Ways of Knowing.* New York: Basic Books, 1986.

Brown, D., Brooks, L., and Associates. *Career Choice and Development: Applying Contemporary Theories to Practice.* (2nd ed.) San Francisco: Jossey-Bass, 1990.

Chickering, A. W. *Education and Identity.* San Francisco: Jossey-Bass, 1969.

Chickering, A. W., and Reisser, L. *Education and Identity.* (2nd ed.) San Francisco: Jossey-Bass, 1993.

Cornfeld, J. L., and Knefelkamp, L. L. "Combining Student Stage and Type in the Design of Learning Environments: An Integration of Perry Stages and Holland Typologies." Paper presented at the American College Personnel Association Conference, Los Angeles, Mar. 1979.

Dill, B. T. "Race, Class, and Gender: Prospects for an All-Inclusive Sisterhood." In L. Stone (ed.), *The Education Feminism Reader.* New York: Routledge, 1994.

Erikson, E. H. *Identity and the Life Cycle.* New York: Norton, 1980. (Originally published 1959.)

Evans, N. J. "Student Development Theory." In S. R. Komives, D. B. Woodard, Jr., and Associates, *Student Services: A Handbook for the Profession.* (3rd ed.) San Francisco: Jossey-Bass, 1996.

Evans, N. J., and Wall, V. A. (eds.). *Beyond Tolerance: Gays, Lesbians and Bisexuals on Campus.* Washington, D.C.: American College Personnel Association, 1991.

Fassinger, R. E. "The Hidden Minority: Issues and Challenges in Working with Lesbian Women and Gay Men." *Counseling Psychologist,* 1991, *19,* 157–176.

Fine, M., and Asch, A. (eds.). *Women with Disabilities: Essays in Psychology, Culture, and Politics.* Philadelphia: Temple University Press, 1988.

Fowler, J. W. *Stages in Faith: The Psychology of Human Development and the Quest for Meaning.* San Francisco: Harper San Francisco, 1981.

Fowler, J. W. "Stages in Selfhood and Faith." In J. W. Fowler (ed.), *Faith Development and Pastoral Care.* Philadelphia: Fortress Press, 1987.

Gilligan, C. *In a Different Voice.* Cambridge, Mass.: Harvard University Press, 1982.

Harris, A., and Wideman, D. "The Construction of Gender and Disability in Early Attachment." In M. Fine and A. Asch (eds.), *Women with Disabilities: Essays in Psychology, Culture, and Politics.* Philadelphia: Temple University Press, 1988.

Helms, J. E. "Introduction: Review of Racial Identity Terminology." In J. E. Helms (ed.), *Black and White Racial Identity: Theory, Research, and Practice.* Westport, Conn.: Greenwood Press, 1990a.

Helms, J. E. "Toward a Model of White Racial Identity Development." In J. E. Helms (ed.), *Black and White Racial Identity: Theory, Research, and Practice.* Westport, Conn.: Greenwood Press, 1990b.

Helms, J. E. *A Race Is a Nice Thing to Have: A Guide to Being a White Person, or Understanding the White Persons in Your Life.* Topeka, Kans.: Content Communications, 1992.

Jones, S. R. "Toward Inclusive Theory: Disability as Social Construction." *NASPA Journal,* in press.

King, P. M. "William Perry's Theory of Intellectual and Ethical Development." In L. Knefelkamp, C. Widick, and C. A. Parker (eds.), *Applying New Developmental Findings.* New Directions for Student Services, no. 4. San Francisco: Jossey-Bass, 1978.

Knefelkamp, L. "Developmental Instruction: Fostering Intellectual and Personal Growth of College Students." Unpublished doctoral dissertation, University of Minnesota, 1974.

Knefelkamp, L., Widick, C., and Parker, C. A. (eds.). *Applying New Developmental Findings.* New Directions for Student Services, no. 4. San Francisco: Jossey-Bass, 1978a.

Knefelkamp, L., Widick, C., and Parker, C. A. "Editors' Notes: Why Bother with Theory?" In. L. Knefelkamp, C. Widick, and C. A. Parker (eds.), *Applying New Developmental Findings.* New Directions for Student Services, no. 4. San Francisco: Jossey-Bass, 1978b.

Kohlberg, L. "The Cognitive-Developmental Approach to Moral Education." *Phi Delta Kappan,* 1975, *56,* 670–677.

Kolb, D. A. "Learning Styles and Disciplinary Differences." In A. W. Chickering and Associates, *The Modern American College.* San Francisco: Jossey-Bass, 1981.

Kolb, D. A. *Experiential Learning.* Englewood Cliffs, N.J.: Prentice Hall, 1984.

Kolb, D. A. *Learning Style Inventory: Self-Scoring Inventory and Interpretation Booklet.* Boston: McBer, 1985.

Krumboltz, J. D., Mitchell, A. M., and Jones, G. B. "A Social Learning Theory of Career Selection." *Counseling Psychologist,* 1976, *6*(1), 71–81.

Langston, D. "Tired of Playing Monopoly?" In M. L. Andersen and P. H. Collins (eds.), *Race, Class, and Gender: An Anthology.* Belmont, Calif.: Wadsworth, 1995.

Levine, H., and Evans, N. J. "The Development of Gay, Lesbian, and Bisexual Identities." In N. J. Evans and V. A. Wall (eds.), *Beyond Tolerance: Gays, Lesbians and Bisexuals on Campus.* Washington, D.C.: American College Personnel Association, 1991.

McEwen, M. K. "New Perspectives on Identity Development." In S. R. Komives, D. B. Woodard, Jr., and Associates, *Student Services: A Handbook for the Profession.* (3rd ed.) San Francisco: Jossey-Bass, 1996.

Moore, L. V. (ed.). *Evolving Theoretical Perspectives on Students.* New Directions for Student Services, no. 51. San Francisco: Jossey-Bass, 1990.

Osipow, S. H. *Theories of Career Development.* (3rd ed.) Englewood Cliffs, N.J.: Prentice Hall, 1983.

Parks, S. *The Critical Years: The Young Adult Search for a Faith to Live By.* New York: HarperCollins, 1986.

Perry, W. G., Jr. *Forms of Intellectual and Ethical Development in the College Years: A Scheme.* Austin, Tex.: Holt, Rinehart and Winston, 1970.

Perry, W. G., Jr. "Sharing in the Costs of Growth." In C. A. Parker (ed.), *Encouraging Development in College Students.* Minneapolis: University of Minnesota Press, 1978.

Perry, W. G., Jr. "Cognitive and Ethical Growth: The Making of Meaning." In A. W. Chickering and Associates, *The Modern American College.* San Francisco: Jossey-Bass, 1981.

President's Commission on Disability Issues. *Reasonable Accommodations: Teaching College Students with Disabilities.* College Park: University of Maryland at College Park, 1990.

Rodgers, R. F. "Recent Theories and Research Underlying Student Development." In D. G. Creamer and Associates, *College Student Development: Theory and Practice for the 1990s.* Washington, D.C.: American College Personnel Association, 1990.

Rubin, L. B. *Worlds of Pain: Life in the Working-Class Family.* New York: Basic Books, 1976.

Rutledge, M. "Faith Development: Bridging Theory and Practice." In J. Butler (ed.), *Religion on Campus.* New Directions for Student Services, no. 46. San Francisco: Jossey-Bass, 1989.

Sanford, N. "Developmental Status of the Entering Freshman." In N. Sanford (ed.), *The American College.* New York: Wiley, 1962.

Sanford, N. *Where Colleges Fail: A Study of the Student as a Person.* San Francisco: Jossey-Bass, 1967.

Scheer, J. "Culture and Disability: An Anthropological Point of View." In E. J. Trickett, R. J. Watts, and D. Birman (eds.), *Human Diversity: Perspectives on People in Context.* San Francisco: Jossey-Bass, 1994.

Schlossberg, N. K., Lynch, A. Q., and Chickering, A. W. *Improving Higher Education Environments for Adults: Responsive Programs and Services from Entry to Departure.* San Francisco: Jossey-Bass, 1989.

Stewart, G. M. "Learning Styles as a Filter for Developing Service-Learning Interventions." In C. I. Delve, S. D. Mintz, and G. M. Stewart (eds.), *Community Service as Values Education.* New Directions for Student Services, no. 50. San Francisco: Jossey-Bass, 1990.

Swezey, E. D. "Grounded in Justice: Service Learning from a Faith Perspective." In C. I. Delve, S. D. Mintz, and G. M. Stewart (eds.), *Community Service as Values Education.* New Directions for Student Services, no. 50. San Francisco: Jossey-Bass, 1990.

Wadsworth, B. J. *Piaget's Theory of Cognitive Development.* New York: McKay, 1971.

Weis, L., and Fine, M. (eds.). *Beyond Silenced Voices: Class, Race, and Gender in United States Schools.* Albany: State University of New York Press, 1993.

Widick, C. "An Evaluation of Developmental Instruction in a University Setting." Unpublished doctoral dissertation, University of Minnesota, 1975.

Worthington, E. L. "Religious Faith Across the Lifespan: Implications for Counseling and Research." *Counseling Psychologist,* 1989, *17,* 555–612.

Chapter Four

Developing Campus-Community Relationships

Catherine R. Gugerty, Erin D. Swezey

In a recent essay, Henry Cisneros, secretary of housing and urban development, asserted that "institutions of higher learning . . . bring formidable intellectual and economic resources to their communities. It is encouraging to report that many institutions are . . . tearing down the wall that separates campus from community, and devoting intellectual and other resources to community building. . . . [Colleges and universities] are deciding that they prefer to live together with their community rather than live apart from it" (Cisneros, 1995, p. 10). As the service-learning movement has matured in the past decade, many institutions of higher education have become active members of their local communities in a variety of ways, with both sharing their human, educational, technical, and fiscal resources. For better or for worse, social issues of crime, violence, inadequate housing, and an underprepared labor pool have compelled several colleges and universities to step down from the ivory tower and become involved in their communities for their own self-interest. In other instances, community members or leaders have reached out to institutions for help in dealing with community problems. In still others, service-learning educators have sought out relationships with the communities surrounding their campuses as rich learning environments for students, as well as opportunities to contribute to community development.

In their enthusiasm to promote student learning and development through service, however, colleges and universities all too often thrust students into the community without adequate planning or community development. Some educators have developed service-learning programs in a vacuum without even consulting the members, organizers, and leaders of the community, yet strong and sustained community involvement by service-learning educators is essential to achieve the reciprocity that is fundamental to service-learning. Collaboration and the ultimate focus on community empowerment are also required for the long-term success of campus-community relationships.

There are basically two levels of campus-community collaboration. The more prevalent is a partnership between a community-based organization and a campus department or office. The other is an institution-wide commitment to collaborate and work with a community (Kupiec, 1993). This chapter examines foundations, approaches, and strategies that underlie both of these types of campus-community relationships.

Getting Started

It is incumbent on each college and university to learn about the community in which it resides or with which it intends to develop a relationship. This involves learning about the history and unique contributions of the particular neighborhood or community. It also entails understanding the rich traditions and values of its various ethnic, racial, and class cultures and how they influence the community. Gathering information about community resources from the community members themselves as well as from the community's formal and informal leaders and from community agency staff, assists service-learning educators in gaining an accurate picture as they enter into community territory.

A good place to begin is with basic facts about a community. Census data, obtained from the library, provide information on racial and ethnic composition, income, educational levels, family status, and stability of residency. This information can be compiled for the development of a neighborhood profile sheet. The library is also likely to maintain a file of newspaper clippings and magazine articles on the community, which may offer historical background, highlight issues the community is or has been dealing with, and identify the gifts, strengths, and talents of the people in the community. Information on a particular community or neighborhood may also be available in city, county, or state government offices. Depending on the history and activities of a particular neighborhood or community, a great deal of material may be available.

Although much information can be gleaned from reading, there is no substitute for oral tradition. Most communities have at least a few long-time residents who can describe colorfully what the neighborhood used to be like, why and how it has changed, how they see things now, and what they predict will happen in the future. Such individuals can be found around the neighborhood and at community meetings. It is worth tracking them down, as well as attending meetings of community and neighborhood associations. Putting themselves in the position of learner, with community members as the experts and teachers, is a significant role reversal for most college and university personnel.

The real history and sense of a community may best be obtained by simply being present in the area. Getting involved in a community activity is one way for college or university service-learning educators and other key players to meet community members informally. In order to prevent making avoidable mistakes, service-learning coordinators need to learn from community members and leaders what has been tried, what has failed, and what needs to be tried or tried again.

Finally, in a reciprocal relationship, the college or university should provide opportunities for community members and leaders to learn firsthand about the institution. Community members and leaders can be invited to an event of interest (a lecture, performance, or exhibit), followed by a reception; represent their constituencies on institutional boards and committees; serve as consultants for service-learning; be a guest lecturer; or cosponsor an educational event for members of both the campus and surrounding community.

Taking Care to "Do No Harm"

Gaining information about a community's history, demographics, culture, resources, and specific service programs is only part of the understanding required to work with the community in the context of service-learning. Each college or university must also go through a process of institutional self-examination of its own philosophy, mission, and approach to community involvement. It is essential that institutions not regard communities merely as teaching or research laboratories, an approach that assumes a false hierarchy of power and perpetuates an attitude of institutional superiority. Questions an institution should ask itself are: Is the purpose of community involvement merely one of institutional self-interest or one of community development and empowerment? Does the institution view itself as a part of the community in which it is located or apart from it? Do its leaders enthusiastically encourage or tacitly condone community involvement?

How an institution approaches or enters into a community is crucial to the long-term success and sustainability of service-learning programs. Having inclusive representation throughout the process and being clear on goals, roles, responsibilities, and definitions builds trust and encourages lasting relationships. Committing the institution to continuous evaluation with the community fosters effective communication and successful accomplishment of mutually defined goals. The Wingspread *Principles of Good Practice for Combining Service and Learning* (Porter Honnet and Poulsen, 1989) provide some direction for authentic, reciprocal community involvement on the part of educational institutions. (The Wingspread principles, which have a program development thrust, are listed in Chapter Two.)

Many service-learning educators, in dialogue with community members, use the medical profession's ethical commitment to "do no harm" as their fundamental guiding principle. Although most institutions of higher education have the best intentions when they embark on service-learning programs, their lack of attention to power differentials and to ethnocentric values creates harm and distrust in many communities.

Educational institutions engaged in service-learning need to be cognizant of false hierarchies of power that perpetuate myths about educational institutions and communities (Mulling, 1995). One prevalent myth that has the potential to affect service-learning programs adversely is that there exist superior and deficient cultures. Belief in this myth can lead students and service-learning educators alike to discount the strengths and resources within the community. Consequently the community can become disempowered and develop a negative self-image as the result of institutional intervention. Students would likely leave the community with an attitude of superiority and a false sense of good fortune (Mulling, 1995).

A second myth posits a superiority of knowledge and expertise. It holds that the best knowledge comes from the most prestigious institutions of higher learning. It assumes that faculty know better how to solve local problems than teachers in underfunded schools, neighborhood association leaders, or those who live in communities dealing with violence and inadequate housing (Mulling, 1995).

According to the third myth, there exists a rigid hierarchy of wisdom, with faculty wiser than students and students possessing more wisdom than the community. In reality, members of particular communities are often in the best position to see their own capacities and needs, and the appropriate course of action is for those from the academy to listen to and learn from community members (Mulling, 1995).

Effective service-learning respects the dignity and self-worth of cultures and individuals, forms multiple partnerships with organizations in the community, and searches for common ground among all involved while gathering resources to be shared by all. Being committed to the principle of doing no harm demands of colleges and universities the understanding of power dynamics that maintain situations of oppression and injustice (wiger, 1995). Service-learning educators must ask: Who possesses the power, who wants power, and how is power used to preserve the status quo? Some community leaders claim that the academy cannot be an authentic partner because of the power dynamic but it can support community development by leveraging the necessary resources for communities to help themselves (wiger, 1995).

In taking care to do no harm, service-learning educators must be sensitive to different cultural frameworks and understand that the community may have definitions of power, leadership, success, service, and even community that differ from its own (wiger, 1995). For example, leadership in some communities is based not on positional status but on relationships and demonstrated wisdom. College and university personnel must seek out and respect community leaders and leadership structures rather than making potentially false and hurtful assumptions.

Institutions preparing to engage in service-learning must struggle with other important questions—for example, Who profits, in both terms of funding and prestige, from service-learning? And for predominantly white institutions, what is the effect of entering into communities of different racial or ethnic composition? Are we builders of a just community on our own campuses before we attempt to build this kind of community beyond our borders?

Working with the Community

In order to develop effective relationships with the community, colleges and universities must wrestle with the notion that educators and administrators must work with rather than do to or for communities and individuals. A key question to be considered is: Who is to be invited to the planning table with knowledge of the community and with vested interest in the proposed partnerships?

Compiling a list of community stakeholders is a starting point. Community members and leaders with whom relationships already exist should review this list and make suggestions. Campus Compact defines stakeholders as "people who will be needed to bring about change, people who will be affected by change and the people who will actively oppose change" (1994, p. 3). Community stakeholders can include members and leaders of neighborhood organizations, social service agencies, churches, schools, local government, and local foundations, as well as parents, teachers, clergy, block captains, librarians, and holders of community history and tradition.

The belief that both the institution and the community have something to contribute and something to gain from each other is a prerequisite to reciprocity. Both partners must believe that they have equal share in the service-learning process. A group that believes itself to be superior will communicate that attitude, consciously or unconsciously, throughout every aspect of the experience. Nothing will be accomplished, and the initial feelings of hope will turn to suspicion and distrust. More often than not, the intended recipients of the service are the ones who suffer the most when this attitude is held. For example, some students who serve at a meal program as their service-learning experience may be reluctant to participate and believe that they would not have to provide this service at all if those being served were employed. The meal guests undoubtedly will sense the students' superior attitude and feel demeaned, foreclosing any possibility of establishing reciprocity.

Communication is the key to the development of a reciprocal relationship. Service-learning educators and community representatives must openly discuss what each can offer the other. The gifts and strengths of each group must be clearly spelled out, and each must understand and articulate its part in the endeavor. Communication must occur often, both formally and informally. Each group must be willing to travel to the other's place of work so that each gains a sense of the nature of the other's work and work environment.

At their initial meeting, community and college or university stakeholders must determine collectively both the process and content of future meetings. Sharing leadership of the process and agenda develops trust and models partnership. Kupiec (1993, pp. 114–118) outlines important process points to consider with community leaders as initial meetings occur—for example, researching and getting to know the interests, history, traditions, leadership, and cultures of the community, as well as institutional self-examination of interests, motivations, and mission. In addition, Kupiec urges partners to discuss their own interests, needs, and purpose for working together. Together the partners should determine priorities and set an agenda, clarifying different "perceptions of time," such as academic calendar versus annual or political calendars (1993, p. 116). Finally, partners should develop together coordinating structures and procedures to determine regular communication, liaison roles, the creation of an advisory board, as well as various responsibilities to be performed. These structures, especially an advisory board, ensure ongoing planning, assessment, and evaluation of the partnership. (The formation and role of advisory groups are addressed in Chapters Ten, Eleven, and Thirteen.)

Defining Capacities, Needs, and Desired Outcomes

Most important to building trust and long-term relationships with the community is the specific agenda brought forth by service-learning educators and their institutions. All too often these agendas have focused on the community's problems, needs, and deficiencies. John Kretzmann and John McKnight (1993) observe that educational leaders and nonprofit service directors enter into a "needs" mapping process with communities, and "as a result, many lower income urban neighborhoods are now environments of service where behaviors are affected because residents come to believe that their well-being depends upon being a client" (p. 2). This deficiency model of community partnership does little to empower communities to help themselves, especially after the institutional presence is gone. Nor does it enable communities to leverage the necessary long-term resources to be managed within the community to solve problems rather than to be controlled from the outside.

Kretzmann and McKnight propose a different approach, which they call *asset-based community development*. They believe that effective community development efforts "are based upon an understanding or map, of the community's assets, capacities and abilities" (Kretzmann and McKnight, 1993, p. 5). The process entails discovering and detailing the gifts, abilities, and resources of each individual, household, association, and institution in the community. Part of the process is determining with the stakeholders how to harness these assets to address community needs and problems. In *Building Communities from the Inside Out,* Kretzmann and McKnight outline three interrelated characteristics of this approach to community development:

1. Obviously enough, the first principle that defines this process is "asset-based." That is, this community development strategy starts with what is present in the community, the capacities of its residents and workers, the associational and institutional base of the area—not with what is absent, or with what is problematic, or with what the community needs.
2. Because this community development process is asset-based, it is by necessity "internally focused." That is, this development strategy concentrates first of all upon the agenda building and problem-solving capacities of local residents, local associations, and local institutions. Again, this intense and self-conscious internal focus is not intended to minimize either the role external forces have played in helping to create the desperate

conditions of lower income neighborhoods, nor the need to attract additional resources to these communities. Rather this strong internal focus is intended simply to stress the primacy of local definition, investment, creativity, hope and control.

3. If a community development process is to be asset-based and internally focused, then it will be in very important ways "relationship driven." Thus, one of the central challenges for asset-based community developers is to constantly build and rebuild the relationships between and among local residents, local associations and local institutions [Kretzmann and McKnight, 1993, p. 9].

To achieve reciprocity, the college or university engaged in service-learning should develop programs that build on community assets and meet community needs as defined by the community.

Kretzmann and McKnight (1993) believe that a community assessment should be a capacity inventory of individuals within the community—those at the center and those on the margin. The inventory should survey skills, community involvement, business interests and experiences, and personal details in order to connect people's skills and capacities with community initiatives and ideas. Pairing community members with college students to conduct such an inventory can promote collaborative relationships if the community members are seen as the experts and if everyone involved is provided proper training. In their handbook, Kretzmann and McKnight (1993) offer several strategies and inventories to be used with particular populations (youth, senior citizens, and people with disabilities), local organizations (neighborhood associations, churches, and cultural groups), and local institutions (schools, libraries, police, and hospitals) in community development efforts.

Local United Way chapters, YWCAs or YMCAs, or other charitable organizations may conduct community assessments and can be sources of helpful information. Service-learning educators and students who participate in these efforts will begin to develop important networks of community members with whom they wish to establish relationships.

Community providers must know and understand the outcomes the service-learning faculty are hoping will result for students, and faculty need to understand the capacities, needs, and goals of the community programs and agencies. Again, sitting down together at the table, preferably at the service site, is necessary. Some faculty use telephone conversations or letters as means of communication with service providers in the community, but these efforts do not provide the best opportunity for dialogue needed to appreciate and grasp what each has to offer the other and to place and orient effectively the students with whom they will both be working. In order for faculty members to gain an understanding of the community and of the goals of the service site, they should participate in a service experience similar to that which they seek for their students.

Service-learning faculty have an active role. They must believe in the educational value of the service-learning experience and take the time that is necessary to make it the best possible experience. Just as faculty must prepare so they can teach effectively, they must lay the groundwork before sending students into the community. By the same token, community service providers must take the time to prepare for the students who will work with them by setting up meaningful service experiences and by educating both the service-learning faculty and the students about the population with which they will be interacting. Most providers see these efforts as an investment that will benefit both them and the people they serve.

Program Development

Once capacities and needs have been assessed and outcomes have been established and agreed on by both the service-learning educators and the community representatives, program development can begin. From the perspective of the college or university, the primary goal of the service-learning experience is generally student learning and development. From the perspective of the community, the goal of hosting service-learning students is to obtain assistance in meeting its immediate and long-term needs. These perspectives are not mutually exclusive; both can be accomplished. Achieving the goals from each perspective is largely determined by how the program is developed. In all cases, ongoing discussions between service-learning educators and service providers are important for assessing mutual expectations and outcomes and addressing any educational opportunities and logistical issues that may arise.

There needs to be a role reversal for both the service-learning educator and the community service provider. The educators need to take time to immerse themselves in a direct service experience, preferably where their students will be or are currently involved. And the service provider in turn should become the teacher and take time to share with students the knowledge he or she has gained by working with the community and organization. This preparation can be done at the service site or by inviting the service provider into the classroom. The service provider should also assist with ongoing reflection. For example, students who write reflection papers can share them with the service provider as helpful feedback about the nature of the students' experiences with the agency and community.

Preparation should also occur at the community service site. During their first experience at a site, students should learn where things are, the procedures, the spoken and unspoken norms of the agency, and the philosophy of the agency in word and in practice. In the second experience, they will have a little more confidence about what they are doing and a better sense of the routine and the staff. Then they can begin to focus on the people they are meeting and their needs.

For a fuller experience, the students should also get to know the neighborhood or the broader community. The community service provider can arrange this kind of orientation, which can be done formally or informally. Perhaps an individual from the neighborhood, preferably someone working in the agency or receiving its services, can be invited to speak with the students at the service site or a neighborhood center. Experiencing the broader community should also include a walking tour of the neighborhood, tapping into the lived experience of a neighborhood resident.

Informal community exploration can be accomplished when students eat in one of the neighborhood diners, shop at the neighborhood food store, or do their own self-guided walking tour. The goal is to spend time in the neighborhood, just being present and letting the community see that the students' interest goes beyond being there as servant. Seeing students, faculty, and staff in the neighborhood when they are not engaged directly in service helps them establish a credibility with the neighbors that cannot be obtained any other way.

Finally, it is important to note that the service experience in itself is not necessarily educational. Both service-learning educators and on-site community service providers must continually challenge students to reflect on and discuss their experiences and share them with those who have and who have not had similar experiences. Asking community members, leaders, and service providers to facilitate or participate in reflection sessions held in the community or on campus legitimizes these members of the community as essential educators in the service-learning process.

Models of Community Relationships

As many colleges and universities begin service-learning programs, they often fall into the trap of being overly focused on logistics or on finding student placements rather than investing the time and effort into developing a lasting relationship with a particular community that will have long-term impact in leveraging the necessary resources to create desired change. Campus Compact's Project on Integrating Service with Academic Study developed a continuum of models for community relationships from discussions, site visits, surveys, and workshops conducted with forty-four colleges and universities. The three models on the continuum depict service initiatives moving from a clearinghouse to partnership to collaboration (Campus Compact, 1994).

In the clearinghouse model, the institution maintains a database of placements to offer to students and faculty and seeks only minimal institutional investment in community relationships. While colleges and universities using this model often do so as a result of limited campus commitment or fiscal resources, a regularly updated database can be an effective means of connecting students and service opportunities. Since the clearinghouse model fosters minimal reciprocal relationships with the community, it is almost solely needs based and does not build on the capacities of the community. This approach can promote the harmful superior-culture myth, false hierarchies of power, and the deficiency orientation to the community because it tends to view the community as an opportunity for student learning and to invest little in the educational process for students. Rarely are community members and leaders tapped as educational resources.

The partnership model emerges when the community or the institution seeks the other to develop a more intentional relationship based on joining resources to meet each other's needs. Attention is paid to the assets of both partners as well as the needs. The partnership model compels the college or university to narrow and deepen its service focus and increase its time investment to a few community organizations or agencies rather than the many agencies usually typical of the clearinghouse model.

In the collaboration model, campus and community become interdependent in some significant ways, explore the root causes of relevant social issues, and agree to implement a common agenda to address these causes. Distinctive to this model is a visible and sustained institutional presence within a particular community, not as dominant partner but as valued contributor to the community development process. The focus is community development as outlined by Kretzmann and McKnight, with student learning or faculty research as a secondary by-product of this assets-based community development. This model demands extensive institutional time and personnel committed to community dialogue, development, and evaluation (Campus Compact, 1994).

As partnership and collaborative models develop between institutions and communities, the sharing of fiscal, human, and technical resources occurs. Partnerships and collaborations can seek joint grant funding for their initiatives and work together to place part-time, full-time, or split-site professionals in community staff positions to perform the administrative functions that accompany service-learning programs. This sharing of staff resources enables a consistent institutional presence in the community and supports financially strapped community organizations. Campus-community collaborations may also lobby elected officials to enact mutually beneficial local, state, and national legislation.

In sustained relationships, colleges and universities provide assistance to communities through professional and graduate programs. Medical, legal, and educational resources are among the assets many colleges and universities can contribute to the partnership. As institutions develop and upgrade computer systems, they can offer computer technology to community programs and provide them with Internet access through the institution's network. This access expands the community's capabilities and enables institutional and community partners to communicate easily. Faculty and students can also go to a community site to develop software or to teach computer skills to agency staff and community members.

Maintaining an Educational Thrust

A focus on education may be the only constant in a campus-community partnership or collaboration. It must take place on every level and throughout every aspect of the relationship. Leaders of both the college or university and the community, agency staff and volunteers, community members, and students must participate in ongoing education.

Service-learning educators who engage in orientation and continuing dialogue with community leaders and service providers about college students as volunteers have been able to develop and maintain lasting and effective relationships that deepen the students' educational experience. These educational sessions assist service providers in becoming aware of and familiar with the developmental issues of college students and how they affect, and are affected by, their involvement with service-learning. Once community partners understand the desired learning outcomes for students, they can be instrumental in helping to achieve them. The Service Learning Model (Delve, Mintz, and Stewart, 1990) described in the introduction to Part Two and the learning and development theories described in Chapter Three are useful in this process. It is also important for community partners to recognize that students have differing amounts of time available, depending on their class schedule and whether they commute, work, or have parenting responsibilities. Service-learning educators should also seek information from service providers about their strategies for working effectively with college students.

Opportunities must be provided for community members, leaders, and service providers to educate students, administrators, and faculty about the agency—its mission, philosophy, structure, staffing, target population, resources, services offered, and particular needs—and the surrounding neighborhood. Service-learning intentionally expands the traditional notion of the teacher. Community members and leaders become important teachers, mentors, and role models for students. Some service-learning faculty share their classrooms with community members and leaders in the effort to integrate practice with theory. This teaching partnership helps students to broaden their perspective about learning and to see the invaluable contributions of those in the community with whom they work.

Assessing and Evaluating Community Impact

Finally, most critical, and yet often overlooked, in sustaining effective service-learning partnerships is evaluation. The consistent and ongoing feedback from members of the community, recipients of the service, and service providers creates the necessary momentum to reshape and redirect efforts, as well as to expand existing programs. In conducting interviews with service-learning practitioners across the country, we found that many readily admitted that evaluation is the weak link to their efforts yet recognized the need to assess the impact of their initiatives with the community.

Many colleges and universities evaluate their community impact through the use of stakeholder feedback groups. Leaders from both the institution and the community who coordinate the service-learning partnership gather together the original stakeholder group established to identify assets and needs for regularly scheduled evaluation sessions. These sessions are generally facilitated discussions of predetermined questions or topics. The frequency and inclusiveness of these sessions are key ingredients to the successful understanding of impact and outcomes, as well as continuous improvement and community development.

Other evaluation methods include both quantitative and qualitative assessments of the specific population being served and related groups. For example, if the service-learning site is an elementary school, the students can be given pre- and posttests as well as interviewed individually or in focus groups. Parents and teachers should also participate in the evaluation.

For each partnership, the specific evaluation methods and

tools should fit the particular initiative or program. Finding community and faculty resource people to work together on the design, implementation, and interpretation of evaluation efforts is helpful. Another strategy for conducting evaluations is to seek out potential facilitators or interviewers who are not immediately involved with the service-learning partnership. Asking community members or nonstudent volunteers to conduct parts of the evaluation process may provide a more objective picture of impact and outcomes. (Chapter Eleven contains additional information on program evaluation.)

Sometimes evaluation results or other circumstances may require a college or university to withdraw from a community relationship. Regardless of the specific reasons for termination of a relationship, the use of Kupiec's (1993) process points and Kretzmann and McKnight's (1993) asset-based community development approach will serve to minimize ill effects. As in the beginning of a campus-community relationship, both parties must come together to discuss their respective and reciprocal interests, needs, and resources in order to clarify immediate responsibilities, perceived difficulties, and future directions. A mutually respected facilitator or mediator can assist if dialogue becomes difficult. (Further discussion of issues related to program termination can be found in Chapter Eleven.)

Conclusion

In their enthusiasm to promote student learning and development through service-learning, colleges and universities often start up programs without sufficient planning or community development. It is all too easy to attempt to develop service-learning programs in a vacuum without the voices and support of members, organizers, and leaders of the community, but strong, sustained community involvement is required to create effective service-learning partnerships. Campus-community relationships based on mutually determined goals, capacities, needs, and strategies can have long-term impact in leveraging the necessary resources to create change. Reciprocity and community empowerment are essential elements for the long-term success of service-learning endeavors.

References

Campus Compact. *Mapping the Geography of Service on a College Campus: Strategic Questions About the Institution, Stakeholders, Philosophies and Community Relationships.* Providence, R.I.: Campus Compact, 1994.

Cisneros, H. *The University and the Urban Challenge.* Washington, D.C.: U.S. Department of Housing and Urban Development, 1995.

Delve, C. I., Mintz, S. D., and Stewart, G. M. "Promoting Values Development Through Community Service: A Design." In C. I. Delve, S. D. Mintz, and G. M. Stewart (eds.), *Community Service as Values Education,* New Directions for Student Services, no. 50. San Francisco: Jossey-Bass, 1990.

Kretzmann, J. P., and McKnight, J. L. *Building Communities from the Inside Out: A Path Toward Finding and Mobilizing a Community's Assets.* Evanston, Ill.: Center for Urban Affairs and Policy Research, Northwestern University, 1993.

Kupiec, T. Y. (ed.). *Rethinking Tradition: Integrating Service with Academic Study on College Campuses.* Providence, R.I.: Campus Compact, 1993.

Mulling, C. "Do No Harm." Paper presented in a panel discussion at the National Gathering: College Educators and Service Learning, Providence, R.I., May 1995.

Porter Honnet, E., and Poulsen, S. J. *Principles of Good Practice for Combining Service and Learning.* Racine, Wisc.: Johnson Foundation, 1989.

wiger, f. "Do No Harm." Paper presented in a panel discussion at the National Gathering: College Educators and Service Learning, Providence, R.I., May 1995.

Designing a Spectrum of Service-Learning Experiences

Colleges and universities should offer a wide range of service-learning experiences intentionally designed for students at different points in their education and at various stages of development. The Service Learning Model of Cecilia I. Delve, Suzanné D. Mintz, and Greig M. Stewart (1990) describes five phases of students' development that result from engaging in the kinds of service-learning experiences described in Part Two of this book. The model is based on four key variables: intervention, commitment, behavior, and balance.

Intervention, the first variable of the model, contains two elements, mode and setting. *Mode* refers to whether the student engages in service-learning as an individual or as a member of a group. *Setting* describes the student's relationship to the client population. The *indirect* setting is one in which students are physically distant from the service site and the population being served. *Nondirect* settings are those in which students are involved at the service site but are not in direct contact with the client population. The *direct* setting involves face-to-face interaction with the client population at either the service site or elsewhere.

The second variable, *commitment,* concerns the nature of the service-learning activity. It is characterized by *frequency,* how often a student engages in the activity, and *duration*. Duration encompasses both the long- or short-term commitment to the activity, and the source of the student's commitment—to the other students involved, the activity, the service site, or the client population.

Students' *behavior,* the third variable of the model, involves both *needs* and *outcomes.* Needs are students' motivations for involvement in service-learning. Outcomes are possible effects of service-learning on students' behavior.

Finally, as described in Chapter Three, a *balance of challenge and support* is necessary for development to occur. Development is encouraged when the student confronts challenges in a service-learning experience, together with supports designed to enable the student to cope with and learn from the challenges (Delve, Mintz, and Stewart, 1990).

The Service Learning Model describes five phases of student development in relation to service-learning. Educators will encounter students in all the phases and will recognize that students' developmental phases are directly related to the nature of the service-learning experiences that are most appropriate for them.

Phase 1: Exploration. According to Delve, Mintz, and Stewart (1990), students in this first phase are "'bright-eyed and bushy-tailed,' eager to explore new experiences" (p. 14). Such students are usually excited about new opportunities, naive about the depth and complexities of the problems that create the need for service, and want to "help" or "get involved." Most students in this phase are involved in one-time or short-term activities that do not involve direct contact with the client population. Their commitment is often to the group sponsoring the activity rather than to the experience or its related issues, and their behavior may be shaped by a desire to "feel good" or to receive a reward, such as a T-shirt, for participating. Because the uncertainties of new experiences can be quite challenging, supports for students should include a high degree of structure and clear expectations.

Phase 2: Clarification. In phase 2, characterized as "the salad bar approach," students explore their various opportunities and begin to make decisions about where and how to concentrate their energies related to service (p. 15). Students in this phase generally engage in one-time service experiences at a variety of sites through association with a peer group. Service can be indirect, nondirect, or direct. Students often develop allegiance to the group, reinforced by a sense of belonging, rather than to a service site, population, or issue. Challenges include the process of eliminating options and choosing among potential service experiences; supports are growing group identity and engagement in structured activities.

Phase 3: Realization. Often a favorite for service-learning educators, students in the realization phase figuratively exclaim "Aha!" as they recognize what service-learning is all about (Delve, Mintz, and Stewart, 1990, p. 15). At this phase, students begin to focus on a particular population or issue and to understand the concept of reciprocal learning. Students' service now reflects a long-term and frequent commitment to a site, activity, or issue. They may serve independently or as a member of a group, and service may be direct, indirect, or a combination of the two. Students' challenges involve deepening exposure to diverse people; interpersonal dynamics among agency staff, volunteers, and clients; and the complexity of the social and political issues that underlie the need for service. Supports important at this phase are structured reflection opportunities and individual relationships with on-site supervisors and campus personnel. Students' potential for burnout as a result of their excitement should be monitored.

Phase 4: Activation. Students in the model's fourth phase generally feel a strong sense of solidarity with the population with whom they work, and become advocates on its behalf. They grapple with the large issues of social justice—racism, classism, and economic inequality. Students likely continue direct involvement with the client population as they concentrate on a salient issue in an indirect way. As in phase 3, they may work independently or with a group concerned with their issue. Commitment is intense, and involvement is at a high level. Such students may frequently voice their lifelong dedication to the issue. Their challenges arise from the injustices they encounter and from the unfavorable reactions they may get from peers and family members to changes in their appearance, lifestyle, and verbal and written expression that result from their intense commitment to their cause. Supports from service-learning educators can help students deal with frustrations, avoid potential burnout, and realize that they can make career and personal decisions based on their values.

Phase 5: Internalization. This final phase describes the few who have fully integrated service into their lives and who make lifestyle and career decisions consistent with the values they have embraced. The choices they make incorporate both personal and community values. The challenges students encounter are those of trying to live a life consistent with their values and the decisions they must make related to career, family, place of residence, and use of money and other resources. Sources of support are the sense of community and solidarity they gain from the depth and consistency of their involvement, and the sense of inner peace that is a result of living consistently with one's values.

The chapters in Part Two describe a spectrum of service-learning experiences that provide the appropriate challenges and supports for students in all phases of the Service Learning Model, from introductory opportunities to assisting students to make career and lifestyle choices that integrate the values acquired through involvement in service-learning. Each chapter cites numerous examples of successful programs and approaches from a broad range of institutional types in all parts of the United States.

Reference

Delve, C. I., Mintz, S. D., and Stewart, G. M. "Promoting Values Development Through Community Service: A Design." In C. I. Delve, S. D. Mintz, and G. M. Stewart (eds.), *Community Service as Values Education,* New Directions for Student Services, no. 50. San Francisco: Jossey-Bass, 1990.

Chapter Five

One-Time and Short-Term Service-Learning Experiences

Mark D. McCarthy

At many colleges and universities, students are introduced to service-learning through participation in one-time or short-term experiences. They take their first steps into the communities around their campuses through such activities as spending an afternoon in a neighborhood cleanup project during orientation week, volunteering at a Labor Day Muscular Dystrophy Telethon event, preparing and serving a meal at a homeless shelter, or joining the members of a residence hall floor in an annual program to assist older adults winterize their homes.

Well-planned and well-orchestrated introductory experiences can serve as a foundation for all other types of service-learning. Indirect, nondirect, and direct modes of service (Delve, Mintz, and Stewart, 1990) provide students with opportunities to reinforce previous service experiences, explore the community in which their institution is located, affiliate and connect with other students to accomplish something worthwhile, gain new insights about themselves and others through experience and reflection on that experience, and clarify which issues and service organizations are possibilities for ongoing service-learning commitments. The first steps into service-learning can help move students to take further action and add focus to their courses of study. By understanding

the various elements that are necessary for a successful introduction to service-learning, students, administrators, and faculty will
be able to design experiences that set the stage for learning, open
the doors to understanding, and increase students' participation
in their own education.

Although college students at all levels (first year through graduate school) can be introduced to service-learning through one-
time or short-term experiences, many of these initiatives focus on
first-year students who come to campus with varying degrees of
community service experience. In his studies of entering college
students, Astin (1991) noted a decline in the expected level of volunteer service involvement as compared with reported community
service participation in high school. More recently Astin, Korn, and
Sax (1994) reported that while 70.1 percent of the entering students in 1994 performed volunteer work in the previous year, only
17.3 percent estimated that chances were very good that they
would participate in volunteer or community service work in college. Giles and Eyler (1994) suggest that this decline in intended
volunteer involvement might be partially due to the uprooting
nature of the college experience for many students, caused by a
number of factors, including entering a new community; losing
family, school, religious, and social group connections that tie students to their communities; and moving away from that which is
known and comfortable to environments that place new and more
complex demands on students' lives.

One-time service-learning events as part of orientation or first-
year experience programs can provide an organizational and supportive context for reattaching students to service and help them
to consider service-learning options in their decision making about
how they will spend their time during college. In their study of the
impact of community service laboratories, Giles and Eyler (1994)
found that service experiences of limited duration may help to
reshape the way students think about obligations and opportunities for service and about the people who need social services.

Goals of Introductory Service-Learning Experiences

Developing goals for one-time or short-term service-learning experiences begins by assessing the motivations and needs of the stu-

dents, as well as the needs expressed by the community. In this process, the contributions and assets that these groups bring to the project or experience are identified and articulated. Determining an appropriate balance of challenge and support to students involved in service experiences is necessary for learning to occur.

In their review of the literature about the traits and motivations of college students who participate in volunteer service activities, Winniford, Carpenter, and Grider (1995) identify two major motivations: altruism (acting with the ultimate goal of helping others) and egoism (acting toward the ultimate goal of increasing one's own welfare). Most studies cite egoistic rewards, such as feeling a sense of accomplishment and satisfaction, gaining skills, and affiliating with others, as critical to initial and continued involvement in service (Serow, 1991). Winniford, Carpenter, and Grider (1995) report that altruistic motivations (helping others, contributing to a community, and acting out of a concern for those less fortunate) are most important to students in their initial involvement in volunteer service organizations, followed by egoistic motivations, which become more important to their continued involvement. Giles and Eyler (1994) describe the need for a sense of efficacy—the feeling that participation in service projects can make a real difference—as an important predictor of student involvement in service.

Recognizing the importance students place on feeling good, accomplishing something, and being seen as fitting in, short-term service-learning activities that result in visible changes or accomplishments (painting over graffiti, cleaning up a neighborhood, or serving food to a hungry person) and support group involvement through residence hall floors or student organizations, orientation, and campus-wide events have a greater likelihood of meeting students' needs and encouraging them to become more involved in service-learning. Providing rewards for participation, such as T-shirts or hats, a postevent picnic, and opportunities to identify and affiliate with a group, are important motivations for students who are participating in the types of service experiences described in the first phases of the Service Learning Model (Delve, Mintz, and Stewart, 1990).

Although effort should be given to create a supportive environment to meet students' needs, sufficient challenge must also be presented to encourage students to question their preconceptions about the causes of personal hardship and the individuals they may encounter (Giles and Eyler, 1994). If a fundraiser for AIDS research or a food or toy collection to benefit homeless families or victims of abuse does not include educational components and opportunities for reflection about AIDS as a disease or the victims of abuse, as well as opportunities to bump up against issues, people, and experiences far removed from most of their daily lives, then students' perceptions about social problems are less likely to change, little learning occurs, and expectations for continued active involvement are limited.

Typically goals for introductory service-learning experiences include establishing a target number of participants, providing information to assist students to understand a social issue or community concern better, introducing students to the city or rural area in which the campus is located, and building a commitment among participants to engage further in service-learning. For new students who may have fears about fitting into the social community of a college or university, service-learning experiences can also offer a sense of shared purpose and larger social impact, especially when programs are designed to permit them to do so at their own pace and support them in ways that nurture "their heart and soul" (Loeb, 1994b, p. 104). Although these goals may also be important to and shared by community organizations and the community members they serve, community representatives may be more concerned about completing maintenance projects, providing enjoyable experiences for the children or older adults who are the focus of their program or organization, or establishing ongoing partnerships with the college and university.

Designing One-Time or Short-Term Service-Learning Experiences

Campus organizers of introductory service-learning projects need to collaborate with community representatives to establish shared expectations for students and community participants that are focused and short term in nature. Developing a plan of action that takes into consideration the interests of the student participants, the amount of time they have available, and the scope and difficulty of the service to be performed, as well as reaching agreement on the ways in which preparation for and reflection on the service experience will be included, are necessary to achieve meaningful, mutually beneficial, and well-designed service-learning experiences.

Planning Process

The establishment of planning teams that include experienced student leaders, community members, and faculty or administrators is critical in designing projects that support student involvement in activities that are meaningful to them and to the community. In fact, *Into the Streets* (1993), a manual written by the Campus Outreach Opportunity League (COOL), describes the formation and maintenance of a leadership coalition as the most important step in program design. The planning team serves as an organizing body and a means to include campus and community members with differing skills, abilities, and resources in determining realistic goals and shared expectations for a service project. Diving into program details is often the first item on the agenda of planning team members, yet building effective coalitions requires taking time to learn about members' varied expectations, values, purposes, and intentions and to develop shared ownership for the goals of a particular project.

In addition to establishing planning teams, effective management of programmatic details related to setting and keeping time lines, volunteer recruitment, publicity and media relations, transportation, site or issue selection, finances and fundraising, food, and liability concerns is essential. Depending on the nature of the experience, the importance of each of these issues will vary, but the development of a project planning and implementation time line that includes the responsibilities and tasks to be performed by the individuals or committees organizing the event will help to ensure the successful accomplishment of the goals. Also, holding regular meetings of the planning team leaders to report on progress made in accomplishing tasks and grapple with problems or conflicts that may have been encountered is helpful in keeping everyone informed, solving problems, and maintaining momentum. Finally, establishing a budget that adequately covers publicity, transportation, recognition awards such as T-shirts, materials and supplies, and food is needed, so that institutional resources can be identified and solicitation of funding and other support can occur. (Chapter Eleven addresses administrative issues related to the design and implementation of service-learning projects.)

Selection of Community Sites, Issues, and Service Tasks

In the exploration phase of the Service Learning Model (Delve, Mintz, and Stewart, 1990), indirect (raising money for a local AIDS project or making Christmas stockings for children in a homeless shelter) or nondirect (cleaning up a senior center or stocking a food pantry) forms of service are often the primary activities or interventions. Introductory service-learning experiences on many campuses also include direct forms of service, such as serving food at a meal program, visiting with the residents of a nursing home, and reading to children in a hospital. One-time projects, like participating in a stream cleanup or organizing an activity for an after-school program, offer students the opportunity to participate with other students and to perform immediately useful tasks without engaging in longer-term political or social action (Loeb, 1994a). As a result of media attention and high school experiences, programs that are connected to issues such as the environment, hunger and homelessness, AIDS, literacy, and youth empowerment generally attract student interest. Students also identify with experiences that help them to connect with other students who share common values and a commitment to become involved. Allowing students to choose activities that match their interests by providing a range of opportunities (Delve, Mintz, and Stewart, 1990) may increase their commitment and enthusiasm for involvement.

Sites and activities selected should also reflect students' busy schedules. Regardless of the nature of students' motivation to serve, event organizers and community agencies need to understand that participating in service is only one of many demands on students' lives as they juggle schedules that may include working; studying and going to classes; commuting; socializing; and attending to family, friends, and personal priorities.

Although the impact of a single project may be small, narrowing the focus of an introductory service-learning activity to one issue—perhaps preparing Thanksgiving dinners for a few families or cleaning up the graffiti on one city block—enables all participants to see tangible, however short term, benefits to the community or individuals served. The limited scope of this kind of activity can be a source of frustration to community agency administrators and community members whose work continues and who often see their needs, problems, and issues as growing and compounding. Thus it is important to define the length of service commitments and anticipated outcomes for both students and community partners.

Campus Culture

The culture of a particular campus—as expressed through its mission statement, demonstrated through its commitment to and history of community involvement, and put into practice through faculty, administrative, and student initiatives—is an additional factor to consider in the design of one-time or short-term service projects. At some institutions, faculty, student affairs administrators, campus ministers, and student leaders offer consistent messages in and out of the classroom about the value they place on service. These messages to new students and student organizations can influence student participation in introductory service-learning opportunities, encourage reflection on service experiences, and help to create a campus culture that emphasizes and encourages service to and with others. Other campuses have norms, perceived and actual, that discourage involvement in activities that focus on anything but making good grades or preparing for a lucrative future career and support detachment from social and political issues. Where these norms exist, it may be helpful to tap into the more pragmatic motivations of students to participate in short-term service-learning activities, such as learning more about the communities in which their institutions are located, gaining leadership skills, earning extra credit, affiliating with peers, and gaining a sense of satisfaction, accomplishment, and enjoyment. Regardless of the students' motivations to participate, well-planned service and reflection activities can move even less-interested students to deeper levels of self-understanding and a greater desire to serve.

Reflection

The following examples of service-learning experiences offer a variety of options for preparation and reflection. Carefully planned reflection should be included in preservice, in-service, and post-service activities to raise students' level of awareness about service-learning, increase their potential for learning, and create positive experiences that lead to further involvement in service-learning.

Preparation and Preservice Reflection

It is important to encourage individual and group goal setting and sharing of expectations for service-learning. The COOL *Into the Streets* manual (1993) points out the importance of creating an expectation that reflection is part of participation. Students need information about the nature of the project they are about to undertake and the clients or populations served. At orientation sessions, agency representatives, community members, and experienced student leaders can also teach students how to act appropriately at a site and prepare them for the possible emotions (frustration, anger, uncertainty, joy, and hope) they may feel during and after their service experiences.

The use of simple written measures of interest and understanding of social issues can be useful tools in helping students to focus on the upcoming experience. Asking the same questions in a postservice measure can also provide information to the students about their learning and to the project organizers about changes in attitudes and knowledge among student participants. In another format, students write letters to themselves about their expectations and hoped-for outcomes that might result from the service experience. These can be distributed after the event and used to facilitate discussion about the expectations and realities of service.

In-Service Reflection

At the start of a service-learning project or event kickoff, students can set the tone for the day by taking five minutes to reflect silently about their reasons for participation and desired outcomes and to think about their roles and relationships with other participants. This type of mini-reflection can be guided through prayer or by a series of questions that call on students to "get into the others' shoes," to "center" themselves in the present, and to put aside past and future issues that may take away from the experience they are about to share.

If group transportation is provided to and from the site, travel time can be used to prepare for and reflect on the service experience and to gather students' feedback on the program. Short evaluations can also be used to collect immediate reactions and names of students who wish to be involved in further service. As part of the Walk the Walk service-learning experience for emerging leaders at Marquette University, student participants walk as a group to a nearby St. Vincent de Paul meal program. This thirty-minute walk through the inner city is conducted in silence as a way for participants to explore their own thoughts and feelings about the issues of hunger and homelessness.

Postservice Reflection

At the conclusion of a service experience, it is important to bring participants together to discuss their activities and to share reactions, emotions, ideas, and questions. After large events, a postevent gathering on campus is a way to celebrate involvement and explore future service-learning opportunities. Small-group discussions focusing on the questions—What actually happened? So what was the significance to me and others? and Now what do I [or we] do?—invite students to reflect on the meanings of service.

Sometimes the extent or significance of a service experience can take time to sink in. The next scheduled organization or group meeting, class session, or floor meeting can be devoted to discussing what surprised participants, whether their expectations were met, and what community needs or issues were presented. After a large campus-wide event, written reflections in the campus newspaper can encourage students to review their own experiences and challenge them to take the next step. Creating a mural that illustrates the service project through words and pictures or putting together a slide show or videotape that captures the people involved in a project and includes comments from students and community members can be used as a way to attract students to a special reunion program of reflection or to promote future service-learning opportunities.

Evaluation

Finally the effective design of any service-learning experience calls for evaluation of the impact of service from the perspectives of both the student volunteers and community agency or individuals served. Although the numbers of service hours and volunteers, gallons of paint used, trash bags filled, or amount of funds raised are useful indicators, measuring student and community outcomes is far more complex.

Students' new knowledge and understandings, changes in their perceptions, and shifts in attitudes about and behaviors toward others who differ from them can be assessed through focus group discussions prior to and after a service-learning experience. Tracking the numbers of participants who commit to and actually engage in additional service through service-learning courses, student service organizations, and other campus volunteer outreach programs also helps to gauge the effectiveness of introductory service-learning experiences. Postevent discussions and feedback sessions with community agencies provide information about the activity from the community's point of view and can help develop community partnerships for future service-learning activities.

Examples of One-Time or Short-Term Service-Learning Experiences

Although the following brief descriptions of one-time or short-term activities illustrate an array of service-learning programs at small and large, public and private, religiously affiliated, and other types of institutions, they are not necessarily representative of all the introductory service-learning programs currently being conducted across the country.

Campus-Wide Events

Campus-wide day-long or weekend service-learning activities are popular at many institutions because they involve hundreds of students with many community members and organizations, attract media attention, result in tangible and visible changes, offer students opportunities to explore social issues, and celebrate campus-community collaboration. National activities such as the Hunger Clean-up, National Youth Service Day, and Christmas in April (a program in which volunteers rehabilitate the houses of low-income home owners) also offer opportunities for institutional recognition for outstanding contributions in terms of participation or amount of funds raised. Neighborhood cleanups and Into the Streets programs introduce students to service and to the communities in which they are living, and celebrate a campus-wide commitment to community action.

Piloted in the fall of 1991 by COOL, the national Into the Streets program grew out of learnings from successful one-day outreach programs with service and educational components that occurred in the spring on many campuses. The goals of Into the Streets programs are based on COOL's "Critical Elements of Thoughtful Community Service" (see Chapter Two) and include the following: empowering the vision of local organizations to expand their programs, recruiting more individuals and developing student leaders for long-term and even lifelong involvement in their communities, and strengthening students' capacity to explore and solve societal problems (COOL, 1993). An essential element of Into the Streets is its emphasis on building coalitions to strengthen community action. In the fall of 1993, over two hundred institutions organized Into the Streets programs, with participants numbering between 150 and 800 in each program. The COOL model for the program and the *Into the Streets* manual (1993) continue to be used in the development of one-day, large-scale service programs at many institutions.

In addition to the half- or full-day event, some one-day campus-wide programs, such as the Hunger Clean-up, include fundraising through the solicitation of pledges, donations, and individual or business sponsors. Like Into the Streets, the purpose of the Hunger Clean-up is to involve more students in service, but this event also attempts to raise awareness about the issues of hunger and homelessness and funds to support meal programs and shelters locally and nationally. Initiated by the National Campaign for Hunger and Homelessness, Hunger Clean-up programs are now locally organized and tailored to meet the needs of the communities in which they are located.

Chandler-Gilbert Community College

This branch of the Maricopa County Community College system is located in a rural area forty miles from Phoenix, Arizona. The Office of Student Life organizes Into the Streets programs several times each semester on Fridays and Saturdays as a way for students and faculty to participate in projects with area Boys' and Girls' Clubs, literacy programs, and Special Olympics events, as well as projects for people who are homeless, nursing home residents, and victims of domestic violence. All students enrolled in English 101 are required to participate in two one-time service-learning experiences and to reflect on and write about them. In addition, faculty teaching psychology, biology, education, math, and music courses link class assignments to participation in Into the Streets programs. By providing a breadth of service-learning options, many of them related to the content of introductory courses, the student life staff and faculty offer choices for students that promote involvement and learning. Preparation for the Into the Streets programs is provided by individual faculty as part of class time and through campus-wide orientation sessions sponsored by the Office of Student Life prior to the programs. Activities that connect students directly with community members are selected whenever possible. The Into the Streets experiences at Chandler-Gilbert serve as the foundation for students' longer-term participation in more integrated service-learning courses offered in subsequent semesters.

Grand Valley State University

Located in Allendale, Michigan, Grand Valley State University offers several activities that have been effective in attracting student involvement in ongoing service. The Office of Student Life sponsors an annual Hunger Theater event, which serves as a way to raise awareness about hunger and homelessness and raises funds for Oxfam America. Students buy tickets to a banquet and are randomly seated in three groups representing the First, Second, and Third Worlds. First World students (10 percent of those at the dinner) are served a full banquet meal, Second World students (30 percent) serve themselves a more basic meal, and Third World students (60 percent) eat rice and drink water while seated on the floor. Following the meal, students from the theater department stage a one-act play related to Third World concerns and hunger and homelessness issues. A powerful reflection discussion follows the play. Student involvement in neighborhood hunger and homelessness programs has resulted from participation in this one-time experience (J. Cooper, personal communication, May 1995). The Hunger Banquet is part of the annual Fast for a World Harvest campaign sponsored by Oxfam America. Planning kits from Oxfam America are available to schools interested in organizing this program.

Marquette University

The 1993 and 1994 Marquette University Hunger Clean-ups received national recognition for having the most participants and for raising the most funds: $16,000 in 1993 and $20,000 in 1994. Marquette is a Jesuit university located in the urban center of Milwaukee. This event is a late-spring tradition at Marquette and annually attracts more than thirteen hundred students, faculty, and children from area Boys' and Girls' Clubs and after-school programs at which Marquette students serve throughout the year. Each year the student planning team members work with community agencies and interview homeless community members to determine the projects or programs to which funds will be contributed. Team leaders receive training about the particular agencies that are Hunger Clean-up sites, and all participants receive on-site orientations to the particular agencies at which they are assigned prior to beginning a morning of service. After the experience, participants return to campus to complete reflection evaluations and join in a celebration that includes music and food.

Course-Related Service-Learning Activities

In order to provide information and real-life experiences for written assignments and group projects and to encourage students to expand their understanding of societal, economic, or urban issues, one-time or short-term (multiple site visits during a semester) service-learning experiences are offered in courses across the curriculum at many institutions. Some courses include assignments such as interviewing homeless persons or residents of a nursing home to gather pieces of oral history, spending part of a day in an inner-city school as part of a research project on public education, or serving food and eating at a soup kitchen in preparation for writing an article for a journalism course. Carefully designed assignments can draw students to experience "the other" and help to inform a paper or project through practical experiences and richer examples.

Exposure to some form of service-learning may assist students to begin making connections between knowing about and doing something about a community issue or problem. Experiences that require students to associate a name and a face with the lives of homeless or mentally ill persons or to shadow a health care professional in an inner-city hospital or hospice can open students' eyes to ethical and moral issues, racism, and economic class differences and motivate them to take further action. To be effective, course assignments should be tied to the goals of the class; include adequate preparation and reflection opportunities; engage students in service activities that are meaningful to the students and the community members toward which their efforts are directed; and be evaluated by faculty, students, and community representatives.

Colorado State University

Colorado State University, located in Fort Collins, offers a variety of service-learning courses and seminars, some of which include required one-time service experiences. As a means to explore the issues of ethics, public service, and the medical profession, students engage in an "alternative weekend service experience" as part of the two-credit Premedical Service Learning Seminar. After studying the history and biology of HIV-AIDS and establishing personal and academic goals to guide their service-learning experiences, students serve in a variety of nonprofit agencies in the Denver metropolitan area that focus on HIV-AIDS prevention, education, and care. Through this mini-immersion experience, seminar students work side by side with people who have HIV-AIDS, health care providers, community leaders, social workers, and clergy.

To assist students in reflecting on their service experiences, they are required to keep journals, write a paper that includes reactions to the experience and explores the realities of medical and social care provided to persons with HIV-AIDS, and participate in class discussions regarding the medical, social, political, and economic issues associated with the disease. Students then combine the knowledge derived from their experience with seminar discussions and research on health education and prepare a presentation for a selected audience of campus and community representatives.

Westminster College

Located in Fulton, Missouri, Westminster College is a small, private, liberal arts college. Going Crazy, Being Sane is one of fifteen three-credit seminar courses offered to first-year students each fall. The seminars meet intensively (three to four hours a day) during the week prior to the beginning of classes and then twice a week for the remainder of the semester and typically include one-time service components, though not necessarily tied to the seminar topic. In this seminar, participation in service is combined with presentations by faculty and guests, class discussions on readings, small-group projects, and reaction papers in an effort to explore mental illness more fully.

To make the study of mental illness real and personal, pairs of students are teamed with a former resident of Fulton State Hospital, the largest psychiatric hospital in Missouri, who now resides in a transitional home. During the first week of the semester, students and patients labeled as schizophrenic participate together in a variety of activities. Patients give students tours of their complex and the Fulton State Hospital, and students give patients tours of the college. They also share several meals and spend recreational time socializing, biking, and cooking. Students write an integrative paper regarding their service project with the residents of the state hospital group home and share their experiences through a case study project, written assignments, and class discussions.

Prior to these experiences, students receive an orientation from hospital staff and read about and discuss the history of mental illness and treatment. At the start of the course, students reported that they made fun of the "crazies" who shared their community. During and after the course the students defended these individuals and educated others on campus about the nature of mental illness (R. Hansen, personal communication, June 1995).

Orientation Programs

The inclusion of service-learning experiences as part of new-student orientation programs is on the rise at all types of colleges and universities. In addition to the first-year seminar courses similar to the Westminster College example, institutions offer prematriculation mini-immersion experiences, day-long service-learning experiences, and cocurricular first-year experience and emerging-leadership programs that include service-learning.

University of Vermont

Since 1991 the University of Vermont has offered a five-day service-learning program for entering students called TREK, which takes place immediately prior to the start of fall semester classes. Up to twenty-four students are selected as TREK participants each summer, and when they arrive on campus in the fall, they are housed together for one week in a residence hall. Through a series of half- or full-day group service-learning activities, TREK participants are exposed to a variety of different service issues and agencies, including Boys' and Girls' Club outings, Salvation Army dinners for people who are homeless, recreational activities at correctional centers and nursing homes, and maintenance work at a local residential treatment center for drug and alcohol abuse.

The program begins with a number of team-building experiences, including a ropes course and recreational activities. Representatives from host sites and the university join the TREK staff in daily reflection sessions to acquaint students with key issues and the need for the service they provide. Mealtimes, which are sometimes shared with community members and served at the sites, are often used as intentional reflection opportunities. A structured reflection workshop on the experience concludes the program.

Early in their college careers, almost all the TREK participants become involved with one or more of the Volunteers in Action programs. Staff advisers to TREK have found that friendships formed during the program often sustain themselves over time, and TREK participants become involved in deeper and more long-term service-learning and leadership during their years at the university. Student participants pay a fee to cover the costs for food and housing during the program. Experienced student leaders are selected in the late fall to plan, organize, and publicize the next year's TREK program (G. Albert, personal communication, June 1995).

Gettysburg College

As part of the annual new-student orientation program held in August, entering students participate in Gettysburg Is Volunteer (GIV) Day, an afternoon of service in the community followed by an evening open house and service fair sponsored by the Gettysburg College Center for Public Service. Gettysburg College, a liberal arts college in rural Pennsylvania, is affiliated with the Evangelical Lutheran Church.

GIV Day is designed to provide challenging and meaningful service-learning opportunities for the students and to demonstrate the college's commitment to the community to being a listening, caring institutional neighbor. Student project directors and staff advisers identify and select about thirty-five project sites each summer. Community organizations provide information about their purposes and needs, proposed project details including equipment and material needs, and the name of an on-site project supervisor. Agencies are also invited to participate in the volunteer service fair as a way to advertise their programs and to recruit first-year students for ongoing projects.

The GIV Day service-learning experience has three components: an orientation to the site, the work itself, and the follow-up reflection. The orientation is provided on site by a representative of the community agency. The work projects, usually two to three hours in length, are designed to accommodate about ten students and a project leader (a faculty member, administrator, support staff, or upper-class student project leader). The reflection occurs immediately after the service and is in the form of a discussion facilitated by the project leader who works with the team at the site. In order to encourage further involvement as a result of this initial exposure to service-learning, GIV Day concludes with the fair, at which over 60 percent of the first-year students participate.

Regis University

At Regis University, located in Denver, Freshman Service Day is a key element of the three-day orientation program. To help students better understand the Jesuit mission of the university—which includes the ideals of developing men and women for others, and leadership through service—students are invited to participate in teams of fifteen to twenty for an afternoon of service in Denver. The experience is designed to connect students with the city and urban issues, develop community among students through identification with a small group, build identity as Regis students in the community through the T-shirts worn by the participants that read "Learning through Service–Regis University," and enable participation in meaningful and fun activities such as neighborhood cleanups, painting projects, or organizing playground activities for schools. Students are introduced to the concepts of service-learning and prepared for the experience at a banquet held the night before Freshman Service Day when they select and sign up for a project. Student leaders accompany the new students throughout the project and lead debriefing reflection sessions on the return trip to the campus, as well as subsequent small-group discussions that are also part of the orientation program.

North Central College

As part of the six-week FYI orientation and transition seminar at North Central College in Naperville, Illinois, three-member teaching teams (comprising a faculty member, a student affairs administrator, and an upper-class student leader) lead groups of fifteen to twenty new students in a five-hour service-learning experience during the first week of classes. The goals of this experience include introducing students to the college's service ethic, increasing students' awareness of social responsibility, building community among the students through a shared experience, establishing informal relationships between first-year students and North Central's faculty and student affairs staff, and providing an introduction to and link with the surrounding community (S. Dodd, personal communication, June 1995). Established in 1993, this service-learning kickoff program has resulted in partnerships with over fifteen community agencies that serve senior citizens, homeless families, disabled young adults, and children.

Preparation and reflection activities are incorporated into the FYI sessions held immediately before and after the half-day service-learning project. In the first FYI class, students are given information about the agency at which they will be serving and learn about the issue or population around which the agency is organized. They also receive a reflection worksheet to complete for the next class. These reflection sheets are then used as a springboard for class discussions of the service experience.

Student Organization or Group Activities

Student organizations and groups such as residence hall units often offer students opportunities to join others in one-day or short-term service-learning experiences. Campus chapters of Alpha Phi Omega, Habitat for Humanity, Circle K, Amnesty International, Best Buddies, and Public Interest Research Groups (PIRGs) offer opportunities for students interested in developing deeper commitments to service or to particular social, environmental, or political issues. At many institutions, these organizations also host events that involve members, nonmembers, and other student organizations in one-day service-learning experiences.

In addition to activities initiated by student organizations, special events or programs organized by student life offices or service-learning centers introduce students to service through a number of experiential and outreach programs. Some institutions, like Regis University, offer monthly projects organized with different community partners that attract the participation of individual students, student organizations, and classes for which faculty incorporate a service-learning experience as an optional course component. Others, such as Marquette and Santa Clara universities, include one-time experiences as a category of involvement in their clearinghouses of service experiences.

Lafayette College

Lafayette College, a private liberal arts college located in Easton, Pennsylvania, has over twenty volunteer programs that meet weekly for service, community building, and reflection. To encourage residence hall floor cooperation and to introduce students to service in the Easton community, Hands Across the Hill is organized by the residence hall floors in the early fall. Children living in Easton are invited to the campus to participate in an afternoon of fun activities sponsored and organized by each of the floors. After the event, Lafayette students reflect on their experiences with inner-city youth during their floor meetings. Participation in the event leads to further involvement of students in community-based tutoring and after-school programs.

Kansas State University

The SAVE student organization at Kansas State University, located in Manhattan, Kansas, provides interaction between students and rural communities located within several hours of the campus. The purpose of SAVE is to join students with elderly and poor residents in neighboring towns in repairing and maintaining their homes, businesses, and parks. Recently SAVE students worked with the citizens of a small community in painting all the storefronts on the town's main street. SAVE members organize several weekend trips each semester to introduce students to the problems and challenges faced by Kansas residents living in rural areas. So that participants can gain a better understanding of where they are going and with whom they are working, students are oriented to the work project and issues of rural communities through on-campus meetings prior to the experience, during the van trip to the community, and on site by community leaders and members. During the trip back to campus, students discuss what happened and how they felt about their participation in the rural community. Some of the participants choose to repeat their SAVE experiences through other similar projects, while others move into leadership and organizing roles to promote the SAVE opportunities, contact community leaders, or lead orientation and reflection activities (C. Peak, personal communication, 1995).

Saint Louis University

The Saint Louis University Community Action Program (SLUCAP) is a student organization offering a variety of one-time or short-term service-learning options for the university community. Student participants serve food in local meal programs, staff overnight shelters, visit and tutor in prisons, work in homes for abused children, renovate houses, and cut firewood for winter fuel. Taking action and reflecting on that action form the central elements of the SLUCAP mission. In addition to serving the St. Louis community, SLUCAP participants come together in small groups prior to and after volunteering to discuss the root causes of poverty and other urban issues, to reflect on their purposes and experiences in service, and to pray and worship together (S. Norman, personal communication, 1995).

Conclusion

The success of one-time or short-term introductory service experiences depends on many factors and is measured in different ways by students, faculty, administrators, community agencies, and, ultimately, the individuals and communities served. Conducting an assessment of students' interests, expectations, and previous service experiences as well as of community assets and needs is an important starting point for developing any service-learning program. Working with community partners to identify tasks and develop shared expectations helps to avoid service that does more harm than good or patronizes community members served. Careful preparation and management of programmatic details and involving students at each stage of the planning process help them to become invested in the project and motivate other students to participate. Selecting meaningful activities for which results can be seen and shared by groups of students helps to ensure satisfaction and build friendships among participants. Providing structured reflection opportunities; clarifying the responsibilities of each person or organization involved; including training, supervision, support, and recognition of students; and developing evaluation mechanisms for both student and community outcomes are important elements in designing and implementing introductory service-learning experiences.

Effective one-time and short-time service-learning experiences provide a balance of challenge (exposure to different people, environments, and issues) and support (thoughtful planning, group activities, student leadership). Although the depth, intensity, and purpose of these experiences are necessarily limited, nevertheless they can result in perceptual and attitudinal changes among participants and inspire their commitment to further service.

References

Astin, A. W. "Student Involvement in Community Service: Institutional Commitment and the Campus Compact." Paper prepared for the Wingspread Conference on Service Learning Research, Racine, Wisc., 1991.

Astin, A. W., Korn, W. A., and Sax, L. J. *The American Freshman: National Norms for Fall 1994.* Los Angeles: Higher Education Research Institute, University of California, 1994.

Campus Outreach Opportunity League. *Into the Streets: Organizing Manual 1993–94 Edition.* St.Paul, Minn.: COOL Press, 1993.

Delve, C. I., Mintz, S. D., and Stewart, G. M. "Promoting Values Development Through Community Service: A Design." In C. I. Delve, S. D. Mintz, and G. M. Stewart (eds.), *Community Service as Values Education,* New Directions for Student Services, no. 50. San Francisco: Jossey-Bass, 1990.

Giles, D. E., and Eyler, J. "The Impact of a College Community Service Laboratory on Students' Personal, Social and Cognitive Outcomes." *Journal of Adolescence,* 1994, *17,* 327–339.

Loeb, P. R. "Greeks and Granolas and Steeps and Slackers." *Mother Jones,* Sept.–Oct. 1994a, pp. 56–63.

Loeb, P. R. *Generations at the Crossroads: Apathy and Action on the American Campus.* New Brunswick, N.J.: Rutgers University Press, 1994b.

Serow, R. C. "Students and Volunteerism: Looking into the Motives of Community Service Participants." *American Educational Research Journal,* 1991, *28*(3), 543–556.

Winniford, J. C., Carpenter, D. S., and Grider, C. "An Analysis of the Traits and Motivations of College Students Involved in Service." *Journal of College Student Development,* 1995, *36*(1), 27–38.

Chapter Six

Ongoing Cocurricular Service-Learning

Cesie Delve Scheuermann

The tradition of cocurricular community service is a long-standing one in higher education. From the YMCA to fraternity and sorority philanthropic activities, from Circle K to organizations affiliated with campus ministries, community service has long been an integral part of student life outside the classroom. Many colleges and universities are seeking to develop more cocurricular service-learning experiences for students, and service-learning educators are attempting to include the key elements of reflection and reciprocity in the design of these programs.

Service-learning outside the classroom is often haphazard, and the quality of the learning that occurs may be suspect if students engage in little or no structured reflection. Moving from community service to service-learning in cocurricular settings requires intentional thought and planning if students are going to move beyond phases 1 and 2 of the Service Learning Model (Delve, Mintz, and Stewart, 1990). Because cocurricular service-learning lacks the structured environment—complete with course requirements and consistent meeting times—that the classroom provides, it requires more effort from student leaders, program directors, and service-learning educators to enable learning to take place. Nevertheless, cocurricular service-learning can be done and done well.

Getting Started, Making It Work

There are six steps in developing ongoing cocurricular service-learning programs: developing community sites, assisting the student or organization in choosing a site, getting the student or organization to make a commitment to a site, preparing the student or organization for service, engaging the student or organization in reflection, and evaluating program outcomes. All six steps are critical for developing successful cocurricular service-learning programs. Each builds on the others to ensure high-quality experiences for all parties involved.

Step One: Developing Community Sites

The community is the primary starting point for any effective service-learning program. Too often programs are developed in a vacuum, and the off-campus community and agencies are consulted only when student placements are needed. In determining how to work with the community, one of the key programmatic decisions that needs to be made is how many opportunities the program will offer.

It is advisable to begin a cocurricular service-learning program with fewer sites, so that greater attention can be paid to each community relationship. Although it may be appealing to tell students that they can be matched with any agency of their choosing, there is an inherent risk of forsaking strong relationships in order to offer a plethora of volunteer opportunities. Choosing fewer sites allows a program to underpromise and overdeliver rather than the converse, which may occur if just lists of agencies are offered. Involving fewer sites means that each student's unique interests or needs may not be able to be met. Nevertheless, students, and in turn the agencies, can be provided with rich, rewarding service experiences if service-learning educators take the time to develop in-depth knowledge and working relationships with each community organization that participates in the program.

An additional reason for selecting fewer agencies for students to work with is risk management. Program administrators will be on much stronger ground if they have prior knowledge of the agency should something go wrong. Many years ago when I worked at Georgetown University's Volunteer and Public Service Center, a number of students under the center's auspices volunteered at a soup kitchen. In the middle of the semester, the student who was coordinating the program came to discuss the students' experiences with me. Though the soup kitchen had not advertised itself as being sectarian, she described religious services that students were pressured to attend after the soup was dished out. In addition, students were getting intimidating telephone calls from the organizers of the soup kitchen, requesting, and often harassing, them to attend more services. It became obvious that, at best, this organization did not have our students' best interests at heart and, at worst, it may have been a cult. In short order, our students stopped going to that site, and I learned a valuable lesson regarding the pitfalls of having too many sites to supervise properly.

Another key issue that needs to be addressed when setting up community placements is determining the criteria for selecting sites. In making this determination, the following questions should be considered: Considering the time of day or night students will serve, is the site in a reasonably safe location? Is the site close by? If not, how can students get there? Does the agency offer opportunities different from other placements? Will students be able to interact with populations or issues that are currently not available to them? Who will be the site supervisors? Are they willing to work with program administrators and students? Do they have a positive attitude toward volunteers? Toward their clients?

It is also important to consider what the program is offering to and asking from the community. Typical concerns that may be expressed by the community are the number of students who will be volunteering, their ability to serve consistently, who will be responsible for them, and what preservice training the students will receive. On the most basic level, agency sponsors should commit themselves to offering students substantive projects and experiences, ensuring that they are reasonably safe, providing them with a person to call if things go wrong, and agreeing to meet with a representative from the college or university in person or by telephone at least once a term. In addition, agency personnel should view themselves as integral to the learning process for students rather than merely as supervisors who assign tasks. Agency sponsors can be responsible for working with the students on program evaluation, leading on-site training sessions, and talking through the students' experiences with them.

Step Two: Assisting the Student or Organization in Choosing a Site

Once sites are organized and agencies ready, students can choose placements. Ideally a staff member works closely with each student or student organization to select a mutually compatible placement for both student(s) and agency; however, this is often unrealistic for the majority of programs since staff and time are limited. A more plausible method of assisting students in finding a placement may be to set them up to do a self-directed search.

In this type of search, students are given a form containing pertinent questions, such as: Why do you want to volunteer? What are your interests? How many weeks or semesters are you willing to commit to a site? How many hours a week do you want to volunteer? Do you want to be within walking distance from campus, or are you willing to drive or take public transportation to a site? Are you willing to participate in three group reflection activities per semester?

Once a student answers these questions, a staff member or a seasoned student leader should review the application with the potential volunteer and steer the student to appropriate sites listed in a database or paper files. Files allow students access to brochures, newsletters, and other information provided by the agency that give a clear picture of what they can expect at the site. In addition to campus resources, students can visit the local volunteer center to learn about other possible sites. Once a student narrows the number of promising agencies, site visits by the student are in order. The student can meet with the supervisor or volunteer coordinator to ask basic questions regarding expectations, supervision, safety, and responsibilities. At this point, the student should be ready to make a commitment to a site.

Step Three: Making a Commitment to the Community Site

As part of a 1994 service-learning project at Willamette University, agency volunteer coordinators who were asked what qualities they looked for in volunteers identified three primary characteristics: reliability, commitment to learning, and compassion ("Volunteer Guidelines," 1994).

As is true of any new relationship, there is a lot of excitement in the adventure of discovery. Making the commitment to a site is generally not difficult for students, but sticking with it after the initial excitement is over can be problematic. Unfortunately students and site supervisors often do not discuss each other's expectations. Students do not automatically understand that, in return for their reliability and hard work, the agency is committed to their learning. Most agency volunteer coordinators are interested in working with students invested in learning more about the agency and the issues and populations that it deals with. Compassion is the third quality that agency coordinators seek. From their perspective, it is critical for volunteers to listen to and be supportive of agency clients.

The attributes of reliability, commitment to learning, and compassion need to be part of the student's decision to engage in service, and they need to be reinforced continually throughout the experience. Volunteer agreement forms can be a simple yet effective way for clearly defining student and agency responsibilities. The agreement can spell out the time commitment a student is willing to make, the responsibilities the student will have, what the agency is expected to provide to the student, and what a student is to do if he or she cannot volunteer at a designated time. The document can be signed by the student, the agency sponsor, and perhaps the college or university service-learning coordinator. Once an agreement is signed, the agency, student or group, and institution should each maintain a copy for future reference. If a problem should arise and either the student or the agency is not fulfilling the responsibilities specified in the agreement, the on-campus coordinator can schedule a meeting to review the expectations of all parties.

Step Four: Preparation

The quality of the service-learning experience for both students and the community depends on whether the students are properly prepared and trained. Some agencies have on-site training programs. More often than not, however, it is up to campus service-learning coordinators to plan and implement training programs, with the assistance of the community agencies. In training, students should learn about the individuals with whom they will work, the issues the agency is concerned with, specific skills they will need, and logistical information. Depending on the agency and the students' role, the training may be one session or ongoing. Basic information that needs to be stressed to all volunteers, regardless of the site where they will work, is the importance of dependability, sensitivity, confidentiality, and basic safety guidelines.

For students new to community service or new to the area, the need to think about their personal safety and the security of their belongings may come as a surprise. Students may be unaware of the basic street rules they should follow, such as taking reasonable precautions, recognizing danger signals, and knowing when to report unusual behavior.

In addition, introducing the concept of reflection to students when they are beginning their service experience will assist them in seeing reflection as an integral part of their work rather than as an add-on. It will also underscore the necessity of reflection as a way to ask questions, raise concerns, and make meaning of their community work.

Finally, preparing students for their work in the community also means helping them understand the issues of diversity they will face. Whether the issues are about race, socioeconomic status, age, or mental or physical abilities, students should be prepared for and open to learn about differences. If they are not, they run the risk of being overwhelmed and as a result may withdraw or inadvertently offend community members.

Step Five: Reflection

If a service-learning program is truly going to encourage students' learning and development, time must be set apart from the service itself to allow students to reflect on their experiences. Outside of a structured classroom setting, however, it can be difficult to get students to spend time talking about their service experiences, their feelings about them, and the issues that underlie the need for service. On the face of it, there may appear to be no tangible incentives to taking time to talk about the experience; some students may merely see it as less time to volunteer, study, or work. This is precisely why it is necessary to build in a reflection component to the service experience before students come in contact with the community. If students know and accept that reflection is an integral part of their experience rather than an afterthought, the chances are much better that they will participate.

When reflection is to take the form of group discussions, the groups should be no larger than ten and meet for no longer than one hour. Some students may be wary of the term *reflection*. For them, the word itself may conjure up notions of a religious experience or forced and uncomfortable intimacy. To engage as many students as possible, words such as *discussion group, check-in time,* or *thoughts and opinions* could be used in place of *reflection* to make students feel more at ease in participating in such a group activity.

Marquette University's Action Program has developed a reflection guide that contains many suggestions that can be easily replicated for a variety of cocurricular service-learning programs. The guide *(Marquette Action Program Facilitators' Handbook,* 1992) contains six elements of reflection intended to help students move from simple observations to more complex analyses:

Orientation: Who am I? Why am I here? What is important to me? Where do I come from?

Observation: What do I see and hear? How do I describe what I see (through storytelling and facing the problem)?

Feelings: How do I feel about what I see and hear? Why do I feel this way?

Interpretation: Why did I see what I saw? How do my values and experiences as part of a certain cultural, racial, ethnic, religious group, etc. shape what I see and hear? What are the barriers that prevent me from changing?

Personal Analysis: How am I part of the problem? How have I worked to be part of the solution? What gifts can I offer or learn? Where can I draw hope and strength? What signs of hope exist?

Social Analysis: What are the social and political roots of the problem? What are the possible solutions? Who holds power in this society? How can we as a group become empowered for change? What agency/institution holds the most hope for changing the current situation?

Other ideas for group debriefing include role plays, reflecting on a pertinent quotation, discussing one of the Wingspread *Principles of Good Practice for Combining Service and Learning* at each meeting, playing a simulation game such as "Bafá Bafá" or "Starpower," or viewing a video such as *A Class Divided* or *Freedom on My Mind* followed by a discussion of implications for service.

If group discussion is not feasible, there are numerous alternative models of reflection. The National Interfraternity Conference (NIC) advises each chapter participating in its Adopt-a-School program to devise five solid approaches to reflection in order to meet the various learning styles of its members. The conference offers the following suggestions:

1. A "reflection box" that volunteers may use anonymously or not, at their choice. Volunteers are encouraged to leave comments for the program coordinator regarding what is or is not going well.
2. A "mid-semester volunteer celebration" to spend time talking about what did or did not work.
3. Using one word to describe the community service experience. Students can explain why they would describe the experience in positive or negative terms.
4. The use of journals. If students feel comfortable having the program coordinators or other volunteers read them, this should be encouraged.
5. "Reflecting with color." Using crayons and magic markers, students reflect on their experience artistically. Students can then explain why they drew a particular image or wrote a certain word or phrase [T. Ledingham, personal communication, June 1995].

As students become more proficient in, and have greater access to, computer technology, reflection can be carried out electronically. On-campus computer discussion groups can be formed and e-mail messages sent by students who would rather write to others at any time of the day or night. An added benefit of using computer technology is that students will have the opportunity to "talk" about their experiences and carry on philosophical discussions not only with students on their own campuses but also with like-minded students from around the nation. Some of the reflection methods described in Chapter Five are also useful in ongoing cocurricular service-learning programs.

Step Six: Program Evaluation

All the efforts to develop a successful program may be in vain if program evaluation is not built into program design and implemented. This is one of the most important aspects of a successful program, yet often the step that is the first to go when time runs out. As budgets shrink and programs are scrutinized, a well-documented and well-evaluated program will be better equipped to justify its existence. In addition, a comprehensive program evaluation ensures that the needs of the community really are being met.

Evaluation can take many forms. Much like the volunteer agreement forms that might have been filled out at the beginning of the semester, evaluation forms should be completed at the end of the semester by both the student and agency supervisor. The purpose of the evaluation is to find out what positive things occurred during the semester and what improvements could be made. As a way of thanking community agencies, site supervisors could be invited to a luncheon followed by a focus group that evaluates the volunteer experience. Students could be a part of these groups or have their own evaluation sessions. In addition, a simple survey can be sent to students and agencies. Surveys are notoriously difficult to collect, however, especially at the end of the semester. It may be wise to offer an additional incentive, such as a small gift or a free meal, to those who return their surveys.

In a creative approach, students enrolled in a research methods class at Elizabethtown College in Pennsylvania take on the role of professional evaluators. Their course work includes studies of the effectiveness of the college's service-learning projects. An annual report can also provide a vehicle to evaluate a program. Occidental College in California requests that student leaders evaluate their programs. The results are then published, along with other relevant information about each program and community site, in the Center for Volunteerism and Community Service's annual report.

Programmatic Examples

This section highlights some programs that effectively combine service and learning in cocurricular settings. The examples represent the many types of programs that are offered in a wide range of institutions across the nation.

Leadership Programs

Many campus leadership development programs embrace the Social Change Model of Leadership, which views leadership as based on a "process predicated on the values of equity, inclusion, and service" ("A Call for Student Leadership," 1995, p. 7). One of the primary values the model emphasizes is citizenship: "Citizenship describes the process whereby the self is responsibly connected to the environment and the community. It acknowledges the interdependence of all involved in the leadership effort. Citizenship thus recognizes that effective democracy involves individual responsibilities as well as individual rights" (p. 7). A broader, less hierarchical, and more service-driven philosophy of leadership development has become the basis for numerous programs.

Ohio University

The Emerging Leader program, sponsored by Ohio University's Leadership Development Program, has four proposed outcomes: to introduce participants to the Leadership Challenge model of leadership effectiveness, to provide opportunities for self-assessment and increased self-awareness in relationship to personal leadership, to introduce the concept and value of service-learning, and to provide opportunities to apply leadership theory to practice. For two hours each week for nine weeks, fifty to seventy-five students learn about leadership and service-learning from campus and community leaders ("Emerging Leaders Planning Guide," 1995). Each term students spend an entire day on a farm in a wetlands area at ReUse Industries, Inc., a privately owned nonprofit corporation that works to recycle products from around the area. Students work to restore the land by painting, pulling brush, and building fence lines. The director of ReUse Industries talks to the students about the importance of local nonprofit agencies and the role students should play as community members. Prior to the service day, students discuss with the director of the Center for Community Service the concept of service-learning and what will be done at the site. After the day-long service and during class time, the director of the center leads the students in reflection and discussion about their experience.

University of Vermont

The Volunteers in Action (VIA) program offers students numerous ways to develop their leadership skills. Students who organize one of the thirteen VIA programs are expected to attend an off-campus leadership retreat in the fall and spring. The fall retreat focuses on team building, the nuts and bolts of running the VIA program, and overall goals and objectives for the organization. The spring retreat covers recruiting new leaders for the programs, a simulation exercise that heightens awareness of social justice issues as they relate to VIA programs, and ways to promote reflection within the individual groups. In order to provide support to students once the school year begins, two students codirect the VIA program. The council director is responsible for organizing volunteer recognition, public relations, budgets, and recruitment. The director of programs is responsible for meeting regularly with program leaders on a one-to-one basis. In addition, student leaders come together for a weekly meeting to discuss matters that affect the entire organization—for example, fundraising, logistics, volunteer management, stress management, and social justice issues (M. Rose, personal communication, November 1995).

Gulf Coast Community College

Located in Panama City, Florida, Gulf Coast Community College develops leaders through the Citizen Leadership Institute. Funded by a grant from the W. K. Kellogg Foundation, the institute "characterizes the citizen leader as a cornerstone . . . a catalyst, a provoker of change, a communicator . . . and a collaborator" ("Building Citizen Leaders," 1994). Students who enroll in the two-credit Citizen Leadership Training Program receive instruction in four basic areas: awareness, transformation, commitment, and action. In the area of awareness, topics that are covered include leadership styles, values, and barriers in diversity; transformation looks at the healthy community, communications in diversity, and listening and questioning skills; while studying commitment, students look at the citizen as change agent; and the action area includes motivating and empowering, persuasion, negotiation, advocacy, goal setting, and action planning ("Building Citizen Leaders," 1994). During the semester, each student is required to work for at least six hours with a service organization in the community.

Religious Organizations

It is the mission of nearly every major campus religious group to provide service and to relate service to students' faith development. Campus ministers often serve as advisers to these organizations.

Vanderbilt University

Described by the university Methodist chaplain as "ecumenical and radically inclusive," Vanderbilt's Room in the Inn program tries to prevent homeless men from literally freezing to death. Every Sunday night during the winter, students pick up fifteen homeless men; bring them to St. Augustine's Chapel; and provide them with dinner, showers, conversation, mattresses, and a morning meal. The eighty students who participate in the program have several opportunities to reflect on their work, most notably at the Sunday worship services where issues raised are incorporated into the sermon, liturgy, and prayers. Students also talk about their experiences and any special concerns at their weekly organizational meetings. The Room in the Inn is a citywide ministry; the Episcopalian and Presbyterian campus ministries also participate (M. Forrester, personal communication, June 1995).

University of Tulsa

Composed of students, staff, and individuals from area churches, the university's Regional AIDS Interfaith Network (RAIN) team provides a ministry of practical support, including transportation, meals, and visiting, to persons living with AIDS. Team members undergo extensive training and commit to attend monthly team meetings. RAIN represents an excellent way in which students can participate in an existing program in the community. Initially the team was watched closely by the citywide RAIN organization because community members were unsure how it would work on a college campus. Because the team is now considered to be one of the strongest in the area, it has been asked to represent RAIN in media coverage (L. W. Baskett, personal communication, March 1995).

Habitat for Humanity

Habitat for Humanity is an expressly Christian ministry inclusive of persons of all faiths that has gained worldwide recognition for its work in building quality homes together with the families who eventually become the homes' residents. It gives students the opportunity to provide physical labor in a group setting on a regular basis. Habitat has an application process for colleges and universities that wish to start chapters. A prospective campus chapter must agree to hold open meetings that include both prayer and time to explore faith in terms of service.

In lieu of creating a campus chapter, many student groups affiliate with an existing Habitat for Humanity chapter in the community. Peter Taylor from Bates College, an adviser to Bates's campus chapter, offers three suggestions on how relationships between the campus and community Habitats can be strengthened: "First, establish solid communication links between the affiliate and campus chapter. . . . Second, seek out additional volunteer opportunities other than on-site construction such as site selection, family selection, family support, public relations, materials acquisition, etc. . . . Third, if the affiliate nearest you is not cooperative, contact another, especially if your institution is in or near a metropolitan area" (Taylor, 1995).

Service-Oriented Student Organizations and Projects

Virtually every college and university has at least one student organization dedicated to community service and one or more ongoing community service projects. Relatively few of these, however, include reflection on the service experiences. Following are some examples of organizations and projects that have developed a reflection component.

University of California at Los Angeles (UCLA)

The UCLA Community Programs Office houses twenty-eight student-initiated and student-supported projects that encompass educational, legal, social, medical, and academic services to underserved communities in the Los Angeles area. The projects are based in part on the premise that "while working with the community, students must consciously make an effort to continuously learn, to question, to analyze, to have dialogue, to listen, to reflect, to be critical, and to do work. . . . Most importantly, students must not assume that they have the answers for their community" ("A Conscious Effort," 1994).

Many of the UCLA projects serve ethnically diverse populations, such as the American Indian Tutorial Project, Asian Dental Care Program, and Black Hypertension Project. Two other programs, Black-Latino AIDS Project (BLAIDS) and Latinas Guiding Latinas, are standouts. BLAIDS works to break down the misconception that AIDS is just a "white, male, homosexual disease." Volunteers are trained to counsel about AIDS and to disseminate information and condoms, where allowed, in the black and Latino communities. Latinas Guiding Latinas (LGL) was formed because Latinas have the lowest educational attainment of any group in the United States. LGL provides university tours, social and cultural events, student-parent conferences, school visits, workshops, professional role models, and ongoing mentorship.

Best Buddies

Best Buddies, an international organization founded in 1988 by Anthony Shriver while he was a student at Georgetown University, matches college students with people who are developmentally disabled to form friendships based on mutual interests. Best Buddies has developed a strong structure for its 180 campus chapters. In order to become a campus chapter, a group must complete an application and commit to be active for one academic year. Student members agree to have contact with their buddies in person two to three times a month and telephone contact at least once a week, participate in two group activities with their buddies per semester, and attend mandatory meetings twice a semester. At these meetings, called "rap sessions," volunteers are encouraged to reflect on their experience and receive support and advice. The student "College Buddy Director" receives extensive training and support from the national and regional Best Buddies offices. Best Buddies sponsors each director to attend its annual national three-day conference.

Ohio University

The Center for Community Service at Ohio University seeks to encourage and support curricular and cocurricular initiatives, promote reflection and scholarship, meet community needs as identified by community members, work collaboratively with campus and community-based organizations and efforts, and routinely evaluate its initiatives ("Our Mission," 1994). Two cocurricular programs of note are AppalAction and Special Needs Athletes Partners Program (SNAPPS). AppalAction was started by a student who realized that after three and one-half years she had not explored the Appalachian culture that was around her in Athens, Ohio. In addition to raising awareness about Appalachian culture, the group has focused on projects such as a river cleanup, painting a high school gymnasium, and washing the windows of the old train depot. Group members meet twice a month to plan projects and discuss issues raised by their presence in the community (Bortle, 1994).

SNAPPS is a joint venture between students and children with disabilities who are mainstreamed into the surrounding communities. SNAPPS trains special-needs athletes once a week for athletic competitions such as Special Olympics. The volunteers also meet an additional night per week to plan for the upcoming week and to discuss meets, activities, and competitions (Stephens, 1994).

Florida State University

Project Amistades, or "Project Friendship," is a service-learning program that links students with service opportunities within the Hispanic migrant community of Gadsden County, forty-five minutes away from the university. Sponsored by the Office of Campus Community Partnerships, Project Amistades consists of five different activities: in-school tutoring, homework assistance, adult literacy class, a migrant health clinic, and Friday Fun Day with games for children. Reflection seminars, to which faculty are invited, are held bimonthly, but getting students to come to reflection sessions has been difficult. However, since the van ride to and from the site is long, the students have ample opportunity then to talk with peers and program leaders about their experiences.

Morgan State University

Sponsored by the Community Service Office, the Kreating Urban Unity Utilizing Morgan and Baltimore Adolescents (KUUUMBA) program is an intensive tutoring program that matches Morgan State students with first-time juvenile offenders from Baltimore. Swahili for "creativity" (and one of the Kwanza principles), KUU-UMBA was founded in 1994 at the request of the Maryland state's attorney's office in Baltimore. Forty-five Morgan State students are matched with ninety teenagers; they meet twice a week for two hours on campus. Together they work to improve the teens' social, reading, writing, and math skills and develop each student's leadership, career, and entrepreneurial potential. The tutors meet weekly to discuss issues that have been raised, develop the program, and attend to basic programmatic issues. Once a month, the teens meet to discuss similar issues (D. Ikhinmwin, personal communication, November 1995).

Residence Halls

Increasing numbers of colleges and universities offer service-learning residence halls or residence hall floors. The benefits of residential service programs include enabling students interested in service to live together, ease of organizing reflection, and increased ability to make a commitment to serving a set number of hours at one or more sites. Rather than creating specific service-learning floors in residence halls, other institutions focus on developing a range of service activities and trying to engage students living in all residence halls in service.

Michigan State University

During Welcome Week, part of Michigan State's orientation program, participating residence halls are assigned a community agency. As part of the reflection procedure, the students in each hall engage in service and take photographs at the service site. Hall leaders, who are trained in using the photographs in reflection activities, may make a bulletin board or put together a scrapbook as a team (Chabot, 1994). A staff member from the Service-Learning Center follows up with the Welcome Week volunteers and enlists them to provide service throughout the year to the community.

Georgetown University

After a few years of decline in numbers, the District Action Project (DAP), a community service residence hall floor project in existence for nearly twenty years, has seen a recent resurgence of interest. Twenty-two students applied to live on the floor and were interviewed by staff members from the Volunteer and Public Service Center and the Campus Ministry Office. Residents must agree to perform five to seven hours of service a week and participate in two retreats and programs developed by floor members. Each set of roommates is responsible for two social, reflective, or service programs per year. Floor members understand they must attend at least two programs from each category per semester. DAP also sponsors campus-wide discussions. Previous topics have included AIDS, domestic violence, the Holocaust and genocide, and faith and social change (C. Koliba, personal communication, October 1995).

Hobart and William Smith Colleges

Residents of the Community Service House, located in a former fraternity house of this upstate New York college, are catalysts for service on campus. Students who wish to live there must apply and vie with two to three times as many students as spaces are available. The application asks students to reflect on their motivations for service, previous service experiences, and goals they have for the Community Service House. The seventeen students who are selected each year must commit to five hours of individual service per week and one community service house project each semester. Previous projects have included a lakefront cleanup, a party for local children, food drives, and a cleanup of a historic opera house. The focal point of each spring is "Celebrate Service . . . Celebrate Geneva . . .," a one-day all-campus service event that has had more than a thousand participants. All house members are on the planning committee, and the Community Service House hosts the planning meetings (L.C. Turbide, personal communication, October 1995).

Fraternities and Sororities

There is no doubt that fraternities and sororities devote a tremendous number of hours to, and raise substantial amounts of money for, their philanthropic causes. A concern of service-learning educators is how to move Greek organizations from simple philanthropy to engaging in service-learning. One national organization, NIC, is instituting service-learning in deliberate ways with its chapters. In 1992, NIC began the Adopt-a-School program that by 1994 boasted 170 college and university participants in partnership with 180 public elementary schools. Over ten thousand college students devote at least one hour per week to work primarily one-on-one with children identified by classroom teachers as at risk. Before students can volunteer, they must attend an orientation and receive training at the school.

Each participating fraternity or sorority chapter receives a packet that outlines COOL's Critical Elements of Thoughtful Community Service (see Chapter Two). Chapters are expected to strive to meet all these elements as they participate in Adopt-a-School. Some of the reflection techniques NIC suggests can be found in the "Step Five: Reflection" section of this chapter. NIC is dedicated to ensuring that the Adopt-a-School program is about learning and that it is a reciprocal program between the college or university and the public school.

I was unable to locate examples of fraternities and sororities outside the NIC program that engage in regular reflection about their service experiences. When an e-mail message was sent out on the Service-Learning Listserv Discussion Group requesting examples, no one responded with program examples, although two messages asked me to pass on any information received.

In lieu of examples, a few simple suggestions are offered to help move fraternities and sororities, and other student groups, from philanthropy to service-learning. A first step is to retitle the philanthropy chair as the service-learning or community service chair. This rewording would send a distinctly different message to the student in that position as to what his or her role could be and should be. Service-learning educators can then provide workshops for these student leaders explaining the service-learning elements of reflection and reciprocity. Once the student leaders understand the basic concepts, service-learning educators can assist them to develop community relationships and opportunities to process service experiences with peers or a facilitator to determine what changes need to be made in the program, in society, or within their own lives to improve the lives of others. Fraternities and sororities have a distinct advantage in that service-learning "can be built into existing programs such as All Greek retreats or workshops, new member camps and orientation programs, Greek leadership classes and mentor programs, and recognition ceremonies and awards" (Albaneso, 1993, p. 6). Greek organizations' philanthropic efforts have long been a powerful force in ensuring the financial health of many nonprofit organizations. It is time to broaden the scope of Greek philanthropy to incorporate service-learning.

Intercollegiate Athletic Programs

Service in athletic programs is gaining more visibility. While many coaches may be reluctant to "share" their athletes during the season, and while care must be taken to comply with National Collegiate Athletic Association resolutions, some coaches are discovering unexpected benefits from combining service and sports, such as increased confidence, motivation, and teamwork. "Although most athletics departments are involved in community service in some way, greater emphasis should be placed on using student-athletes and coaches to promote the responsibilities of citizenship and public service" (Gerdy, 1993–1994, p. 32).

University of Redlands

The head football coach at the University of Redlands assigns the team captains the task of locating an agency, such as an elder-care facility or children's hospital, to adopt for the year. According to Tony Mueller of the university's Community Service Learning Office, "The success has been positive in unexpected ways. . . . The team is less nervous for a game if they spent that day volunteering. . . . The team also invite the elderly and at-risk youth to attend games where they get great seats and meet the [university's] president" (T. Mueller, personal communication, June 1995).

University of Maryland at College Park

Each semester, twenty-five junior and senior student-athletes who maintain at least a B cumulative average in their field of study participate in Team Maryland. Sponsored by the university's Athletic Department and the Center for Political Leadership and Participation, Team Maryland sends student-athletes to local schools and community organizations to give motivational speeches. The student-athletes are enrolled in a course offered through the center, which is located in the College of Behavioral and Social Sciences. During the class they are professionally coached in public speaking and have an opportunity to discuss their community experiences.

University of Nebraska

A similar program at the University of Nebraska does not offer credit but is successful nonetheless (Fernandez, 1994). The Husker Outreach Program has developed a partnership with another campus service organization, the Golden Key National Honor Society, whereby students go to area schools to give motivational speeches on topics such as the importance of being drug and alcohol free and the value of staying in school. According to Keith Zimmer, assistant director of academic programs for the University of Nebraska's athletics department, the collaboration with the honor society is crucial: "It's important that the kids see that you don't need to be just an athlete to make a difference" (K. Zimmer, personal communication, November 1995). In the spring, the Husker Outreach Program focuses on the School Is Cool Jam. More than eleven thousand school-age children fill the university's arena for a ninety-minute program of educational and motivational speeches, entertainment, and athletic demonstrations.

Conclusion

The benefits of developing a strong cocurricular service-learning program can last a lifetime for student participants. Students become more aware of the community around them, the campus becomes the front door to the community, and their world becomes a much larger place.

The bases of any effective service-learning program are preparation, training, and reflection. This chapter has highlighted some ideas on how to develop service-learning programs in the cocur-ricular arena, along with examples of colleges, universities, and national organizations that are meeting the challenge to provide high-quality service-learning experiences outside the classroom setting. Since most students discover service-learning through a cocurricular program, it is critical that colleges and universities accept this challenge.

References

Albaneso, V. "Volunteerism and Community Service Redefine Leader-ship." *Perspectives,* Summer 1993, pp. 4–6.

Bortle, C. "AppalAction Explores Appalachian Culture." *Community Connection,* Fall 1994, p. 4.

"Building Citizen Leaders: A Model for Community Colleges." Panama City, Fla.: Citizen Leadership Institute, Gulf Coast Community College, 1994.

"A Call for Student Leadership." *NASPA Forum,* 1995, *15*(8), 6–7.

Chabot, J. *Welcome Week Orientation Venture Grant Final Report.* East Lansing: Service Learning Center, Michigan State University, 1994.

"A Conscious Effort . . ." Los Angeles: Community Programs Office, University of California, Los Angeles, 1994.

Delve, C. I., Mintz, S. D., and Stewart, G. M. "Promoting Values Development Through Community Service: A Design." In C. I. Delve, S. D. Mintz, and G. M. Stewart (eds.), *Community Service as Values Education,* New Directions for Student Services, no. 50. San Francisco: Jossey-Bass, 1990.

"Emerging Leaders Planning Guide." Athens: Ohio University Leadership Development Program, 1995.

Fernandez, S. "An Emphasis on Altruism." *Chronicle of Higher Education,* June 8, 1994, pp. A24–A26.

Gerdy, J. "Restoring Trust in Higher Education: Athletics' Role." *College Board Review,* Winter 1993–1994, *170,* 22–32.

Marquette Action Program Facilitators' Handbook. Milwaukee, Wisc.: Marquette University Action Program, 1992.

"Our Mission." *Community Connections,* Spring 1994, p. 2.

Stephens, I. "SNAPPS Trains Special Needs Athletes." *Community Connections,* Fall 1994, p. 7.

Taylor, P. "Habitat for Humanity." Service-Learning Listserv Archives, June 1995.

"Volunteer Guidelines." Salem, Ore.: Willamette University Community Outreach Program, 1994.

Chapter Seven

Service-Learning in the Curriculum

Sandra L. Enos, Marie L. Troppe

By integrating service-learning into the curriculum, educators do far more than give students opportunities for hands-on experience. They are providing students opportunities for encountering competing definitions of the common good, diverse viewpoints on the root cause of social problems, and questions about who and what knowledge is for. Courses employing service-learning encourage students to ask the larger questions that lie beyond the bounds of most traditional courses. Not only does service-learning have the potential to help students learn the content in a particular discipline, it also asks students to consider the context of a discipline and how its knowledge base is used in practice. Service-learning provokes intellectual struggles that result from testing abstract concepts with those who are affected by practical implementation of those concepts. Students find themselves having to explore ideas through the filters of many different constituencies, which results in confronting multiple layers of meaning.

Key Issues in Curricular Service-Learning

Curricular service-learning works best when it is used to meet course objectives. If service is an add-on that is not designed to advance the objectives of a course or does not help students learn course content, it degrades the academic integrity of the course. By integrating service-learning into a course, faculty are forced to reconsider their course aims. As faculty begin to evaluate the links they wish to make between the service experience and the academic content of their courses, they are also prodded to consider a wider range of course objectives. In most courses, the focus remains on academic content; however, faculty may choose service experiences that are linked to values related to such educational goals as environmental consciousness, multiculturalism and diversity, peaceful resolution of conflict, and community building. Service-learning also induces faculty to consider how their discipline, as well as their own teaching and research, relate to social issues and problems. Service-learning is about more than students' learning; it is also about effectively meeting community needs and applying intellectual expertise in a way that adds value to service.

Course objectives may also incorporate moral development, civic literacy, or the development of critical thinking skills. Because these aims are often considered general goals for undergraduate education, many faculty members have not stated these explicitly as course objectives. The thoughtful incorporation of service-learning into a course prompts faculty to think more broadly about desired course outcomes. Depending on the institutional setting, service-learning can also be used to assist the college or university in working on issues of importance to the campus community, such as retention, racial conflict, and town-gown relationships.

Because service-learning requires additional resources, including faculty time in supervising students and working with community partners, faculty and academic administrators may question whether the benefits of curricular service-learning outweigh the costs. Although there is some research on the effects of community service and service-learning on career, moral, social, citizenship, and leadership development, few studies have examined the effects of service-learning on academic development. Since 1993 researchers have begun to examine this question more seriously (Boss, 1994; Cohen and Kinsey, 1994; Markus, Howard, and King, 1993; Miller, 1994).

Markus, Howard, and King (1993) used an experimental model to study college students in a contemporary political issues course. Students in the service-learning sections reported that the course helped them apply concepts to the real world. They were more likely to attend class sessions and achieved higher course grades. Cohen and Kinsey (1994) studied an undergraduate mass communication and society course. Students found the service-learning component most helpful in understanding two key course concepts: audiences and messages. They found service less helpful in understanding a third course concept, institutions. In testing the effects of service-learning on college ethics students, Boss (1994) found that service-learning methods effectively moved students into the postconventional stage of principled moral reasoning. Miller (1994) noted that service-learning undergraduate students in two psychology courses reported that they were better able to solve real-world problems. These comparative course section studies, though not definitive, suggest that service-learning enhances academic development.

In 1994 Dwight Giles and Janet Eyler of Vanderbilt University undertook a national research project comparing impacts of different models of service-learning programs on students. One model used is service as part of an academic course. In interviews with "benchmark" and "novice" students in community service, researchers compared students' problem analysis, rating the analysis on its coherence and complexity and on whether the focus of their analysis was abstract and systemic or concrete and personal. They concluded that the major gap in knowledge is in the cognitive elements of social responsibility and the cognitive impacts of service-learning and that future research needs to go further in specifying these elements and developing better ways to measure them (Giles and Eyler, 1994).

Some faculty fear that service-learning will dilute the academic rigor of a course. To the contrary, however, these programs can intensify the level of intellectual effort students invest. Doing service in the community, when combined with the critical dialogue that faculty should facilitate in any course, draws students closer to, not further away from, the center of the course content they are supposed to be studying in the first place.

David Droge (1995) at the University of Puget Sound explains the hesitancy with which some faculty approach service-learning: "'Rigor' is traditionally defined as including books, library research and tests and excluding other opportunities for learning which are seen as 'softer' and therefore not rigorous." Hesitancy arises because "service-learning is less amenable to the standardization and predictability of the traditional academic classroom and calendar." Furthermore Droge points out some dilemmas for evaluation of service-learning: "Standards for evaluation of student assignments probably vary more widely than in traditionally organized courses. Students may encounter insights or understandings in their service experiences which are outside the realm of existing knowledge in a discipline or outside the experience of the instructor or both." Ultimately service-learning challenges faculty to reconsider their constructions of control and authority in the classroom and beyond: "Participation in service-learning necessarily involves some sharing or relinquishing of control by the people offering courses. How we deal with the 'unpredictability' of the world outside the classroom, how we capitalize on learning that might emerge when it is not on the syllabus for that day, how we balance our enthusiasm for service-learning with our obligations to teach our disciplines, how we anticipate a situation in which we might become the 'students' of people enrolled in our classes—these questions get to the heart of how we perform as teachers. To polarize the situation as 'rigorous' versus 'soft' ends a conversation which needs to begin."

The requirements of service-learning courses should be explicitly stated in course catalogs. Faculty should also clearly define learning objectives and service expectations and brief students about requirements and options in the first class sessions.

Curricular Service-Learning Options

Service-learning is not destined to be used in every course, but it is possible to incorporate it in any discipline. In each discipline, faculty must be able to answer the following questions: What purpose does this discipline serve in society? What does its knowledge base offer ordinary citizens? How can service be used as a text to illuminate the concerns of this discipline? In the process of their reflection, faculty will probably discover several ways to link service to the discipline under consideration. Service-learning has even been used in classics courses in which students compared community and family life in ancient Athens with that of a contemporary

American city. No one model of integrating service into academic study fits every discipline or every institution. Strong service-learning programs offer a variety of options and give faculty and students enough flexibility to achieve desired faculty course objectives and student development outcomes. The needs of communities must also shape the development of service-learning courses.

Fourth-Credit Option and Stand-Alone Service-Learning Modules

The fourth-credit option and the stand-alone service-learning module are examples of curricular service-learning options that are not integral to the design of a particular course. The fourth-credit option enables students to add a fourth credit to a regular three-credit course by contracting to do a significant number of hours of community service (usually forty to fifty-five hours per semester) and relating the service to the course. The fourth credit is awarded for the demonstration of learning that results from the service rather than for the service itself. Typically students complete a learning contract, which must be approved by both the faculty member and the service-learning center. Most faculty require students to keep a journal and complete a reflection paper or project that synthesizes the service experience with the course content. Loyola College of Maryland, Pennsylvania State University, Georgetown University, and a number of other institutions operate effective fourth-credit option programs.

One advantage of the fourth-credit option is that students do not have to wait for faculty to initiate a service-learning component in a course. Students can be the initiators and often even end up introducing faculty to service-learning. The professor may then begin to offer the fourth-credit option more actively in subsequent courses or may decide to redesign a course to integrate service fully. The assistant director of the Volunteer and Public Service Center at Georgetown University, Chris Koliba, notes that since non-service-learners are mixed with service-learners, the service-learners become advocates inside the classroom for this type of educational experience. All fourth-credit-option students at Georgetown must attend a midsemester seminar-like session with students from the other participating courses. Students are asked to reflect on why they chose to do the option, how the service is linked to the course, and to define service-learning in the light of their experiences. This session promotes the notions that service-learning is applicable in a variety of learning settings and that it transcends the classroom to become a part of one's lifelong learning process (Koliba, 1995).

One of the drawbacks to using the fourth-credit option is that the fourth credit is an add-on, not an integral part of the course. If faculty members do not invite the service-learning students to share their community experiences because they feel the other students will be left out of the discussion, the service-learners will fail to reap the benefits of regular group reflection. If professors do invite such discussion, it might take some time for the non-service-learners to become acclimated to the type of discussions that the service-learners initiate. Faculty members who lack knowledge of local community agencies but who approve the option in response to student requests leave students to rely on their own resources or the advice of the service-learning center for help in selecting a suitable placement. If the college has a service-learning center, this arrangement can work well. If not, the fourth-credit option may not be feasible.

Whereas the fourth-credit option adds a service component to an existing course, other options stand apart from courses altogether. Mesa Community College in Arizona coordinates a stand-alone module of service-learning that entails fifty contact hours at a site per credit earned. Students can earn a maximum of three credits per semester in this program. The student doing the module has two supervisors: one faculty member and one at the site. An elective, the module is a set of assignments rather than a course. Assignments include developing a learning plan, journal writing, three reflective sessions led by staff at the Center for Public Policy and Service, and a final analytical paper. Students choose the discipline to which they want this credit to apply and then are referred to an appropriate faculty member in that field. This option offers students the flexibility to link service-learning to any subject and affords faculty the opportunity to explore service-learning pedagogy on a limited basis, without reworking an entire course or teaching load. This stand-alone option, however, could be labor-intensive for faculty monitoring more than one student at a time since the students may choose individual projects that differ from each other completely. Another disadvantage is that, aside from the three reflection sessions, there is no group classroom interaction from which students often derive meaningful learning.

The Joint Educational Project (JEP) at the University of Southern California is another credit-bearing service-learning experience that is not integral to a course. JEP staff, supplemented by the extensive use of trained student program assistants (PAs), work with seven hundred to a thousand students per semester to provide links between their courses and work in community settings. JEP has developed relationships with a wide variety of service sites. PAs introduce the JEP in courses at the beginning of each semester, match interested students with placements, support students through reflection workshops, observe students on site, and prepare reports for faculty members. It is the faculty members, however, not JEP, who award credit to students for their participation. A distinctive feature of the program is the discipline-based questions that have been developed by JEP to help students structure reflection on their experiences and to assist faculty in making connections between course content and students' service. The advantages and limitations of this approach are similar to those of the fourth-credit option. Additionally, JEP staff cite the difficulty of getting faculty to become active agents in linking academic study to experiences in the community (R. Cone, personal communication, 1995).

Introductory Service-Learning Courses

Introductory service-learning courses enable students to serve while surrounded by the support of peers and faculty. Having the opportunity to discuss what they see and hear in these new experiences may prevent the reinforcement of negative stereotypes about people who are different from themselves. Rather than highlighting one specific issue, such as literacy, homelessness, or unemployment, students can learn about several of these issues and the relationships among them in an introductory course. Such a course might focus more on the service experience than on learning a particular discipline, but it might also motivate students to pursue further service-learning opportunities. Introductory service-learning courses, since they are not as content focused as discipline-based service-learning courses, might not be suitable for academic majors whose curricula prescribe a tightly specified course of study. For example, introductory service-learning courses might be considered interdisciplinary and therefore might not fit into the program of a premed student who has to fulfill a rigid set of science requirements.

Brevard Community College in Florida offers a three-credit Community Involvement course in which students do thirty-two hours of service and spend thirty-two hours in a seminar. The course develops students' skills and understanding of the community through reflection and action. In pairs, students select and research a relevant social problem. They then deliver a fifteen-minute presentation to the class and submit a five-page research paper. In addition, class participation, three exams, and homework assignments determine grades.

Michigan's Albion College offers a one-credit course, Volunteerism, Community, and Citizenship. (One credit at Albion equals four credits at most other schools.) Students spend thirty hours at a community organization. The course investigates the evolution of public service and volunteerism. It focuses on the potentials and limits of volunteerism, as well as the balance of individual needs with service to community over one's life span. (Chapter Five describes other courses offering introductory service-learning experiences.)

Courses Linking Service and Leadership

Courses linking service with leadership are offered at many colleges and universities. The Jepson School of Leadership Studies at the University of Richmond has several such courses. One course, Leadership and Social Movements, helps students understand the leadership of social movements and their own role in them. Students learn about the social movement origins of many concepts that have since become commonplace in formal organizations in other sectors, mechanisms of unjust subordination against which leaders of social movements act, and strategies they use to bring issues into the political system. The course requires students to work with the leaders of a movement organization. For example, students choosing to study advocacy for people with mental disabilities might work with a mental health consumers' association.

Another University of Richmond course, Leadership in Community and Volunteer Organizations, imparts a general understanding of the nonprofit sector and its contextual variables that have an impact on leadership. In this course, students must conduct an administrative task with the staff member of a community or volunteer organization.

The University of Colorado at Boulder selects sixty incoming students to join the Presidents Leadership Class (PLC), a four-semester leadership curriculum that engages students in different kinds of service-learning. Typically, five hundred students apply to this program, which includes a $500 per semester scholarship to those selected. PLC students earn three credits for attending weekly lectures and recitations, which involve service-learning. Each of the four semesters focuses on a particular theme: developing a personal leadership style and the ethics of leadership, community issues and leadership, global issues and leadership, and multilevel issues in leadership, respectively. In the second semester of the sophomore year, PLC students participate in a Walkabout internship involving twelve to fifteen hours of service per week. In the past, students have taught students with physical disabilities to ski, performed marketing studies for fledgling nonprofit organizations, and served as legislative aides at the state level. (The PLC's Walkabout internship is further discussed in Chapter Nine as an example of a program designed to assist students to make career decisions based on organizations' values and styles related to leadership and community service.)

The Maryland Leadership Development Program, housed in the Office of Campus Programs at the University of Maryland at College Park, offers a series of four credit-bearing leadership courses open to all students. One of these courses, Leadership and Community Service, integrates the concepts of civic leadership and community service. With the assistance of the Community Service Programs office, students select sites where they can engage in direct service. In addition to a weekly minimum of five hours of service, students do readings, participate in class discussions, keep a reflective journal, and write a biographical paper about a person, analyzing his or her leadership style and commitment to service. The course is taught by members of the staff of the Office of Campus Programs.

Service as a Required or Optional Course Component

Courses at many institutions include a service component that is used as the basis of papers, class presentations, and other assignments. The focus of such courses is generally on student learning about an issue, reflecting on the cognitive and developmental aspects of the experience, and linking the experience with academic content rather than on substantial community outcomes. In these courses, students engage in a variety of service work, including providing meals in a soup kitchen, tutoring children at risk of academic failure in elementary and middle schools, and cleaning up playgrounds and other public areas. These courses exist throughout the curriculum. For example, at Florida International University in Miami, students provide approximately ten hours of service in courses in world nutrition, social welfare policy, introductory writing, and others. Service may be substituted for other course requirements. In some cases, students may elect to write a synthesis paper based on their service experience instead of a customary research paper. Such students write descriptive and analytical reports identifying issues, programs, and problems faced by clients and those addressing community needs.

At Indiana University–South Bend, sociology professor Scott Sernau's Family course requires four to eight hours of service in a family-related organization. Service options are predetermined with community agencies, with students involved with home-based day care for migrant children, parenting education, educational enrichment for institutionalized children, and other projects. Students use these experiences to write short papers linking service with course work, examining how the agencies respond to community needs and noting unmet needs and problems.

The service experience is optional in a course at Rhode Island College entitled Learning by Doing: A Workshop in Sociology. In this course, students learn fieldwork techniques while providing service of their own design. Students not taking the service option are required to complete a final paper that incorporates library research and interviews of staff members at community agencies. The aim of the class is to document and critically examine how agencies and workers define social problems and then to relate that analysis to client and public understanding of issues. Discussions in class bring together in-depth work by some students in specific settings with the broader perspective of class members involved in developing an overview of services in the community. Linked to key sociological concepts of meaning making, the presentation of self, and the social construction of reality, students develop perspectives on the nature of the helping relationship as it is manifested in both individual acts and in organizational approaches to defining and responding to social problems.

Determining whether to make service a required or an optional component is an important decision. Managing a course in which two-thirds of the class choose the service option differs significantly from a course in which all the students are required to incorporate service. The same issues that arise in fourth-credit-option situations, in which the class contains some students doing service and others not, also apply here.

Either way, making service a course component rather than its primary focus may make it easier to introduce service-learning to students and faculty because the requirements for implementation are less demanding than for other options. Creating one or two projects requiring service in the community consumes less of the professor's time than does monitoring an entire term of community placements. For example, asking students to interview a homeless person or a child with a disability once is less complex than providing companionship to or programming activities for those individuals over a whole semester. The benefits of such an option, however, are limited. The brief exposure to service might reinforce students' negative stereotypes regarding populations typically in need of service, and reflection might not prod students into sufficient intellectual analysis to have any significant impact on them. In addition, it is important that faculty design service-based written assignments and more traditional written assignments to be equally demanding.

Service as a Significant Course Requirement

In some institutions where service is a significant course requirement, with the service an integral and time-intensive part of the course, a set of criteria has been developed for official designation as a service-learning course. The Lowell Bennion Community Service Center at the University of Utah has established the following criteria for its designated service-learning courses:

1. Students in the class provide a needed service to individuals, organizations, schools, or other entities in the community.
2. The service experience relates to the subject matter of the course.
3. Activities in the class provide a method or methods for students to think about what they learned through the service experience and how these learnings related to the subject of the class.
4. The course offers a method to assess the learning derived from the service. Credit is given for the learning and its relation to the course, not for the service alone.
5. Service interactions in the community recognize the needs of service recipients, and offer an opportunity for recipients to be involved in the evaluation of the service.
6. The service opportunities are aimed at the development of the civic education of citizens even though they may also be focused on career preparation.
7. Knowledge from the discipline informs the service experiences with which the students are involved.
8. The class offers a way to learn from other class members as well as from the instructor [*Service Learning Scholars Program*, n.d.].

A faculty steering committee at Colorado State University has developed similar essential characteristics for course inclusion in its Service Integration Project. (These characteristics are enumerated in Chapter Two.) Monthly sessions for faculty interested in service-learning provide a forum for discussion of how to integrate these characteristics into courses. Criteria like these should help distinguish service-learning courses from other types of active learning but should not be so rigid as to stifle faculty creativity. Most important, such criteria should be developed by faculty on the campus where they are to be used, not adopted in entirety from another institution. Once such criteria are developed, a faculty body should be created to review and approve proposals for courses to be designated as service-learning courses. Approved courses should then be identified as service-learning courses in course catalogs and schedules of classes.

When a course carries a significant service requirement, often the faculty member has experimented with lesser service requirements until the course has evolved to the point that it is integrally built around service. At the Maine College of Art, Art in Service is a three-credit elective course that teaches students to explore creative responses to the needs of their communities. Students create and lead art programs at hospices, neighborhood centers, homeless shelters, hospitals, and other sites based on the premise that artists have unique skills that are necessary to create a healthy community. Regina Kelley, who teaches the course, believes in the arts' power to transform the way people experience catastrophic illness. She says that artists take mental images and make them concrete. Visualization—in this case the creation of images that express individual attitudes toward illness and recovery—can greatly relieve the stress of those with chronic illness. Kelley believes in the importance of visualization because creative acts become models of how to grow or change. Since visualization is an important concept in art courses, the benefit of service-learning is helping students to experience and teach visualization in many different settings.

Francis Johnston at the University of Pennsylvania, who teaches Anthropology and Biomedical Science, also integrates a significant service component into his course. Through group projects, students in the class work with students at the Turner Middle School in West Philadelphia to understand the relationship among diet, health, nutrition, and growth. The Turner Nutritional Awareness Project offers an opportunity for students to apply theory by engaging in community health enhancement. Readings and class discussions focus on theories of health and disease; the evaluation of health; nutrition and growth status at the aggregate level; and the formulation, application, and evaluation of intervention programs. Sixteen students teach principles of nutrition to sixth-graders, four students evaluate dietary intakes, three students measure and analyze heights and weights, and three students work on a lunchroom project.

Using service as a significant course component can exclude students who work or have otherwise busy schedules, because they may not be able to take courses that require a substantial amount of service. Many faculty, however, prefer this type of service-learning because it transforms their teaching of the disciplinary content of the course and it enables students to see the connections between service and course concepts more readily.

Service-Learning in the Core Curriculum

Campus Compact's 1994 member survey revealed that of the 114 colleges and universities reporting that they had revised their core curriculum in the previous five years, 39 percent included service-learning in these revisions (Cha and Rothman, 1994). The main benefit of integrating service-learning into the core curriculum, which is far easier to accomplish in smaller institutions, is that more students have the opportunity to experience service-learning. Before deciding to integrate service into the core curriculum, administrators and faculty must determine whether enough appropriate service opportunities exist in the community for the student body and whether sufficient faculty and staff support can be provided.

A general education requirement in effective citizenship at Alverno College in Milwaukee educates students for service to the community. By developing and acting on a vision of public good that enhances the individual and society, students become aware of the inherently public character of their roles as workers, citizens, and neighbors. They foster the habit of viewing their experience from their perspective as both individuals and community members. Faculty infuse the study and practice of the four components that comprise effective citizenship—awareness, information gathering, judgment, and leadership and community involvement—across the curriculum, in all disciplines, from first through senior year, and they serve as mentors in both curricular and cocurricular learning experiences (Cha and Rothman, 1994). Students initiate applied research projects designed to meet the information needs of community groups, such as evaluating the effectiveness of community programs.

Every first-year student at Willamette University in Salem, Oregon, takes the World Views Seminar, a course that explores worldviews according to a different theme every four years. Two recent themes have been the Latin American world and the Middle Eastern world. Over half of the World Views sections include service-learning through one-time projects. For example, during the Latin American theme, one group of students explored rain forest issues in Latin America through reading and by conducting a local environmental project. Another group served Hispanic migrant farmworkers in nearby Woodburn.

Community Service Writing is a joint project of Stanford University's first-year English program and the Haas Center for Public Service. In the first six years of this project, over seventeen hundred participating students engaged in writing projects for more than one hundred agencies. First-year English students choose community service agencies and receive writing assignments from those agencies, including newsletter articles, press releases, grant proposals, and brochures. Because they write for an audience in addition to the instructor, students find the program prepares them well for the kind of writing they will need to do in their future careers.

The long-established PULSE Program at Boston College offers a number of service-learning courses. One of these, Person and Social Responsibility, fulfills the entire philosophy and theology core requirement of this church-affiliated college. The course runs for two semesters, and students earn twelve credits. The field placement component puts students in direct contact with people experiencing the consequences of injustice, such as poverty, prejudice, delinquency, or alienation. Using traditional and contemporary works of philosophy and theology, students explore their responsibility for overcoming social injustices.

Service-Learning as a Graduation Requirement

In 1992 the faculty of Centenary College of Louisiana added service-learning to its graduation requirements. All students complete a thirty-hour-minimum service-learning project: a project under the direction of the college's service-learning director, an academic departmental project, a service-learning module, an academic course with a service component, or a preapproved independent project. Similarly Waynesburg College in Pennsylvania has a general education service requirement in place. Students spend thirty hours in service, complete weekly journal entries, participate in a seminar discussion, and submit a final paper. At Warren Wilson

College in North Carolina, students complete twenty hours of service each year. This graduation requirement, in place for over thirty years, involves evaluation of the service by an on-site supervisor. Students attend regular seminars, and the service plus a pass-fail grade are recorded on the student's transcript.

Beginning in the fall of 1995, North Carolina Central University instituted a graduation requirement of 120 hours of service, which are recorded on transcripts. Students register each service experience with the Community Service Program Office and keep journals and portfolios as documentation. First-year students fulfill their service-learning requirement through a course, Personal Growth and Development.

At Portland State University service-learning courses are required for graduation. These are incorporated into the first-year seminar and throughout the curriculum. A two-course capstone experience embracing both service and academic applications completes undergraduate education. Portland State occupies a somewhat unique position in that it has restructured its curriculum to redirect and focus university work on the community and showcases service-learning as a key building block of the curriculum.

Service-learning requirements for graduation have been hotly debated and in some cases have been the subject of legal challenges. Proponents argue that requiring service-learning has the effect of making it a central rather than marginal element of a college education and that it represents an important opportunity to enhance student learning and development and to instill values of civic responsibility and social consciousness. On the other side of the issue are those who argue that forcing students to do "volunteer" work may provoke negative reactions from students and may in fact result in harm to the community if students unwilling to serve treat community members inappropriately. Opponents also claim that supporting large numbers of students in service-learning experiences presents management nightmares that undermine the real ends of service. Establishing service-learning as a graduation requirement necessitates careful planning. As Levison (1990) cautions, institutions adopting service-learning requirements need to consider not only their institutional missions and their philosophical reasons for establishing this requirement but also the location of the school, the ability of the community to accommodate volunteers, and a host of logistical concerns. Additional issues include faculty development and support for incorporating service-learning into the curriculum and the necessity of comprehensive evaluation of the impacts of service-learning on student learning and development, as well as on the community and the institution.

Course Clusters Involving Service-Learning

Course clusters, a set of courses grouped together to promote the creation of learning communities of faculty and students, are becoming increasingly popular. Clusters consist of two or three courses linked by common themes, shared assignments, classroom activities, and other special projects. The students and professors in a learning community explore ideas from different perspectives and make connections across disciplines. Closed clusters signify that students are required to register for all courses that comprise that cluster. In open clusters, students may register for individual courses within a cluster, or for the entire cluster.

We are not aware of any institution other than Bentley College in Massachusetts that integrates service-learning into course clusters. Bentley typically offers five course clusters, several of which include service-learning. Three of the clusters were specifically designed for first-year students. One of them, Computers, Communication, and Society, is a closed cluster consisting of two courses: one in expository writing and one in the principles of computing. As students develop skills in academic writing and computing, they also examine the impact of computers on people who are homeless and disenfranchised. Students teach residents of a homeless shelter how to use the Internet and other computer applications. Readings include essays on poverty, computer literacy, and the social impact of information technology.

The Bentley Service-Learning Project (BSLP) offers a suggested sequence of service-learning course clusters in a list distributed to first-year students. The sequence begins with a first-semester introduction to a community agency and continues with a placement in the agency through the sophomore year, a semester project at the agency in the junior year, and a more intensive service internship at the agency in the senior year. The BSLP employs students on service scholarships to act as liaisons between agencies and faculty teaching service-learning courses. In addition, BSLP staff offer faculty development workshops on service-learning and seek regular feedback from community representatives through the work of several advisory committees.

Because they are usually team taught, course clusters require much more collaboration among faculty than is generally practiced at most institutions, and faculty already spending extra time to team-teach cluster courses might not feel able to devote additional time to service-learning. Integrating service-learning into course clusters seems to be worth the extra effort, however, because of the ability of service-learning and course clusters to provide intensive interaction that enables students to integrate knowledge from more than one discipline while working with other scholars to solve multifaceted problems and to answer complex questions. Taken together, service-learning and course clusters have the potential to reinforce each other powerfully.

Disciplinary Capstone Projects

The purpose of disciplinary capstone projects is to integrate students' cumulative knowledge in a specific discipline and demonstrate that integration through a project. When combined with service-learning, such capstone projects can be outstanding learning experiences. In 1991, the Brown University Center for Environmental Studies began to develop programs to include service to and collaboration with residents of low-income neighborhoods in Providence, Rhode Island. One of the stated objectives of these activities was to integrate service, teaching, and scholarship. By 1994, the center director had hired a community environmental service (CES) coordinator to organize the course-based service-learning activities for environmental science majors.

The Environmental Problem-Solving course is required for environmental science majors to help them prepare for the senior thesis. Mostly juniors take the course. They meet twice a week as a whole group and once a week in smaller groups. In spring 1992 this class consulted with community leaders and took twenty-four blocks of Upper South Providence (Providence's lowest-income neighborhood) as its service area. Each student recorded baseline data for one block on such topics as the condition of housing, extent of lead contamination in soil, quality of open space, and health of street trees. One student group coordinated a house-to-house analysis of the risk to health from exposure to lead in dust and soil. Students discovered that lead levels in playgrounds and vacant lots were much lower than expected and did not present a significant risk, while lead concentrations in recently renovated houses were at dangerous levels. As a result of this new program, the number of students choosing to write theses on urban environmental issues has sharply increased. CES links selected individual students with community groups. These students then collaborate with community groups on topic definition, research design, and results dissemination for their theses.

At the University of Utah, students selected as "service-learning scholars" engage in four hundred hours of community service, take fifteen credits of service-learning courses, and complete a capstone project that integrates all of these elements. Their transcript notes their status as service-learning scholars, and the scholars are recognized at commencement. Sixty-five students participated in the scholars' program in 1995. Many relate their capstone projects to their major in creative ways. For example, the capstone project of one student who worked extensively with people who are homeless culminated in producing a children's book about homeless children that was written to counter stereotypes. A 1995 engineering graduate worked with an elementary school service-learning project that transformed an urban site into a nature park. He designed the grading required to install an accessible walkway over the sloped area of the park.

This capstone project approach to service-learning helps students to make deep connections between service and their discipline, to understand the relationship of scholarship to service, and to learn how to integrate service into their chosen career. Service-learning in disciplinary capstone projects works best in combination with other service-learning options that can serve as preliminary stepping-stones for students. Institutions that are just beginning to incorporate service-learning might not want to start with this approach.

Research as Integral to Service

Participatory action research and service-related research make the study of community problems and the application of research findings to the solutions the center of service-learning activities. The intent of participatory action research is to change a system while studying it. The researcher does not set the agenda; rather the community—the group affected by the change—does. The results are used to contribute to a body of knowledge and to be acted on. Because it emphasizes action by the affected group, participatory action research can help students understand the connection between service and citizenship. The service provided, research, does not achieve the desired result by itself. Empowering the affected group to conduct research and use research results as advocacy tools represents the real intent of participatory action research. Students involved in participatory action research have greater opportunity to view service as fostering capacity rather than dependency. Since they begin without a preordained agenda, participatory action research projects often lay the groundwork for extended collaboration in the future. Community members favor this approach because it tends to be more sensitive to their agendas and does not amount to research "on" them. Participatory action research, however, does not neatly fit an academic schedule, and community and scholarly agendas do not automatically merge. It takes a significant amount of time to build relationships in the community and to establish trust and a common agenda.

At Drexel University in Philadelphia, sociology majors must take nine to fifteen credits of participatory action research. These credits are not courses; they are entirely devoted to specific projects supervised by a faculty member. Students become involved in projects during their sophomore year, and many build on their projects to develop a senior thesis. In one project, students worked with a group of senior citizens at a neighborhood community center to conduct a needs assessment of the elderly population in the community. The results improved recruitment practices for the senior activity program and, in turn, improved its funding opportunities. Another group formed a reading group at a local library. Students and community members together read a published ethnography of the neighborhood of these residents, who then, as the subjects of the ethnography, wrote responses to it. In an approach similar to the one at Drexel, the University of Pennsylvania Department of Anthropology offers two participatory action research tracks—one in physical anthropology and one in cultural anthropology.

In the 1993–94 academic year, Cornell University students and other concerned citizens worked on a participatory action research project that documented the extent and nature of employment discrimination in their county. They researched the historical and contextual influences of discrimination in order to develop educational materials for all sectors of the local community around Ithaca, New York. In the same year, Regis University in Denver focused a participatory action research project on a lower-income, ethnically mixed, inner-city neighborhood. The project drew on existing campus-based service-learning programs to create research teams that conducted in-depth interviews with neighborhood youth and adult residents, community leaders and activists, and local police officers. These interviews uncovered perceptions and concerns about youth-on-youth crime and opened lines of communication among various groups. The project concluded with a public forum in which the research teams presented their findings, participants discussed the issues raised, and all involved worked on possible solutions and future agendas for campus-community collaboration.

In an upper-division oral history course taught by Beverly Washington Jones at North Carolina Central University, students engage in service linked to research. In the two-semester course, students learn oral history skills and apply these techniques to chronicling the Jim Crow era in the South, a project supported by the National Endowment for the Humanities. These skills are then passed on to community members who are tracing the history of their local churches and community service programs. Connections are also made to researchers in other universities in the area who are engaged in documentary work on this period.

Jose Calderon and Betty Farrell teach a two-semester Community and Social Responsibility course at Pitzer College in California in which students are assigned as participant observers and fieldworkers in the local school district. The district serves a diverse population comprising primarily Latino and Asian children.

Research by the students discovered significant patterns of ethnic segregation that shaped interaction in the classrooms. This research formed the basis for a component of a program passed by the school board of a more culturally sensitive curriculum and a revision of disciplinary procedure. In the second semester, students work with teachers to develop multicultural lesson plans.

The acquisition and passing on of skills related to research can be an important service to the community, especially if the community members clearly desire and seek the ends of the research effort. This blending of research, service, and teaching requires careful planning and organization. Students must be prepared within the time frame of the semester to identify and respond to community needs, and the field of research and its purposes must be worked out with community members. In some instances, the students' research is clearly linked to faculty members' research or community involvements. In order to encourage and support faculty involvement in participatory action research or other community service, institutions must recognize such work in the promotion and tenure process. (Chapters Twelve and Fourteen further address this issue.)

Service-Learning Internships

Metropolitan State University in Minneapolis has developed nearly twenty group internship projects in which students provide needed community service and take complementary courses in which they reflect on theoretical and philosophical aspects of their experiences. Internships include academic work in photography, applied psychology, community health, family studies, English, and other disciplines. Group internships also are organized around issues, with students working in the same service site or in the same issue area. Enrollment in these courses is usually no more than eight to ten students. Special attention is paid to developing university-community partnerships with organizations that serve as hosts for the students' work. Seminars provide students with opportunities for reflection about cross-cultural issues, challenges in research design and development, the application of theory to real-world situations, and other topics. Reflection seminars are specifically focused around critical issues and internship opportunities. (Chapter Eight contains a fuller discussion of reflection in internships.)

Susquehanna University in Pennsylvania offers the Psychology Practicum. Students choosing this internship are placed in an array of agencies dealing with child welfare, criminal justice, child health, and other issues and provide up to 125 hours of service per semester. In class meetings, students examine the contested nature of the helping relationship and explore the nature of service. In final papers, students are required to examine key issues facing the agencies and their clients, identifying psychological literature that suggests answers to the problems at hand.

For institutions with internship programs, service-learning may not appear to be an innovation or a new learning opportunity that may require special attention and planning. Although there are elements common to both types of effective programs, such as careful selection of the site, clear and compelling projects for student assignments, and supervision and monitoring of student work, service-learning can be distinguished in several ways. The opportunity for structured reflection with an emphasis on ties to the academic curriculum, so that students see connections between their actions on the job and their work in the classroom, is one important distinction. Another distinction relates to some of the purposes that many argue are the ultimate goals of service-learning: the development of civic responsibility and moral character. While internships may serve to clarify students' career interests and provide practical job-related experience, these outcomes may be ancillary benefits of service-learning but not its central aim.

Service-Learning Majors and Minors

In 1993, Providence College opened the Feinstein Institute for Public Service and began to offer a major and minor in public and community service studies. The first of its kind in the nation, this program was piloted with a group of eighteen students. The Feinstein Institute is guided by the principles of understanding human diversity, engaged citizenship, social justice, and human solidarity. To fulfill the major, students complete thirty-six credits (twelve courses), distributed as follows: a core of four courses, a specialized track of three courses, three courses in leadership skills and fieldwork experience, and two semesters of a capstone experience. For the specialized track, students choose from among the following courses: Not-for-Profit Management, Humanities, Social Science/Policy Analysis, and Environmental Problems. The minor requires six courses (eighteen credits).

Slippery Rock University in Pennsylvania offers a community service and service-learning minor, which consists of twenty-one credits. Students must take the following six courses: Citizens and Public Affairs, Introduction to Public Administration, Introduction to Public Policy, Organizational Development, Management Issues in Community Service, and Non-Profit Organizations; one of two courses in the Organizational Structures and Norms category; and a practicum. The practicum consists of ten hours of fieldwork per week and is designed to teach students the responsibilities, policies, structures, norms, and functions of community service organizations. It also explores the relationships among organizational dynamics, service delivery, and intellectual theory. Most courses in the minor engage students in service-learning.

Majors and minors in public service or community service-learning require a strong core of faculty with expertise in this emerging field to teach the specialized courses involved in these new programs. Partly because these programs are still few in number, educators continue to debate, without a definitive answer, whether service-learning represents a method or a content area in education. As a method, it shares much with other forms of experiential education; as a content area, it needs additional clarification to distinguish it from areas such as nonprofit management. No matter which way this question is answered, these majors and minors will offer students an opportunity to learn about and reflect on the issues surrounding the professionalization and routinization of human services before they enter nonprofit careers and repeat such patterns. Also, these academic programs might do much to overcome the separation between service and more traditional careers. Too often students view their choices as either-or; a student chooses between, say, the social work profession and being a lawyer or between teaching and becoming a stockbroker. In contrast, such programs will enable students to practice their professions, whatever they are, creatively, as a service to both privileged and disadvantaged members of society. (Chapter Nine elaborates on how students can be encouraged to integrate the values they acquire through service-learning into career and lifestyle decisions.)

Other Examples and Applications

The examples presented indicate the range of service-learning options that exist at colleges and universities, but the list is not exhaustive. Service-learning is also being incorporated into teacher education (Augsburg College in Minneapolis), social work education (Johnson C. Smith University in North Carolina), competency-based course work (Alverno College in Wisconsin), smaller campus learning communities (Arizona State University), residential programs (University of Colorado at Boulder), honors classes (Rutgers University in New Jersey and University of Colorado at Boulder), and graduate business education (University of Wisconsin at Madison).

Conclusion

A growing number of institutions and faculty are responding to the call for service-learning in the curriculum. Although service has been increasingly visible on campuses in the past twenty years, moving service-learning into the curriculum marks it as central rather than marginal to an institution. Given that service-learning helps students and faculty integrate context with content, explore competing definitions of the common good, question the uses of knowledge, and confront multiple layers of meaning, it makes sense to place service-learning at the core of our institutions. As research validates the academic benefits of service-learning and additional evaluation instruments are developed to measure those benefits, we hope that a majority of educators will affirm the importance of curricular service-learning.

Service-learning represents both a return to the foundations of American higher education and a push into the future. Thus, service-learning encounters both eagerness to innovate and resistance to change. Nevertheless, service-learning is leaving its mark on research, teaching, and service in the 1990s. The extent to which it can respond to and resonate with some of the key issues that face higher education, including curricular reform, changing demographics, and communities in crisis, may determine whether its impact is brief and marginal or long-lasting and deep. Service-learning is by no means a panacea, but it does offer opportunities to fulfill important educational and service missions through its incorporation into the curriculum.

References

Boss, J. "The Effect of Community Service Work on the Moral Development of College Ethics Students." *Journal of Moral Education*, 1994, *23*(2), 183–198.

Cha, S., and Rothman, M. *Service Matters: A Sourcebook for Community Service in Higher Education*. Providence, R.I.: Campus Compact, 1994.

Cohen, J., and Kinsey, D. "'Doing Good' and Scholarship: A Service-Learning Study." *Journalism Educator*, 1994, *4*, 14.

Droge, D. "Rigor." *Service Learning Listserv Archives*, Mar. 16, 1995.

Giles, D. E., and Eyler, J. "The Impact of a College Community Service Laboratory on Students' Personal, Social, and Cognitive Outcomes." *Journal of Adolescence*, 1994, *17*, 327–339.

Koliba, C. "Fourth Credit Option." *Service Learning Listserv Archives*, Feb. 13, 1995.

Levison, L. "Required Versus Voluntary: The Great Debate." In J. C. Kendall (ed.), *Combining Service and Learning: A Resource Book for Community and Public Service*, Vol. 1. Raleigh, N.C.: National Society for Experiential Education, 1990.

Markus, G., Howard, J., and King, D. C. "Integrating Community Service and Classroom Instruction Enhances Learning: Results from an Experiment." *Educational Evaluation and Policy Analysis*, 1993, *15*(4), 410–419.

Miller, J. "Linking Traditional and Service Learning Courses: Outcome Evaluations Utilizing Two Pedagogically Distinct Models." *Michigan Journal of Community Service Learning*, 1994, *1*(1), 29–36.

Service Learning Scholars Program. Salt Lake City: Lowell Bennion Community Service Center, University of Utah, n.d.

Chapter Eight

Intensive Service-Learning Experiences

Gail Albert

For students, moving from one-time or limited service-learning involvement to an intensive or immersion experience presents powerful possibilities for learning and development. Immersion in an unfamiliar culture, which can occur near or far from home, presents students with the opportunity to work with people whose experiences and perspectives differ from their own. Ultimately they can develop a sense of solidarity with the people they work with and an understanding of the issues that drive their lives. They can see and act on the problems communities face, engage in dialogue and problem solving with the people most affected by the issues, and question why the problems exist. Through this process, they begin to see how classroom theory applies to real-world issues and to recognize the interdisciplinary nature of problems and solutions. In dialogue and reflection with their service hosts, students become aware of the long-term implications posed by their actions, analyses, proposals, and decisions. They can wrestle with the complexities of the social fabric and grapple with profound challenges to social justice, such as racism, sexism, poverty, oppression, and the distribution of power. These experiences often lead students into a lifelong commitment to socially responsible citizenship.

Intensive service-learning programs in which students immerse themselves in the community they serve include both curricular and cocurricular models and can take many forms: alternative breaks, summer experiences, internships, independent study, action research, and national or international service. Program goals may be primarily academic or developmental and may emphasize civic and citizenship values, commitments to faith or social justice, personal and leadership development, disciplinary or interdisciplinary knowledge, or application of theory to practice.

Although the terms *intensive* and *immersion* have slightly different connotations, they are used interchangeably in this chapter. Service-learning is considered intensive when students dedicate themselves to a service experience for a significant portion of their time—more than ten hours a week—for a sustained period such as a semester or summer yet continue to live the balance of their lives within a familiar environment. An immersion experience offers the opportunity not simply to work in but to live the life of a community for a period of time. These experiences may be brief, as short as a week in duration; or they may extend for a summer, a semester, or longer. With these experiences, an unfamiliar culture becomes the setting for all facets of the student's life. It is clear that a semester of study, home stay, and service in a Mexican village constitutes immersion. Yet, for a student raised in a small midwestern farming community and attending a local college, a semester-long, ten-hour weekly internship in a multicultural neighborhood in Washington, D.C., could also be an immersion experience.

There are a number of particular challenges facing educators in developing intensive service-learning programs: designing programs to achieve desired outcomes, assessing student motivation and readiness, choosing sites that both serve the program's objectives and address the needs identified by the people being served, structuring reflective components to yield real learning and development, providing appropriate postexperience counseling to help students productively integrate the changes they have experienced into their lives, and carrying out effective assessment and evaluation for both students and communities. Through a discussion of these challenges using institutional examples of service-learning programs with different objectives and models, strategies for meeting these challenges are explored. The discussion culminates with a case study that describes how one program integrates the various program elements and addresses its challenges.

Designing Programs for Specific Student Outcomes

A wide range of student learning and development outcomes is attainable through well-designed and carefully implemented intensive service-learning programs. These include civic education or education for citizenship, personal and spiritual development, critical thinking, values clarification, integration of theory and practice, application and enrichment of content-based knowledge, and career and practical skills.

The more intensive a student's service-learning experience is, the more profound and complex are the possible outcomes. The service-learning educator's role is to articulate the program's intentions clearly and to address them in each critical element of the experience. Programs with civic intentions should provide students with the opportunity to discover how they can act on their sense of social responsibility to be active in a community. Programs with intentions of social justice should facilitate in-depth examination of the status quo, analysis of the sources of power, and community problem solving to effect change at the roots of problems. Programs that intend personal development outcomes need to provide an appropriate balance of challenge and support to enable students to work on their individual developmental issues, and programs with desired professional development outcomes need to incorporate strategies that offer students opportunities for values clarification, refining personal and career choices, and practicing professional skills.

Spiritually and morally based programs should employ methods that help students examine their relationships with a higher spiritual power, the world, and people like and different from themselves. They may reflect on concepts that are integral to their particular religious orientation, like compassion, justice, and service. They may include prayer, meditation, and the study of liturgy or philosophical materials that foster religious or spiritual growth and commitment. Discipline-based academic programs will have their intentions tightly integrated with course content, giving students the opportunity to use theoretical models, apply knowledge and skills, and test hypotheses in the context of real social problems.

It would be surprising if programs achieved only those outcomes they intended. Students can hardly emerge from intensive service-learning without experiencing personal growth and clarification and without gaining new knowledge in several areas. Spiritual development and commitment to remain involved in community service often result from these experiences, regardless of program intentions. Thus, this discussion of programming to intention is not to suggest that service-learning educators should attempt to limit outcomes for students but rather that the focus and design of a program provide particular support for the outcomes it is intended to achieve. Whatever the intended outcomes, the issues of program design that follow are important.

Student Motivation and Readiness

Using the Service Learning Model, one could assume that students who choose to become involved in intensive experiences have progressed to or beyond realization, the third of the model's five phases, merely by deciding to participate in extended, direct service to a single issue or community. This would imply that they are ready for the transformative "Aha!" experience that often accompanies immersion in a culture or an issue (Delve, Mintz, and Stewart, 1990, p. 15). This assumption may be accurate for some students, but many are motivated to participate in intensive service-learning experiences for a variety of reasons, not all of which are consistent with having reached a certain phase of the Service Learning Model.

When asked why students become involved in immersion experiences, several service-learning program directors I interviewed reported that their students do so for various reasons. The students often have experience in community service, but not necessarily with service-learning. Their motivations are not limited to those characteristic of the mid- to late-developmental phases of the Service Learning Model. For example, student applications for an intensive service-learning program at the University of Vermont frequently cited wanting to "do something useful" or "giving back to others less fortunate" as their reason for wanting to participate, hallmarks of the exploration phase (Delve, Mintz and Stewart, 1990).

Break Away, a resource organization for alternative breaks located at Vanderbilt University in Nashville, Tennessee, notes that many students describe their experiences as "fundamentally life-changing and the 'best week they've ever had'" (Willette, Magevney, and Mann, 1994, p. 2). As word about the "best week" phenomenon spreads rapidly on a campus, alternative breaks become popular and appeal to students similar to those in the exploration phase, for whom service as part of a group is both fun and unintimidating. They, like participants in some summer programs, may be seeking an adventure, a brief exposure to another culture, or something different from previous vacations, where they also might "do some good." Yet the same trips will also appeal to students at more advanced stages. The more complex the issues addressed, the more direct and focused the service, the more the appeal will extend to students in the realization, activation, and internalization phases, and perhaps the less they will appeal to students in earlier phases.

Curriculum-based alternative breaks, independent studies, action research, and internships suggest additional student motivations: academic interest in the service issues, desire for preprofessional skills and experience, and resumé building. Interns and independent study students at Augsburg College's Center for Global Education in Minneapolis often enroll because of an interest in issues of the developing world (K. Lutfi, personal communication, March 1995). Many students who choose internships have completed their course requirements and prefer to do something more practical than enroll for a course in which they are not particularly interested. Others, returning from study abroad, have discovered out-of-classroom learning and wish to continue to experience it; service is not their primary motivation. Stipends, educational vouchers, and the promise of work experience may influence participants volunteering in national service programs like AmeriCorps. One student interviewed by the program directors of Santa Fe Community College's national service demonstration program told them that AmeriCorps and higher education represented a way out of his involvement in a street gang (E. Bryer and M. Machen, personal communication, November 1995).

Break Away suggests that diversity in gender, year in school, ethnicity, sexual orientation, religion, socioeconomic status, and academic focus among student participants enriches the experience for all (Willette, Magevney, and Mann, 1994). The diversity of students' levels of experience can also be tapped to enrich the experience for all students. As a result of their exposure to one another in the active experience, students with less-developed approaches to service can observe their more advanced counterparts interacting with the community. In the Santa Fe Community College program, the AmeriCorps members represent a microcosm of the socioeconomic and ethnic diversity of Santa Fe, but "two-way mentoring works" as cross-fertilization occurs between those who are more academically knowledgeable and those who are more streetwise (E. Bryer and M. Machen, personal communication, November 1995).

More experienced students have the opportunity to serve as role models and to "teach" as they articulate the depth of their personal service-learning journeys in both casual and structured reflection settings. Thus, service-learning educators should design activities to capitalize on the range of students' experiences. Differences can be used to aid the learning process by creating student teams for reflective or curricular assignments, fostering students' teaching students through student-led projects, assigning students to facilitate reflection exercises, and employing a student leadership model, where more experienced students assume major responsibility for group leadership and reflection.

Recognizing that students may be seeking a variety of outcomes and may present themselves at different developmental stages raises questions for service-learning educators related to recruitment strategies: How will the program description used for recruitment affect who applies? Should prerequisites that will limit participation, such as previous service-learning experience, language or practical skills, or academic background, be required?

Service-learning educators must determine if the nature of the planned experience suggests limiting participation to those with a predetermined level of experience. If so, then the parameters for selection must be predefined, and the application or interview process must address them. Alternatively a program might choose to bring all participants to baseline qualifications by providing pre-service training. For example, L.E.A.D. (which stands for learning, environment, action, and discovery) at Western Washington University intentionally recruits students representing a variety of majors and values to coordinate environmental service-learning activities at local schools. The program makes no assumptions about their understanding of either environmental education or service-learning. Instead the first months' training focuses on basic skills (T. Pickeral and J. Morisette, personal communications, March 1995).

Site Selection and Planning

The community site, the service activity, and the scope and quality of students' interactions with community members significantly affect the nature of their reflection and resultant learning. Talking, sharing perspectives, working, and problem solving with those whose lives students touch are vital catalysts for reflection. Although many settings offer rich opportunities for interaction, reflection, critical thinking, and learning, some issues and sites may require greater student preparation and support than others.

As the Service Learning Model suggests, students in the early developmental phases may adjust more easily to a site where the preponderance of activity is physical and group based and interaction with problems and issues comes through observation (Delve, Mintz, and Stewart, 1990). With this group, casual or structured dialogue with community members will be more appropriate than intense, one-on-one involvements. Environmental work and building projects work well at this level, while interventions with individuals in a group home for pregnant drug addicts and their babies might be less suitable for students without significant additional experience and preparation.

In selecting a site, it is critical that service-learning educators follow the fourth of the Wingspread *Principles of Good Practice for Combining Service and Learning:* "An effective program allows for those with needs to define those needs" (Porter Honnet and Poulsen, 1989). An excellent example embracing this principle in practice is the program coordinated by Dé Bryant at Indiana University–South Bend. When asked how she identified sites for her community psychology action research program, Bryant responded that she did not choose her sites; they chose her. By establishing an active presence in her community through attendance at community events and literally "standing on street corners" to listen, respond to questions, and distribute fliers, Bryant learns about community needs and sustains a dialogue with community members. Her projects emerge from this "fact finding," which also helps her monitor changes in those needs (D. Bryant, personal communications, June, October 1995).

Selecting a site to meet both program and community needs can be challenging when the site is remote from the organizer's home base. Often site contacts evolve from established connections with a given community. For example, the director of volunteer services at Johnson State College in Vermont organized an alternative break in the Jamaican community where she had served as a Peace Corps volunteer. Her students helped paint and decorate the school built during her Peace Corps service (E. Hill, personal communication, June 1995). Educators who have not themselves established relationships with potential service-learning sites should attempt to identify faculty and staff colleagues who have such relationships through past experiences. Religiously based institutions may find projects through their faith community.

Faculty who engage students in action research or independent study often have established connections through their own research endeavors. Word of mouth through professional networks is an excellent way for program directors to share information about service sites. Internet discussion groups can be helpful in assessing sites, since few programs have the budgetary resources to scout potential sites personally.

Many programs take advantage of Break Away's SiteBank, a computerized national database of community, religious, and public organizations that invite groups to serve. Other organizations offer individual and group summer and longer-term service-learning programs. The Higher Education Consortium for Urban Affairs (HECUA) based in Minneapolis–St. Paul offers both local and international internships and field experiences. Most HECUA interns identify their own service sites, although HECUA can offer leads based on past experiences (E. Bejarin, personal communication, June 1995). The Partnership for Service-Learning, based in New York, works closely with local representatives in their overseas and South Dakotan host communities. They employ in-country professional academics to teach courses and an on-site program director who is an official of the host university. Their agency placements "grew out of the community and have stood the test of time in their usefulness to local people" (Partnership for Service-Learning, 1995–96).

Reflection

Reflection in intensive service-learning programs can be both structured and unstructured, but it should be continuous. The circumstances and relationships students encounter in immersion programs typically generate profound dissonance with their traditional ways of thinking. For the less-experienced service-learner, this dissonance may result in serious questions about values, justice, power, faith, and their views of reality and self. Reflection should be designed to help students recognize and integrate their learning, work on personal developmental issues, define their personal service ethic, and deal with their discomfort and dissonance.

More experienced service-learners may have already grappled with important questions and made significant personal choices based on their reflection. Through their participation, they may be trying out their service ethic in practice and seeking solutions to problems they have chosen to address. As one student reflected:

> After last year's ASB [alternative spring break] I came home and started asking myself questions like "Why is the world like it is?, Why are all the people on the trip white women?" Now this year, people are asking me those questions. This year, one woman asked me, "Why can't I take this [crack] baby home? Nobody else wants her." The questions just keep getting bigger and bigger. I thought, "Why did *I* go?" "Why do *I* have to go to do this?" It really affected my outlook on the way things are here and in the world. I discovered I don't know the answers. I do have some answers about what I can do. But when students come to me, I decided that it's not *my* job to tell them *my* answers—they have to find their own answers, which may be different from those I've found [University of Vermont focus group participant, 1992].

Ram Dass and Paul Gorman summarized this process by citing service as "'an endless series of questions,' puzzling and insistent. It not only raises questions, it helps to answer them. Service is a curriculum" (cited by Albert, 1994, p. 97). Reflection is the essential tool of this curriculum, the one that facilitates the connection between the experience and the intention, the experience and the learning.

Tools for structured reflection in immersion programs are similar to those used in less intensive service-learning. Group and personal journals, artistic expression, dialogue around focus questions, and readings contribute to the reflective process. In curricular models, readings, presentations, projects, research reports, and other written assignments can serve as catalysts for reflection. However, the type of immersion experience may dictate the use and nature of additional reflective methods. Many service-learning educators take advantage of Break Away's training workshops on reflective strategies.

Reflection Formats

It is important to set the context for reflection by providing students with the opportunity to examine their preconceptions or expectations before they embark on a service-learning experience. Students can write a letter to themselves, seal it, and leave it with their group leader. When they return, their letters are "delivered," students reread them, and then, either orally or in writing, reflect on what they have learned and how they may have changed their outlook. Alternatively, students may choose a partner from the group to exchange letters with and then reflect together when they return.

During the service experience, group meetings offer the opportunity for students to participate in "rounds" to share their experiences and reflections. Group journals are another effective tool for reflection. The journal may be a traditional notebook, kept in a central and accessible place. Students add their reflections to the journal and have the opportunity to reflect on or engage in dialogue with others' reflections while retaining a degree of privacy or anonymity. Another format for a group journal is a banner of newsprint stretched across the wall of a common space. These rounds or journals can be unstructured or structured by defining a question of the day or by creating sections that focus on particular questions—"Who did I learn something from today?" or "How does the concept of justice relate to today's experience?"

Reflection often can be stimulated by activities involving students and community members. These can range from sharing meals or recreational activities to more formally structured events like a panel of host community members discussing issues relating to their community and facilitating dialogue with the student group in response.

In all interactive reflection activities, it is useful for the group as a whole to define the rules of the interaction. Typically these include guidelines for ensuring mutual respect, like giving everyone an opportunity to speak, agreeing or disagreeing with others' ideas without judging them as individuals, and using first-person statements to express one's point of view.

Curricular programs often begin the reflective process with class meetings focused on course material prior to the service engagement. Class meetings during and after service involve more intense reflection on the relationship of content and experience at the service site. At Augsburg College's Center for Global Education, where the program focus is on peace and social justice as the means to a more just and sustainable world, students in the Gender and the Environment course travel to Mexico, where they live with families for four weeks and undertake independent study or action research. Faculty serve as facilitators for reflection, while community members are the real teachers. Returning to Augsburg, students enroll in four courses per semester that are integrated around similar themes (K. Lutfi, personal communication, March 1995).

Regis University in Denver, where the program intention is to examine the relationship of faith and service in Jesuit practice, requires every student to enroll in an upper-level religion course that focuses on social justice, faith, oppression, and related issues. Assignments include reading and discussion of such texts as John Kavanaugh's *Faces of Poverty, Faces of Christ* (1991), Martin Buber's *I and Thou* (1958), and various papal documents. Participants also convene in site-specific groups to address trip preparation and social issues pertinent to their host communities. Class meets for seven weeks prior to and twice following the service project. During the trip, students gather nightly to process the day's events and discuss topics that relate directly to the course intentions—for example, "What is the First World impact on a Third World economy?" or "What is the role of faith in a Third World nation?" In the final academic segment, each student submits a research document concerning his or her host population (J. Birge, personal communication, March 1995). Xavier University's program begins with three weeks at its Cincinnati campus, followed by ninety days in Nicaragua, which includes classes in language, theology and culture, Central American politics, and service-learning. Students live with host families. On their return, during the last week of the semester, they complete their courses (S. Namei, program description, November 1994). Similarly Kansas State University wraps up its summer program with classes: teams of students take a preparatory course, spend eight to ten weeks working in a local or international community, and return to a fall reflection course (P. Bennett, personal communication, June 1995).

Using Housing Arrangements to Encourage Reflection

Students may plan, travel, and undergo orientation and preservice training together, and then serve at individual work sites or undertake independent studies at sites remote from their peers. Some programs and communities hosting immersion programs arrange group housing in the site communities, which offer opportunities for participants to reconnect with their group for unstructured reflection. Students in Regis University's Romero House Project live together in the Denver barrio with a house manager and the Jesuits who cofacilitate their course and spiritual journey. By living among those they serve, even students in a program based close to home can develop a reflective environment. Service-oriented residence halls can provide similar benefits on campus.

An alternative to group housing is to match participants with community hosts. The University of Vermont's spring break program in Belize placed students with families representing the three local ethnic groups who were collaborating to create an ecotourism site in their local rain forest. Students took advantage of their daily van ride to the service site to engage in group reflection. The Partnership for Service-Learning often uses the host-family format. The host families are members of the community although not necessarily part of the particular population served. Host-family arrangements offer excellent informal venues for sharing perceptions and broadening perspectives of all involved. In some countries, where volunteer service is seen as a uniquely American phenomenon, families can gain new insight into the social issues of their own country by hosting a student. These conversations enrich students, who, in turn, reflect anew on the meaning of service.

Reflection in Internships

Internship programs take various forms. Some offer parallel, discipline-based courses; others have interdisciplinary reflective seminars where students can share their observations. These may run simultaneously with the service experience or occur prior to or after it. Many programs use journals, unstructured or structured with focus questions, as well as readings, writing, and oral reflection. These tools may be employed singly or in combination.

Strong internship programs require clearly articulated expectations for students, site supervisors, and program coordinators. It is highly desirable for the site supervisor to serve as a mentor. In this role, the supervisor can help the student reflect on the organization's history, structure, and funding sources; explore its internal politics; examine the larger social issues that affect its service and constituents; and understand the personal motivations and challenges experienced by others who spend their lives in that kind of work.

Students' potential for success is increased by a strong learning contract outlining personal goals and a work plan or agreement specifying service goals developed in collaboration with the site supervisor. The documents can be revised as circumstances change, but having an agreement provides intentionality to the work experience and a foundation for reflection, evaluation, and personal development.

At Spelman College in Atlanta, sociology students may enroll for fifteen-hour-per-week, semester-long internships. The intention of the internship is to increase students' knowledge of the use of sociology in a community context. Students complete an internship agreement and ask their agency supervisor to provide a job description. Reflection assignments include a thorough agency analysis examining history, objectives, client characteristics, organizational structure, and funding. From their journals, students submit weekly reports to the faculty adviser and write a paper relating sociology to an aspect of the internship experience. Students devise analytical questions about their experience, answer them descriptively, and connect larger sociological questions and concepts to their descriptive data. Finally, all students participate in a seminar, which serves as a venue for discussion of their observations and presentation of their research reports (H. Lefever, syllabus, March 1995).

Students who participate in the Community Service Learning Project at Northeastern University in Boston work at their host agency for forty hours per week for twelve weeks and take part in group service projects. All students, faculty, and project staff participate in the two-day training, which is designed with the intention of developing self-respect and compassion for others. Students also engage in leadership and diversity training, do problem-solving exercises, and complete journal-writing and reading assignments. Two-hour weekly reflection sessions provide the opportunity for discussing broad social issues, critical social analysis, developing understanding of the nonprofit sector, and personal reflection. The capstone assignment is presentation of a final project in which students reflect on and evaluate their experience.

Students in the University of Vermont Field Studies Service-Learning Internship Program may select their ten- to forty-hour-per-week internships from positions posted by local agencies or apply to agencies across the United States or abroad. The program requires a one-hour presemester orientation to set the context for reflection, and a call to the service-learning adviser in the third week. Students are encouraged, but not required, to maintain more frequent contact with the adviser. They keep a personal journal of their experience, which becomes a resource for their internship essays. The "portable curriculum" for reflection is the *Service-Learning Reader: Reflections and Perspectives on Service* (Albert, 1994), which was developed for that program and recently published by the National Society for Experiential Education. Chapters address service-learning, diversity, values development, philosophies of service, agency ecology, concepts of community and individualism, ethics and decision making, and global awareness. The interdisciplinary curriculum intends to develop students' capacity for critical thinking, self- and social awareness, and community responsibility. Students respond to a choice of focus questions related to *Reader* articles with a series of personal, reflective essays. They react to the readings in the context of their chosen question and illustrate why they believe as they do, using examples from their internship (and other relevant) experience.

HECUA offers internships in Minneapolis–St. Paul, Latin America, and Scandinavia with a focus on social issues in urban environments. Although programs have specific themes, the underlying intention is to "promote understanding of the human condition as the foundation for exercising local and global responsibility" (E. Bejarin, personal communication, June 1995). Students engage in twenty-hour-per-week internships coupled with a twice-weekly, day-long seminar. One seminar session consists of readings and discussion around internship themes, such as labor, the economy, community development, and the environment. The second is field based and addresses similar content, using the city and its people as text.

Reflection in National Service Programs

National service, exemplified by AmeriCorps, is another type of immersion program. Many AmeriCorps participants are college students who are taking a year or more off from full-time scholarship or participating as part-time corps members while they continue their education.

A number of AmeriCorps programs intentionally use service-learning strategies to encourage participants to concentrate on visible, demonstrable outcomes and to reflect on the systemic and institutionalized social ills that required their intervention in the first place. If participants vaccinate inner-city children but do not ask why the children did not receive adequate preventive medical care before or if participants teach adult literacy but fail to ask why the adults never learned to read, then the national service program may fail in its intention to build civic responsibility because it will have failed to engage participants in reflecting on their role as informed and active citizens to work to resolve social problems.

Corps members in the Southern Minnesota Youth Works *AmeriCorps program's Mankato Cluster participate not only in

AmeriCorps-mandated training but also in sessions on such topics as citizenship development, HIV-AIDS awareness, diversity, and service-learning. The service-learning training aims to encourage students to understand that both service and learning should be outcomes of their work. Corps members deliberately practice service-learning as they work in teams to plan one-time group service events. Using reflection from the planning stage onward, they develop community contacts, prepare modules that require dialogue and interaction to learn about related issues, and engage in postevent processing that serves as both evaluation and reflection. By including community site supervisors and staff in training on how to facilitate service-learning, the program also encourages infusion of service-learning strategies at the worksite (C. Murphy, personal communication, June 1995).

The Santa Fe Community College demonstration project already mentioned was granted funding from both the AmeriCorps and Learn and Serve America programs. With this dual focus, program directors have been able to make service-learning an integral part of their effort. AmeriCorps members tutor and mentor public school students during and after school. Learn and Serve participants may work in the schools or in other service programs. Some choose direct service related to their degree programs, while others work in organizations to recruit and organize other volunteers. Although Corporation for National Service guidelines did not support students to earn credit toward their degrees for their national service, the program director effectively negotiated that students could earn up to six credits for their nine hundred hours of required service (M. Machen, personal communication, November 1995).

Santa Fe's reflection takes many forms. The Learn and Serve participants begin by completing a form asking them to reflect on their reasons for service, their personal goals, and their preferred worksite. They also complete a service agreement with their agency. Once they have registered, they receive a journal with a syllabus of journal topics that need to be addressed weekly. Students also complete reflection forms about their agencies, which are kept on file for others to access. All of them are also enrolled in a related service-learning course, where they integrate their service experience with course content through reflection.

Santa Fe's AmeriCorps members' journals ask them to reflect on questions about their placements and the issues they observe there. The project coordinator reads the journals and responds to student reflections using sticky notes, so as not to intrude on the personal nature of the journal. She finds the journals to be an effective way for her to understand the challenges the students are facing and helps them express feelings they might not be able to verbalize comfortably in an interpersonal setting. Students also contribute reflections for progress reports that are required by the corporation. The project director and coordinator believe that many of their students have developed an ethic of citizenship. Of the students who completed their service last year, many continue to serve their agencies or other ones addressing similar issues; several are mentoring the new corps members (E. Bryer and M. Machen, personal communication, November 1995).

Campus Corps, a new program in Montana, expects to enroll twenty members representing community and tribal colleges and universities from throughout the state. Their mission is to promote service-learning on their campuses and to recruit students as volunteers for community projects appropriate to their local communities (A. Vernon, personal communication, October 1995). All members are required to maintain a log of their experiences, challenges, and learning situations, to help them focus on their personal, professional, and academic goals (A. Vernon, personal communication, October 1995). The logs will include not only reflections but also correspondence and materials the members develop. The project director will monitor the logs monthly, and the campus-based supervisor will review them weekly.

Pennsylvania's statewide Penn Service Scholars involves 145 participants who are part-time AmeriCorps members and full-time students at thirty-one colleges and universities. The institution-based programs vary in their activities and their reflection requirements; however, the grant requires all members to keep a journal and to take at least one service-learning course. The participants have monthly regional meetings where reflection focuses on both training and the service being performed. A three-day annual conference provides opportunities for reflection and training, and students meet monthly with their campus-based supervisor.

At the University of Pennsylvania, one of the Service Scholars institutions, the service-learning course students take must be in a discipline related to their service, which is the creation of a university-assisted community school. The reflection format varies with the course. For some a research paper becomes a reflection tool; others engage in problem-based learning, which examines the causes of, and proposes workable solutions to, community problems based on their research and experience. Student papers then become the legacy of the program, forming a library of experience to which other students can refer in developing their own research proposals (A. Cohen, personal communication, October 1995).

Coming Home: Supporting Students at Reentry

Once students complete or return from an intensive service experience, it is critical that they have the opportunity to continue the reflective process. In spite of the "high" they may feel, the community solidarity they may have enjoyed, and their sense of accomplishment in the work they have done, they often experience contradictory and disturbing feelings. Their traditional classes may now seem to lack relevance, sensitivity, and context (Willette, Magevney, and Mann, 1994, p. 37). My conversations with students reveal that some seriously question their lifestyles and privileges and feel uncomfortable resuming previous habits and relationships. They may find it difficult to communicate the depth of their experience to those who did not share it and may be hurt or angry when friends and family seem unmoved, lack understanding, or tire of hearing their stories. As a result, students may judge friends and family harshly for their insensitivity to issues for which they themselves hold new awareness. Many deeply miss their hosts and communities and feel guilty for abandoning their new-found friends. Often they feel overwhelmed by the scope of problems or pain they have witnessed and feel personally responsible for finding solutions.

Break Away notes how well-designed curricular programs provide excellent opportunities for postexperience support. Such courses enable students to reconnect with their peers, while course content provides "an outlet for . . . thoughts and reflection in an environment that has tools to address the root causes of the social issue they explored. Instead of feeling apathetic to their studies, students can see their learning as a part of the solution . . . [allowing them] to vent feelings, test theories, construct solutions, and plan further action" (Willette, Magevney and Mann, 1994, p. 38).

Other strategies include special gatherings for students who shared an intensive experience to participate in group reflection, trade photographs, and simply reconnect. Some groups engage in one-time service-learning experiences as a means of reunion and of continuing their commitment. It is also helpful when programs offer postservice activities that encourage continued community involvement. A resource fair with representatives of local agencies, community members from different helping professions, and individuals representing AmeriCorps, Volunteers in Service to America, and the Peace Corps can offer students new outlets for their commitments.

The Institute for International Cooperation and Development (IICD) of Williamstown, Massachusetts, is a private, nonprofit educational program that offers solidarity work programs in which participants volunteer in community-based development projects in Third World countries. IICD involves groups of ten or twelve participants and a teacher in a preparation period, during which participants define together and learn what they need to get ready for service, and an international period, when they perform their service and meet together in groups with the teacher. In the follow-up period the group returns to Williamstown to reflect on their learning and to develop their journals, photos, and videos into books, articles, films, or exhibitions, which they then share with audiences in K–12 schools, colleges and universities, prisons, and soup kitchens, as well as with civic and church groups. By spreading awareness about the issues they have observed, students can articulate and reflect upon their experiences (Institute for International Cooperation and Development, 1995–96). (Chapter Nine addresses how to assist students in making career and lifestyle choices based on the values they acquire through service-learning.)

Assessment and Evaluation

When a program's desired outcomes inform its structure and strategies, assessment and evaluation follow easily. Both are continuous processes that comprise the program's own course of reflection. Just as students need to engage in reflection throughout and beyond their service, program staff and faculty must provide continuous feedback to students and communities.

The reflections students share in class and in journals and papers can help provide qualitative assessment and monitoring of both student and community outcomes. These reflections, however, offer only the student perspective.

A work plan or contract developed by service-learning program coordinators and community representatives that contains clear expectations can provide quantitative and qualitative criteria for measuring service rendered. Additional mechanisms also must be established to communicate with the community to ensure the efficacy and relevance of the service. Although paper evaluation can provide important documentation, it is also critical to maintain an active and open relationship with the community hosts, for nothing is better than strong interpersonal relationships.

Programs address liaisons among the sending institution, the student, and host agency in different ways, but each partner has an important role in the evaluative process. Ideally the three parties would meet together periodically to review progress and reflect on the overall experience. HECUA has such a trio meeting at least once during the semester, as does Spelman's sociology internship program. In reality, however, not all programs have the resources to achieve that ideal. As an alternative, periodic monitoring through written assessments, meetings or "calls home" with students, and regular communication with host agencies is helpful. Many programs provide evaluation forms for mentors or agencies to complete with their individual interns at defined intervals so the feedback can be applied during the term of service.

Additional Challenges

Immersion programs present other challenges to service-learning educators. Many community colleges, urban universities, and other institutions with large numbers of part-time students report that immersion programs are difficult to plan for their students, who tend to be older, work at least part-time, have more family responsibilities, and take fewer classes per semester. These institutions find that the most successful way to overcome these obstacles is to integrate service-learning into traditional courses (G. Robinson, personal communication, June 1995).

Funding issues can affect participant diversity by limiting participation to those who can afford it. Some programs charge fees to cover program costs and offer scholarships to those who need them. Others make fundraising part of the commitment required for participation, keeping registration fees low and equitable by making up the difference between fee and cost with monies raised. Team fundraising projects can build group solidarity, but they also have the potential to consume energies and overshadow critical planning, orientation, training, and reflection activities.

Careful planning should outline anticipated in-transit expenses, define bookkeeping systems, and designate how fiscal responsibility will be allocated. Higher education institutions can also take advantage of the federal work-study program by allowing students who are eligible for financial aid to earn their work-study allocation for the work they do with an eligible community organization. In this way, students who must work to help support their education are able to use their work time in service to the community.

Cross-cultural and language training are critical to many international programs, and perhaps to some domestic ones as well. In curricular models the training can be integrated with course work and become part of the orientation and reflection process. Much cross-cultural education will occur within the service environment. However, when students are inadequately oriented to what they should expect at their service site, culture shock could impede their ability to adjust, contribute fully, or learn from their experience. Site leaders, whether staff or students, need to be trained and sensitive to warning signs of culture shock, homesickness, stress, host-student mismatch, and so forth, and be capable of the intervening with advising, support, referral, mediation, or change, as appropriate.

Political sensitivities are essential, especially in international settings. Dé Bryant at Indiana University recounted how her Social Action Project in Nigeria chose the acronym SOCACT after rejecting SAP (Social Action Project) because it was identical to that of the highly politicized Social Adjustment Plan, which was unpopular in their host community. HECUA, as part of their preproject planning in Bogotá, Colombia, maintains an ancillary site in Ecuador to which student service and learning activities can move hurriedly in the event of local unrest. Domestically, one program with environmental concerns was required to refrain from using the word *activist* to describe individuals whose names appeared on a list of contacts students were to use in gathering information about water-related issues (R. Cairn, personal communication, October 1995).

Other challenges involve logistical details, such as travel, housing, meals, immunizations, passports, liability issues, policies regarding alcohol and other drug use, personal safety, and emergency response. (These issues are addressed in Chapter Eleven.)

A Case Study

The objective of Dé Bryant's SOCACT, which began at Indiana University–South Bend in 1990, is to foster "the growth of effective and competent communities" (D. Bryant, course syllabus, 1995–96). SOCACT is a community psychology course that engages students, as members of a field team, in creating community change by learning to design, implement, and disseminate applied research projects that address "psychological and sociological problems in living associated with urban decline" (D. Bryant, course syllabus, 1995–96). The texts used for the course are discipline based.

The theoretical intent of the interventions is to examine "networks and how they function to spread innovation . . . [and] how culture (social norms about the way society functions) influences the creation of an intervention" (D. Bryant, personal communication, November 1995). The outcome of the research is used "to design more effective community interventions here in the U.S. and in Nigeria" (D. Bryant, course syllabus, 1995–96). Bryant differentiates her research approach from other empowerment research by her intent to focus on process, or the "way connections are made and between whom information flows," as opposed to outcome, where often we learn only about "why empowerment has failed" (personal communication, November 1995).

The project activities, which were the outcome of two years of "'fact finding' to understand how the communities defined their needs" (D. Bryant, personal communication, October 1995), take place in Benton Harbor, Michigan, and Aba, Nigeria. Bryant's means of keeping in touch with the pulse of the community is to play an active role in it. She attends meetings, talks to elementary school classes, emcees at events like a fundraiser for the National Association for the Advancement of Colored People, and actively listens as she participates to understand the spoken and "unspoken issues that always underlie the events that unfold in a community" (D. Bryant, personal communication, October 1995).

Field teams operate in three- to five-week immersions at each site. Their projects are predefined by the host community and tend to be interrelated and support each other as they build community: the Youth Community Theater deals with issues related to esteem, identity, and psychological development; an intergenerational program explores cultural heritage as it relates to life satisfaction and locus of control and creates plays for the theater group; Partnerships in Achievement engages youth in using their culture and heritage to develop basic business and personal skills, while the monies earned in their business ventures support the theater. An international pen-pal program links people in the United States and Nigeria through various media to explore the role of culture in identity and self-esteem; Education 2000 works to establish a public library in a Nigerian community and develop and implement a model primary school to generate a curriculum without culture bias.

The projects have long-term goals that extend far beyond the time frames of the classes that work on them. They are designed with the expectation that they may have a seven- to ten-year development process, after which the projects are to be turned over to community leadership. Team members make extended commitments to the project, and as they complete their term, new members cycle in smoothly as the project continues.

Most students pursue the course and fieldwork simultaneously. An unusual feature of this program is that students who participate in fieldwork are required to make a minimum commitment of three semesters; those who cannot make this commitment, for reasons of time or money, may participate as support staff. Support staff work for at least one semester, helping with literature searches on Nigerian culture and history, cross-cultural psychology, social movements, and race relations; keeping a newspaper archive from both sites; and assisting with project functions like data coding and clerical support (D. Bryant, course syllabus, 1995–96).

Student motivation for joining the project seems to fall into three categories: those searching for something relevant to study, those seeking research experience with practical application and relevance, and those who volunteer as support staff because they want research experience but cannot make the longer commitment. About one-third of the students participate without enrolling for credit, simply to gain experience (D. Bryant, personal communication, June 1995). Participants represent a variety of disciplines, and many have no previous applied research experience; the community projects use their varied backgrounds and talents.

Formal reflection and project progress assessment occur in required team meetings in which Bryant guides the discussion as members of the group report about their experiences and raise questions for discussion. As facilitator, Bryant keeps discussion flowing, ensures participation by all who wish to speak, and "detects *subrosa* topics that may exist" (D. Bryant, personal communication, October 1995). The goals of the reflection are twofold: to enhance the effectiveness of the service activities and to facilitate the learning and development of the students on the team.

Qualitative data collection in the Intervention Team Log, which forms the basis for the research, is also a powerful group journal because the data (observations on how communities react to and grow with their projects) must be articulated clearly enough to be analyzed by a volunteer coder. The research data also become a record for general assessment and evaluation of the community intervention and provide the core of the research on how community development and social change take place.

Team meetings provide the venue for Bryant to assess student progress qualitatively. The assessment is based on criteria clearly defined in the syllabus, where she acknowledges that "progress, then, is a matter of process. It involves problem solving, brainstorming, tenacity, consistency, patience, and (no small amount of) creativity" (D. Bryant, course syllabus, 1995–96). The course description and syllabus clearly articulate the community-building goals of the team research project and stress a clear interdependence among team members for the success of the project. Full responsibility for team outcomes is assigned to the students.

Grading is based on attendance at weekly meetings (forty points), submission of research data (forty points), and satisfactory progress on the community project (twenty points). Progress is demonstrated not so much by the project's completion, for, as Bryant acknowledges, "the amount of control each person has over their work will vary" (D. Bryant, course syllabus, 1995–96). Rather it is demonstrated by the student's engagement in the process and by meeting the attendance and data submission requirements, which would be difficult to accomplish "without having done the work" (D. Bryant, course syllabus, 1995–96).

Among the challenges this project faces are political sensitivities and funding requirements. Bryant's campus provides funding for SOCACT's local work, and the Indiana University system helps to support its international work. The intervention project has also been supported by contributions from locally based corporations and religious and civic groups. Unexpected costs that emerge as projects develop are covered about equally by all support services. Students generally need to contribute about half their costs for international travel. Another challenge Bryant cites is to "meet the real hunger students have to learn more about how to do this kind of community work" (personal communication, June 1995). Sometimes she must work with students to balance their involvement in SOCACT with other demands.

Conclusion

Intensive service-learning experiences offer outstanding opportunities for student learning and development in many domains, as well as for community development. Clarity regarding the program's desired outcomes, when it infuses the program at all stages from planning to reflection to postservice evaluation and support, will enhance the outcomes, for both participants and the communities served. To attain program potential, critical components must be addressed: service and site planning, participant recruitment, reflection activities, reentry support, and outcome assessment. While immersion programs may attract participants with diverse experience and developmental readiness, thoughtful planning can use these differences to increase the learning and development for participants at all levels. Questioning, problem solving, teaching, observation, reflection, role modeling, and dialogue all contribute to the learning and developmental process. When students and community members interact in these capacities and the service is rendered in the glow of such a reciprocal relationship, the outcomes can be transformative for all involved.

References

Albert, G. (ed.). *Service Learning Reader: Reflections and Perspectives on Service*. Raleigh, N.C.: National Society for Experiential Education, 1994.

Buber, M. *I and Thou*. New York: Scribner, 1958.

Dass, R., and Gorman, P. "Reprise: Walking Each Other Home." In G. Albert (ed.), *Service Learning Reader: Reflections and Perspectives on Service*. Raleigh, N.C.: National Society for Experiential Education, 1994.

Delve, C. I., Mintz, S. D., and Stewart, G. M. "Promoting Values Development Through Community Service: A Design." In C. I. Delve, S. D. Mintz, and G. M. Stewart (eds.), *Community Service as Values Education*. New Directions in Student Services, no. 50. San Francisco: Jossey-Bass, 1990.

Institute for International Cooperation and Development. *Global Education*. Williamstown, Mass.: Institute for International Cooperation and Development, 1995–96.

Kavanaugh, J. F. *Faces of Poverty, Faces of Christ*. Maryknoll, N.Y.: ORBIS, 1991.

Partnership for Service-Learning. "A World of Challenge . . . A World of Opportunity . . . A World of Difference." New York: Partnership for Service-Learning, 1995–96.

Porter Honnet, E., and Poulsen, S. J. *Principles of Good Practice for Combining Service and Learning*. Racine, Wisc.: Johnson Foundation, 1989.

Willette, Z., Magevney, M., and Mann, L. *Curriculum Based Alternative Breaks: The Manual*. Nashville, Tenn.: Break Away—The Alternative Break Connection, 1994.

Chapter Nine

Integrating Service-Learning Experiences into Postcollege Choices

Irene S. Fisher

People live richer, more useful, and more fulfilling lives when they are able to avoid segmented thinking and view career, relationship, location, and lifestyle choices as a coherent whole. Commitment to community service and social justice is a way of life that all individuals can choose rather than an option in only certain social-work-type careers or as a separate activity to be done around the edges of other commitments.

Students involved in service-learning have opportunities to engage in reflection processes that facilitate their learning about the larger social issues behind the individual and community needs they address. As students use journals, in- or out-of-class group discussion, and other creative ways to reflect on service, communities, and related social issues, a personal foundation develops from which life choices can be considered. Elements of these reflective processes that ask students to recognize the skills they bring to and develop in the service experience, assess their own learning and development, and contemplate the meaning of social responsibility are particularly well suited to help students lay the groundwork for later personal career and life decision making.

The stage at which students begin consciously, and often franti-
cally, to consider postgraduation choices provides a rich opportunity for personal introspection on the values they have recognized,
developed, or lived through their service. This is also a critical time
for the service-learning educator to encourage students to think
more deeply and seriously about how they will integrate these values into whatever future paths they select and create supportive
personal networks that can help them live and develop these values throughout a lifetime. Ideally this occurs after several years of
progressively more challenging service and reflection, so that students' decisions are part of an ongoing personal development
process.

Efforts to assist students with career and lifestyle choices should
be incorporated in the service-learning experiences discussed in
Chapters Five through Eight and grounded in the theories of student learning and development outlined in Chapter Three. In
addition, specific programs and activities designed for the final
months of the college experience can assist students at this critical
decision-making point. The choices students make and subse-
quently live are, in a very real sense, key outcome measures for the
success of service-learning.

If one accepts the view that people in all professions and occu-
pations can live a lifetime of service, then any career path can
become an opportunity to be an advocate for service, community
involvement, and social justice. The task for service-learning educators wishing to help students make choices consistent with their
values and personal interests is not only to help them identify their
own career interests but also to help them see how a particular
career choice provides options for service.

For program planning purposes as well as to assist individual
students, service-learning educators must be aware of postcollege
options for students and some issues related to each of these
options.

Postgraduate National and International Service

Many students choose to spend a year or two after graduation from
college in full-time national or international service as a change of

pace before beginning graduate school, a new experience before entering a career position, an opportunity to focus their energies and skills on service for an extended period of time, or a combination of these. A number of national service options are available to students who did not participate in service-learning in college, as well as to students who want to build on their collegiate service-learning experience in a full-time, challenging postgraduation service experience. These positions are generally low in pay but rich in other less tangible rewards. Full- and part-time service opportunities are available through AmeriCorps programs, funded by the Corporation for National Service, which include AmeriCorps* VISTA and the National Civilian Community Corps. The range of work settings and responsibilities is very broad. A distinctive feature of AmeriCorps programs is that participants earn a modest living allowance and a postservice stipend to help pay for future higher education or vocational training or repay student loans. Other opportunities for national service are offered by such organizations as Teach for America, Jesuit Volunteers, and the Lutheran Volunteer Corps, as well as through a variety of institutional programs.

Students who have been challenged by global internships, study-abroad programs, or cross-cultural service-learning experiences as undergraduates frequently seek additional short- or long-term international service opportunities. Students who lack these pregraduation experiences might also have interest in these programs as a personal challenge or as a way to compensate for not participating in these options as undergraduates. The Peace Corps is perhaps the best known of a wide array of international service opportunities. Habitat for Humanity, World Teach, Jesuit Volunteers: International, and the Overseas Development Network are other organizations that focus on placing individuals in service settings around the world. (Appendix B provides further information for service-learning educators and students about the programs noted here.)

Graduate Education

When students who have been engaged in service-learning consider graduate school as a postbaccalaureate option, a number of issues can arise that merit their reflection on service and career connections. Service-learning educators can encourage students to think about graduate school as both a place to continue their service involvement in another educational setting and as preparation for a career path to further service.

Undergraduates seeking service-friendly graduate programs should be encouraged to review catalogs and ask questions of graduate recruiters about their graduate programs' learning goals and the research interests and community service involvements of program faculty and students. As more and more alumni of service-learning move into graduate programs, they may well become the best advocates for service-learning at that level.

Individually Created Graduate Service-Learning Opportunities

Students in graduate programs in most disciplines can seek ways to connect their academic study with service to integrate service-learning into their graduate education. Ideally this effort would be supported by graduate programs that place a high value on community involvement, service-learning educators who understand the potential linkages between community needs and graduate students' learning and development, graduate faculty who have research and service connections with the community, graduate student organizations that offer service opportunities related to the discipline, and service-learning options within the graduate curriculum.

The minimum essential ingredients to allow the connection of service and graduate study in a program are a student's intense interest in service-learning and a supportive faculty adviser who will assist the student to meet program requirements and personal learning goals through engaging in service-learning. With personal interest and faculty support, for example, a master's candidate in statistics might conduct a survey for residents of an inner-city neighborhood to learn their views of how a vacant building could best be used and prepare a report for the neighborhood association. A graduate student in ergonomics might design a special chair that would enable nursing home patients to stand up without assistance. An education administration student might assess the need for and create an after-school tutoring program in a local elementary school.

Graduate Programs That Support Service

Graduate programs are increasingly seeking to attract students with interest and experience in service-learning. Some programs proudly publicize the service opportunities they offer students. For example, the Stanford Graduate School of Business advertises in its M.B.A. program catalog that over two-thirds of its students volunteer in one or more service activities each year. The Stanford Management Internship Fund uses donations from M.B.A. students working in the for-profit sector to supplement the lower salaries of first-year students who take summer positions in government or nonprofit organizations. A New York University School of Law publication proclaims that what distinguishes this institution from its peers is its setting and the extent to which it encourages students to value public service.

The University of Washington, in partnership with the Health Education Center system in the state, sponsors the Rural/Underserved Opportunities Program for students between their first and second years of medical school. Students are placed in community settings to work one-on-one with community members and to carry out community-wide health education and disease prevention programs.

At the University of Arizona in Tucson, the Commitment to Underserved Populations (CUP) program was initiated by medical students seeking to serve local communities, particularly the Native American community. The program sponsors a range of credit-bearing and cocurricular service opportunities for students in the summer and during the academic year. Twenty grants from the Pew Charitable Trust were recently awarded to health professions schools to integrate service into their programs.

Some professional organizations offer service opportunities to graduate students preparing to enter the professions they represent. The American Medical Student Association sponsors a number of programs for medical and other health professions students to gain service experience in underserved, culturally diverse settings. For example, the Health Promotion Disease Prevention project places medical, nursing, dental, and physician assistant students in community clinics during the summer in community outreach and health education projects. Its adolescent substance abuse program, Coaching Adolescents Towards Careers in Health, pairs medical school–based student chapters with local public schools.

Graduate student organizations may also offer opportunities for service and community involvement. Public-interest-minded students at Harvard Law School, for example, have organized an annual auction for the past three years to raise funds for their summer public interest work. Harvard Law School's Student Public Interest Network sponsors a mentorship program for students interested in pursuing public interest work. And Providing Unpaid Legal Services offers Harvard Law students the opportunity to volunteer at nonprofit and government agencies in the Boston area. The Public Interest Advising Office helps students make connections to these and other opportunities.

Graduate Programs That Relate Directly to Service

Although service-learning can be integrated into any graduate program and any program may be viewed as preparation for a lifetime of service, a few newly developing graduate programs focus specifically on service-related fields, such as nonprofit and voluntary organizations and philanthropy.

The Indiana University Center on Philanthropy offers a comprehensive program of study, research, teaching, and public service, with the goal of increasing the understanding and practice of philanthropy. Several degree programs are now available, including the nation's first master of arts in philanthropic studies, based in the School of Liberal Arts. Several dual degrees have been proposed. Such options would allow a student to pursue both a master of arts degree in philanthropic studies and a master's degree in another discipline.

Graduate programs in philanthropic studies or nonprofit management are offered at the Mandel Center at Case Western Reserve, the Institute for Non-Profit Management at the University of San Francisco, the Center for the Study of Philanthropy at the City University of New York, and Duke University. Many other institutions offer a concentration in public or nonprofit management within their management programs.

The Partnership for Service-Learning, a New York City–based organization that fosters the union of academic study and community service in higher education and provides service-learning opportunities in international and intercultural settings, is creating a master of arts program in international service, which will be offered by Roehampton Institute/Surrey University in London. The anticipated starting date is fall 1997.

Assisting Students in Making Career Choices

Private, nonprofit, and public sector careers can all offer opportunities for service and the pursuit of social justice. Nonprofit and public sector choices are more frequently designed specifically to serve these ends, but a careful career search can identify for-profit organizations that offer opportunities for civic and community involvement. Service-learning educators are in a unique position to make students aware of these opportunities and to encourage them to consider the pros and cons of careers in the three sectors.

Private (For-Profit) Sector Careers

Students considering careers in the private, for-profit sector need to think critically about how to incorporate the values they acquire through service-learning in an organizational setting that may or may not share those values. Because for-profit companies offer the majority of jobs, probably many students will find themselves either temporarily or permanently employed in this sector. Service-learning educators can help students think about issues and questions to raise during a job search process or after becoming employed.

Assessing Corporate Mission and Values

Imagine a student with career and personal interests in improving the environment who applies for a position with a mining or timber company or a new graduate who was involved with a homeless shelter and is now applying for a position with a local financial institution. Job seekers expect the prospective employer to assess their qualifications for the position. The service-learning educator can help students view the interview process as an opportunity for two-way assessment, allowing the job applicant to find out about corporate social responsibility policies and other issues pertinent to their own employment decision. The graduate interested in improving the environment might ask a timber company interviewer about the company's timber replacement policy. The applicant for a position with a local bank might ask about how the bank works to ensure compliance with community reinvestment requirements. Any applicant might ask about a company's financial or human resource contributions to the surrounding community, efforts the company has made to improve its internal environmental practices, or opportunities for employees to be involved in community service, during or outside of work hours. Additional information about company social responsibility policies is also available through annual reports and other corporate publications, past or present employees of the firm, career counselors, trade association publications, and press coverage.

Identifying Corporations That Support Employee Community Service

An increasing number of corporations offer employees opportunities to be involved in community service during work hours. Xerox Corporation allows employees to apply for a one-year paid leave to perform community service after three years on the job. About four hundred Xerox employees have participated, with projects ranging from work in homeless shelters and on American Indian reservations to participation in AIDS-related programs. Timberland, a New Hampshire manufacturer of outerwear, offers employees thirty-two hours of paid leave time per year to participate in one or more of five community projects organized by the company. Some law firms have pro-bono policies, which spell out the firm's practices for use of attorneys' time for public interest work in relation to billable hours. Mike Stevenson, manager of information services at the Center for Corporate Community Relations at Boston College, indicates that among companies granting released time for community service, most allow a maximum of two hours per week (personal communication, 1995).

Many companies organize and encourage community service activities for employees on their own time. Electronic Data Systems in Virginia recently developed a partnership with a local middle school as one project to meet its stated community affairs mission.

Chase Manhattan Bank held its first Global Day of Service in October 1995, giving employees in forty cities and thirteen countries a chance to help their communities. Allstate Insurance Company in Northbrook, Illinois, was one of six companies that received the Points of Light Foundation's 1995 Award for Excellence in Corporate Community Service. More than 75 percent of Allstate's 46,255 employees participated in its Helping Hands program last year. Projects included providing food for soup kitchens, neighborhood revitalization, and community-wide disaster preparedness. Fannie Mae in Washington, D.C., another award winner, involved 36 percent of its employees through the We Are Volunteer Employees program in projects that included mentoring teens, visiting nursing home residents, and delivering meals to people homebound with HIV-AIDS. Corporate Volunteer Councils in many cities work in partnership with United Way agencies or volunteer centers and facilitate involvement of area corporations in meeting community needs.

Building Corporate Support for Social Responsibility

Service-learning educators can assist students to realize that once they are employed by a corporation, they can encourage their employer to develop ways in which both the company and individual employees can become responsive to and involved in the community. The support of the chief executive officer and other corporate leaders is essential if a company is to develop and sustain a commitment to community service. Employees seeking to increase the corporation's interest in and commitment to community service and socially responsible corporate practices can work through employee organizations or the management hierarchy of the company to encourage this perspective. Even new employees can use the insights they acquired through service-learning in college to help the corporate leadership to realize the possibilities and potential benefits of involvement in community service. Often an employee can be an effective advocate for corporate social responsibility in ways that make sense within the nature of its work and location. For example, a food manufacturer or distributor can develop a partnership with local homeless shelters to make regular deliveries of overproduced or overstocked foods. A health management organization or private hospital can offer free health education, screening, and immunizations in local communities.

As more college graduates with a service ethic move into the for-profit sector, it is optimistic but reasonable to believe that employee workplace change efforts could focus on such goals as released time for community and public service, company policies regarding responsiveness to community needs, and employee service projects organized during work hours but carried out in non-work hours.

Careers in Nonprofit Organizations

Service-learning educators often find that the students who become deeply engaged in service-learning develop strong interests in careers in the nonprofit sector. Nonprofit organizations generally address a particular social or environmental need through direct service, advocacy, public education, grass-roots organizing, or a combination of these activities. Careers in nonprofit administration, program planning and implementation, and financial development are available in nearly all communities. The challenges to students seeking careers in the nonprofit sector will be finding and competing for the limited number of positions and living with the insecure funding and lower salaries that are sometimes, but not always, associated with these careers.

Service-learning educators should make an effort to keep abreast of job openings within the nonprofit agencies with which they work and develop ways to convey this information to students. When they develop a personal network of individuals involved in the community, they are in an excellent position to learn about open positions and to connect job-seeking students to them. Speakers from local nonprofit agencies could be invited to the campus to discuss employment opportunities with interested students.

Student volunteers should also be encouraged to make personal contacts with agency staff to learn about their work and identify job openings. The student who volunteers in a family services organization could discuss careers in social work with the social worker who heads the organization. The student who organizes other students to volunteer at a shelter for families who are homeless can ask staff there about career options that focus on homelessness. Many communities also have volunteer clearing-houses, United Way agencies, information and referral resources, and other organizations that are knowledgeable about nonprofit organizations in the area. These provide a good starting point for students seeking information on available positions.

Students interested in nonprofit work frequently voice the dilemma they see between their desire for success as defined by position, money, and power and their desire to make a "real" difference through full-time community work, so frequently available only with low pay in tenuous organizations dependent on fundraising efforts. These dilemmas are heightened by other factors, such as parental and peer pressure, the need to support themselves as well as family members, and debt acquired from educational and other loans. Students may be aware that they have the personal attributes necessary to achieve success in high-paying careers, and they may know from personal interactions with nonprofit agency employees that the hours are often long, the demands heavy, and the pay scale lower than in the private sector. Information about nonprofit organizations that do not fit this image can help broaden the picture but cannot eliminate this very real dilemma. Service-learning educators can encourage students pondering these issues to talk with community members who have faced them and found satisfying personal answers, as well as offering their own personal examples and support.

Public Sector Careers

Many of the issues concerning nonprofit sector careers are also applicable to careers in the public sector. Students seeking public sector employment will need to learn about the precise hiring schedules and procedures of the governmental jurisdictions, school systems, and individual agencies in which they are interested. Students may also benefit from reflective discussions about the role of government in addressing social and environmental needs, especially in this time of loud and frequent criticism of government at all levels. Service-learning educators can work with public policy centers at their institutions to develop campus forums on public policy issues that lead students to reflect on how their sense of civic responsibility and public service relate to these issues. In addition, they can advocate for the development of service-learning courses in government and political science and create opportunities for students to experience government at work.

Students considering public sector careers should be encouraged to learn about the opportunities for appointed and civil service positions and the different processes for seeking each. For example, students might be encouraged to become involved in a political party or an individual candidate's campaign as a route to an appointed position in the public sector. Service-learning educators should also suggest that students work with the campus career center to find out about local, state, and national governments' hiring procedures for civil service positions. Students who are interested in social problems and the role of public policy in addressing them may be well advised to consider elective office at some point in their lives. (Appendix B lists resources on nonprofit and public sector careers that service-learning educators will find helpful for students considering career choices.)

Integrating Personal Values into Any Career

Service-learning educators can help students understand that any career choice can be a venue for living one's values of civic engagement, social justice, democratic participation, and personal responsibility. From this perspective, physicians, dentists, and other health care professionals can serve some people free or at reduced fees or can organize other professionals to respond to international health care crises. Restaurant owners can make regular or seasonal contributions to local food banks. Utility company executives can support public policies that prevent utility shut-offs in low-income households during cold winter months.

One of the most natural ways to help students who are engaged in service-learning see firsthand how civic-minded citizens in any occupation can serve their communities is to have them ask a retail or corporate representative for contributions to their service projects. Each request to a restaurateur for a pizza to feed volunteers, to a hardware store for a chain saw to cut wood for Navajo elders, or to a physics professor to offer a science enrichment program in a school in a poor immigrant neighborhood offers an opportunity for students to observe individuals in all walks of life as they support (or do not support) community service. A discussion after such an experience can help students reflect on how they can integrate these examples into their thinking about their own future careers.

Personal Decisions and Life Choices

Mary Catherine Bateson, in her wonderful book *Composing a Life,* suggests that career decisions are best viewed as part of an integrated whole in a life that is continually improvised from the basic building materials of work, home, love, and commitment. Bateson, an anthropologist, questions the traditional life-planning view in which the choice of academic discipline sets the stage for a preplanned, lifelong, straight-line career pathway. Reality, she asserts, illustrates a much richer and more complex pattern of choices made over time within a rich context of constancies and innovation. She traces these complexities through the lives of five diverse women (Bateson, 1990).

Students looking forward to a life based on the values they have developed through service-learning might well benefit from Bateson's integrated view of life. Her book provides a foundation for understanding that the ability to live one's values related to service exists in a context of relationships, work responsibilities, and competing demands for time for family, community, and self. Realizing that they will need to consider these issues on an ongoing basis, as well as at critical junctures such as the completion of an undergraduate degree, can help students develop a context and a holistic approach to making life decisions.

The Service Learning Model reveals that college students in its advanced stages often face challenges as they exhibit an active commitment to the population they serve and begin to raise the larger societal questions of racism, classism, and economic justice. Such students feel resistance from family members and friends, who may not understand why they spend so much time with the issues they care about and the people they serve. They describe the disjuncture between their own developing interests and significant others who simply do not understand the changes in their behavior. They also indicate that their sources of support are community members and individuals on campus who share their concerns and commitments (Delve, Mintz, and Stewart, 1990).

Graduates who pursue their values in other career and life settings undoubtedly will face similar challenges to their involvements
and passions, but now without the supportive environment offered
through campus service-learning programs on a daily basis. Students will need to understand the importance of developing personal relationships with others who share their values to help them
balance the challenges they will encounter in environments that
are less supportive of their pursuit of social justice and moral commitments.

Anne Colby and William Damon (1992), addressing questions
of moral development, offer insights on the importance of creating a community of like-minded people for ongoing personal support. Their findings are useful to service-learning educators
wrestling with how to help students live consistently with their
social justice values. In their research, Colby and Damon interviewed people identified as living lives of high moral commitment.
One of their findings was the importance of associates, or interaction with a supportive group, who played an important role in their
interviewees' moral development over a lifetime.

The issue of support and shared values is critical as well when
students consider long-term personal relationships, such as the
choice of a spouse or partner. Lowell Bennion, the lifelong community servant for whom the community service center at the University of Utah is named, regularly advised students that they should
never marry someone until they have done a service project with
that person. Some may view this advice as quaint, but it underscores the need to explore personal values as part of the development of long-term relationships.

Service-learning educators should also work with students to
help them make thoughtful decisions about where to live and
work. A rural setting, for example, offers different opportunities
and challenges from an urban setting, and some social problems
are more evident in certain parts of the United States or the rest
of the world. Frequent moves from one location to another offer
opportunities to learn about the assets and needs of various types
of communities. On the other hand, becoming an active member
of a single community over time offers the potential to build strong
relationships and make a significant personal contribution to community development.

Creating Opportunities for Reflection on Career and Life Choices

Service-learning educators can and should design ways to encourage students to reflect on key career and life choices in a variety of settings. Programs that provide these opportunities throughout the college experience, as well as at critical career decision points, will increase the likelihood that students involved in service-learning can integrate their learning into their life decisions.

Providing opportunities throughout college for students to reflect on service experiences and their meaning forms the essential base for pregraduation strategies to help students consider career and life choices. These opportunities to reflect on questions and developmental issues related to career and lifestyle decisions in individual and group reflection as early as the first year are vital.

Structured Reflection Forums

Service-learning programs can structure and strengthen students' reflection on career and life planning by offering sessions specifically designed and timed for this purpose. Many formats to achieve this goal can be used; two models are examined here.

Through the Visiting Mentor Program, the Haas Center for Public Service at Stanford University invites individuals from the community to help students consider career and lifestyle issues. The purpose of the program is to enable experienced persons from various careers in the community and public service to interact with students informally. Mentors, who live on campus for about a week, participate in structured activities, such as residence hall discussions and consultations with student groups, and talk with students individually. Discussion topics include how the mentors chose their career field; how they balance career, family, and other responsibilities; and how they maintain their values and ideals even if working in a corporate environment. Mentors have included an African American community organizer from Los Angeles, a superintendent with the National Park Service who has been very involved with issues of community access to parks and environmental decision making, and a Washington, D.C., physician who works with poor and homeless patients.

The Presidents Leadership Class at the University of Colorado at Boulder offers another model for students to consider career choices related to their personal values. A goal of the program is to help students design their own perfect job based on their career interests and personal passion. The program's thirty-five-member board of trustees serves as a network to place students in internships in the second semester of the sophomore year. During the Walkabout semester, students work twelve to fifteen hours per week on a project of consequence while they study the leadership style of their Walkabout organization. They can also develop learning goals related to how their values for social justice and community service fit into the work setting as they experience it. When they complete the internship, students make presentations on the work they did and their analyses of the leadership styles of their organizations at a "Walkabout Weekend."

Career Center–Service-Learning Program Partnerships

Almost all campuses have a career center or career services office, and the service-learning program may be housed within this office. If it is not, partnership initiatives can enhance the capacity of both the service-learning and career centers to assist students in making thoughtful career and life choices.

At a minimum, service-learning educators can assist career center librarians to acquire and promote resources, such as those listed in Appendix B, and publicize the availability of the resources and other offerings of the career services office. Career center staff can present workshops to familiarize students with these materials or discuss opportunities for nonprofit careers. More active partnerships can hold special forums developed specifically for students active in service-learning. These forums might be reflective in nature, offer practical ideas for resumé writing to present service experiences most effectively, give information on service-related fields, or involve a combination of these approaches.

The Metro Volunteer Program and the Career Center at the University of Houston, for example, created a program, Work for a

Change: A Volunteer and Career Opportunity Fair, that is similar in format to many volunteer fairs. This one focuses on career opportunities by requesting that participating agencies send representatives who can talk to students about career planning, professional career tracks in their fields, and their own career experiences. Fair planners also invite organizations that go beyond the more traditional agencies and include groups such as Accountants and Lawyers for the Arts and the Chamber of Commerce. The fair offers breakout sessions to explore topics like "How to Do Well by Doing Good" and "What Is the Independent Sector?"

Career Exploration Internships

While many service-learning internships can serve as opportunities for career exploration, some internships are structured specifically to meet career exploration objectives. For example, at Michigan State University, staff members of the service-learning center work with faculty to determine career-related learning objectives for various academic disciplines and then try to match those objectives with community needs identified by agencies in the community. When a match is made, placements are developed and publicized to the students, who apply for the placements and can take them for credit or no credit. Service-learning center staff help the faculty members and agencies work effectively together to establish goals and to evaluate outcomes of the placements for both students and agencies. Sophomore students from any academic department at the State University of New York (SUNY) at Brockport may register for internships in their field. They are matched with a faculty adviser, keep a reflection journal, and attend related workshops. Students complete 125 hours of service and earn three credits. The community service office at SUNY Brockport is located in the career services department, and as a result, most of the service-learning programs have a career focus. Ninety percent of the students registered for the career exploration program work with nonprofit organizations. To the extent that concepts of civic responsibility and social justice as well as discipline-based knowledge become part of the reflection process, such internships can help students see how these complement one another and inform future career choices.

Helping Students Build Resumés with Service-Learning Experiences

Students who are progressively more involved in service-learning throughout their college years gain a wealth of experience that can be very attractive to graduate admissions committees and employers, yet students often lack the knowledge of how to translate this experience into a resumé. Service-learning educators can help students by encouraging them to record regularly their community involvements, their accomplishments, the skills they used in a given project or program, and the dates of important projects for future use in resumé writing. This record will enable students to create resumé entries that emphasize their leadership roles and concrete accomplishments—for example: "Served as group leader of seven people in Habitat for Humanity project, helping to build six homes in one week for low-income people"; "Worked 150 hours in a homeless shelter, interviewed ten shelter residents, and wrote a reflective paper on public misunderstanding of the homeless population."

Considering how to describe their service-learning experiences on their resumés, students can also be encouraged to broaden their reflection to what they have learned about issues, social institutions, communities, and community-based organizations; planning, organizing, and evaluating projects; motivation, supervision, and collaboration; leadership and followership; and the relationships of power to race, class, and gender. Although such learning may not appear on a resumé, it certainly can become part of students' decision making about future career paths.

Letters of Recommendation as an Opportunity for Reflection

Service-learning educators spend a significant amount of time writing letters of recommendation for students applying for employment and for graduate programs. Student requests for recommendation letters from these individuals are frequent because of the close relationships that develop between students active in service and service-learning faculty and program staff. Students often have stronger relationships within the service-learning setting than anywhere else on campus. The rich relationships that give rise to the request for recommendation letters can offer a comfortable and safe opportunity to discuss students' ideas and plans for the life choices they are making.

Staff members in the Lowell Bennion Community Service Center at the University of Utah regularly engage in extended conversations with students triggered by requests for recommendation letters. Discussions focus on how the students intend to integrate the values and skills learned through their service-learning experiences with their graduate study or employment. Students are asked to write a brief statement summarizing their current thoughts on how they will achieve this integration. For example, how can a student's social justice ethic be integrated into work toward a master's degree in business? How can a concern for people who live in poverty be meshed with a career in law?

In the context of a trusting relationship, at a time when choices are imminent, this type of introspection can help the student focus on big-picture issues, as well as the more concrete and immediate tasks of pursuing classified ads and constructing resumés. With some encouragement, faculty advisers, career counselors, student services staff, and chaplains might be willing to use similar ideas.

Alumni Organizations

The development of alumni community service programs appears to be receiving increased attention on college campuses. As more recent graduates who have developed the habit of service become active in alumni groups, this kind of program is likely to continue to grow. Such programs can provide crucial lifelong connections for those former students who have chosen a lifetime involvement in service and can perhaps help alumni at any stage of life reconnect with their collegiate commitments to social justice. Although most of these programs do not feature structured reflection opportunities, there are some notable exceptions.

The Education in Action Program at the University of California at Los Angeles invites alumni employed in service-related fields to work with students, offering an opportunity for discussion, reflection, and idea sharing. This program is similar to the Alumni Social Concerns Forum at the University of Notre Dame, which offers an annual three-day retreat for alumni working with social issues, faculty, staff, and students to engage in service and service-related discussion. Several service-learning programs, such as at Notre Dame, Stanford, and the University of Utah, in partnership with their institutional alumni associations, have created summer service-learning fellowships that immerse students in full-time service in another city with an active alumni chapter. Selected students work in a community service agency, interact with alumni chapter members, keep reflective journals of their service experience, and return to active participation in the campus service-learning program after their summer of service.

Conclusion

In *The Good Society*, Robert Bellah (1991) powerfully describes how the major societal institutions, within which all of us as individuals are embedded, affect the perceived life choices and actual life experiences of each person and the shaping of our society. Higher education, as a major social institution, has a unique and critical responsibility to prepare active and socially responsible citizens. The need for colleges and universities to prepare individuals with not only knowledge and capability but also with the desire to apply their knowledge and capability to make our global society a better place is painfully evident.

The mission statements of many institutions of higher education reflect this responsibility. Service-learning programs offer a unique way to enable institutions to fulfill this mission, as well as to meet other goals for student learning and development.

How students fulfill their responsibilities as citizens through their lifestyle and career choices is a measure of an institution's social responsiveness. To this end, information has been presented on various graduate education and career options for students, how service-learning educators can and should work with students to make well-reasoned decisions, and examples of programs that colleges and universities have developed to assist students as they make critical life choices. The decisions that service-learning educators can assist students to make will have a profound impact on the future of communities and the world.

References

Bateson, M. *Composing a Life.* New York: Plume, 1990.

Bellah, R. *The Good Society.* New York: Knopf, 1991.

Colby, A., and Damon, W. *Some Do Care.* New York: Free Press, 1992.

Delve, C. I., Mintz, S. D., and Stewart, G. M. "Promoting Values Development Through Community Service: A Design." In C. I. Delve, S. D. Mintz, and G. M. Stewart (eds.), *Community Service as Values Education.* New Directions for Student Services, no. 50. San Francisco: Jossey-Bass, 1990.

Part Three

Organizational, Administrative, and Policy Issues

Although there is no single correct model for service-learning programs, a number of administrative issues undergird all successful service-learning efforts. The principles and program examples set out in Parts One and Two are necessary but not sufficient for the design, implementation, and evaluation of service-learning experiences. In fact, effective organization, administration, and policies may be the most crucial factors in the initiation and sustainability of service-learning. The chapters in this part of the book address management issues related to starting a service-learning program, supporting all the types of service-learning experiences described in Part Two, and institutionalizing service-learning to ensure that programs are sustainable over time. The final chapter presents a mandate for action to secure the future of service-learning.

Chapter Ten

Starting a Service-Learning Program

Diana A. Bucco, Julie A. Busch

In developing any new initiative, it is tempting to jump into program development without putting in the time and effort to lay the groundwork for a program that is sustainable over time. However, the history of service-learning is fraught with examples of programs that started out strong and eventually weakened or disappeared as a result of failure to build a firm foundation. Many of the approaches and suggestions we present are based on our extensive experience working with numerous colleges and universities to develop high-quality service-learning programs. The focus of this chapter is starting a program with the intention and capacity to grow and become institutionalized.

Assessing Institutional and Community Contexts

To be successful in the long run, a service-learning program must be connected to the mission of the institution. In fact, service is mentioned either directly or indirectly in the mission statement of virtually all colleges and universities. In addition, the institution's commitment to service is often articulated through admissions literature and the admissions process, presidential speeches, and alumni publications. How service fits into the institution's mission

depends on the nature of the institution. Religiously affiliated institutions, community colleges, urban universities, and land-grant
institutions all have central but varying service missions. In developing a program model, it is important to take a close look at the
institution's mission statement and to craft a service-learning mission statement that links the program's focus to the institutional
mission.

Institutional environment and culture are important contexts
to consider in starting a service-learning program. The extent of
presidential commitment; the degree of support of key administrators; the institution's academic focus; campus traditions; openness to innovation; faculty morale; and the emphasis placed on
research, teaching, and service can all dramatically influence a program's development. An institution whose faculty are accustomed
to collaboration and where innovative teaching is rewarded may
be receptive to service-learning. On the other hand, low faculty
morale, budget cutbacks, and competing priorities can create a
climate that does not favor service-learning.

Understanding the nature of the student body is equally critical. For instance, community colleges draw students who are
already part of the local community, while the students in private,
rural, residential colleges typically have little or no prior association with the community in which the institution resides. As a
result students at different types of institutions may have different
motivations for participating in service-learning. Students who
attend college in their own community may want to apply their
newly acquired knowledge to address local issues and concerns.
Students who are new to an institution and a community may see
service-learning as an opportunity to learn about their new environment. Whether the majority of students attend part-time or full-
time, whether they are of traditional age or older, and their
employment status are all factors that will influence their participation in service-learning.

Initial research should include an assessment of what community service and service-learning initiatives already exist within
the institution and who are potential program supporters. The catalog, student handbooks, and faculty and student newspapers can
provide some clues to how service is already incorporated into the
curriculum and the cocurriculum, natural linkages, and ways

the institution values service. For example, the catalog may reveal that the education and social sciences departments have some courses with service-learning components, and newspaper articles may highlight outstanding student and faculty service.

Every institution is likely to have a core group of students who are involved in community service. A good way to find them is through service-oriented student organizations, such as Circle K, Habitat for Humanity, and Best Buddies. Identifying advocates within the fraternity and sorority system will also help to expand the base of student support. The most effective programs recognize students as key partners in the service-learning process from the outset.

If curricular service-learning is a goal, faculty must also be involved from the start. The support of respected faculty brings credibility and integrity to the program. In addition to faculty in the traditional service-friendly disciplines, it is worthwhile seeking faculty allies in other disciplines, such as engineering, biology, and computer science.

Administrative support provides the infrastructure necessary to start and develop a service-learning program. Key supporters can typically be found in student affairs, campus ministry, the career center, student activities, public relations, alumni affairs, institutional advancement, financial aid, and internship programs. Administrators know the processes for accessing institutional resources and services, such as campus vans, space for training and events, printing and mailing services, press releases, and fundraising. Using the experience, knowledge, and networks available to these individuals can positively influence the overall impact of service-learning on the campus and in the community. Top-level administrative support is crucial to building a sustainable program, garnering financial and public support, and encouraging the involvement of all members of the campus community. Because of the power and influence available to higher-level administrators, they can be key in shaping the agenda and long-term success of a service-learning program.

Effective service-learning is designed with community needs and capacities as central. Potential community partners to be consulted in the earliest phase of program development include residents, city management, community-based organization staff, public school personnel, local foundations, and businesses. The community should have responsibility for identifying service initiatives that meet its own needs while complementing learning outcomes.

Developing a Programmatic Framework

Tapping into the resources of state, regional, and national organizations, as well as other institutions, can assist substantially in the development of a program model. The institution or individuals may already have memberships in organizations such as the National Society for Experiential Education, the American Association of Higher Education, or the Campus Outreach Opportunity League. Building a library of books, publications, and training materials is inexpensive and worthwhile. Taking a group to visit service-learning programs at neighboring institutions enables program organizers and supporters to observe models, begin to develop a network, collect information and ideas, and build enthusiasm. Active discussions of service-learning occur on the Internet and at the state, regional, or national conferences offered by many of the organizations listed in Appendix A.

Establishing Goals, Focus, and Expectations

In initially conceptualizing the program, it is essential to develop desired outcomes for students, the community, and the institution. Potential student learning and development outcomes include deeper knowledge of course material, sharpened critical thinking, leadership development and ethical decision making, self-esteem, understanding of citizenship and social responsibility, and multicultural education. Among possible community outcomes are better understanding of community assets and needs, community empowerment, improved delivery of services, access to institutional resources, and more effective advocacy for underrepresented and underserved groups. Finally, outcomes for institutions can include better community relationships, increased community recognition of the value of higher education, and opportunities for faculty to enrich their teaching and research, as well as increased student learning.

It is also important to set both short-term and long-term goals. Keeping these visions in mind helps program development stay on track. Nevertheless, the plan should allow enough flexibility to take advantage of unexpected opportunities that may arise if they fit into the long-range vision for the program. It is all too easy to become sidetracked by opportunities that initially seem intriguing but are likely to end up being more of a drain on the program than an enhancement. For example, applying for a grant that would provide funds but require the program to develop in a direction tangential to its mission may not be wise.

One of the early programmatic decisions is how centralized or decentralized the service-learning program will be. The most centralized programs are involved in all linkages between the institution and the community and coordinate, or assist in the coordination of, all service-learning experiences. In this way, program coordinators can develop more intensive community partnerships and can monitor the outcomes of service-learning experiences for students and communities more closely. This approach, however, is often more suitable for a small, rural institution than a large, research university in an urban setting. Academic departments and other units at large institutions are likely to have developed connections in the community already and may not be willing to relinquish control of their projects. In this situation, attempts to centralize service-learning can be counterproductive.

Another early decision is whether the program will have a curricular, cocurricular, or dual focus. The choice has immediate implications for where the program will reside in the organizational structure of the institution. If strong academic linkages are central to the program's mission, housing it within an academic department, dean's office, or provost's office should be considered. Establishing it at the provost level may provide for more opportunities to make a broader impact, since the program will not be viewed as the initiative of one department. On the other hand, this can also have the effect of giving service-learning the appearance of being an administratively driven effort and may consequently alienate some faculty. In other situations, locating the program within a specific academic department may be advantageous because of the prestige or positive image of a certain discipline or department. St. Edwards University in Texas initially targeted curricular integration of service-learning in one academic department and then expanded the program by having the faculty in that department provide workshops for faculty in another academic department.

If the program will have a cocurricular focus, a variety of student affairs areas could be a likely home, such as student activities, residential life, commuter services, or the office of the dean of student services. At institutions with strong religious and spiritual traditions, the chaplain's office or campus ministry could be considered. Programs with a dual focus can be housed in locations ranging from an academic or student affairs unit to the president's office. Some programs have a dual reporting line to both academic and student affairs.

Each new program must also determine its orientation to the community. Some service-learning programs choose to begin as a clearinghouse of volunteer opportunities throughout the community and over time move toward developing partnerships with selected community agencies. Concentrating on the development of reciprocal relationships with community partners at the outset will pay off in long-term dividends of higher-quality service and learning. One of the greatest challenges is matching community needs with learning outcomes. A common understanding of meaningful service-learning needs to be established early by all partners. Striking the appropriate balance between service and learning often needs to be revisited throughout the development of the program.

Comprehensive programs include a wide range of service-learning opportunities that vary in duration, intensity, and required commitment. The developmental framework of the Service Learning Model (Delve, Mintz, and Stewart, 1990) suggests that a continuum of service-learning experiences should be offered to students in various stages of development. One-day or short-term experiences allow students to explore service-learning and introduce them to the combination of action and reflection. Long-term opportunities enable them to make a sustained commitment, begin to understand the concept of reciprocity, consider the underlying causes of social problems, learn about themselves in relation to the world, and make a significant contribution.

Since student involvement in service-learning prior to as well as during college may vary substantially, service-learning opportunities offered should eventually accommodate their wide range of experience. However, initially focusing energies on a couple of prototype opportunities may be more feasible and can serve as an incubator for long-term development. New programs often make the mistake of taking a shotgun approach, offering as many opportunities as possible rather than being strategic and intentional about which opportunities to offer.

Service-learning programs from the beginning should work with all partners in the service-learning relationship—students, the community partner (school, community-based organization, or agency), members of the community being served, and the faculty or staff members coordinating the learning—to set and articulate expectations for all the partners. Clearly defining expectations and relationships early greatly increases the probability that a high-quality, meaningful, and sustainable service-learning program will develop.

Expectations for students should delineate application and selection procedures, time commitment and duration of the experience, supervision and reporting lines, training, orientation, reflection, evaluation, the location of the service site, transportation requirements, and potential risks. Students should also have a sense of their potential learning outcomes from the experience and should assist in defining these for themselves. The community partner needs to know its role in the application, selection, orientation, training, supervision, monitoring, and feedback process of both volunteers and those being served; its financial and human resource commitment to the program; its role in reflection activities; and how ongoing evaluation will be done. Community members should understand where and when service will occur, how to provide feedback, and the role of reciprocity in the relationship. Faculty or staff members coordinating the program must understand how learning goals for the students interweave with needs of the community and how essential their role is to communication flow, quality control, continuous evaluation, overall supervision and monitoring of the program, and ensuring a safe and meaningful experience for both the students and the community.

Selecting a Program Name and Location

One of the decisions that typically takes considerable time and energy is the naming of the program. A name that can bring credibility, recognition, and accessibility needs to be chosen with awareness of institutional and community culture and politics. The name should be concise, inviting, and reflective of the image the program hopes to attain, and it should remain appropriate as the program grows—for example, Office of Community Service-Learning, Center for Service-Learning, Service and Action, Center for Values and Service, Integrating Service and Academic Study, Faith and Justice Institute, and Center for Peace Studies.

The physical location of the program's office needs to be accessible to all of the stakeholders: students, faculty, staff, and community members. The office should be easy to find and located where all stakeholders will feel comfortable and welcome. Picking a site in an area highly trafficked by faculty and students creates visibility. Since community members will need access to the office, parking should be taken into consideration. This also is a key factor for an institution with a large commuter population or where car or van transportation will need to be provided to the service sites. Proximity to other campus offices and services is another factor. When selecting a location, it is worthwhile to consider one in the community rather than on campus. An on-campus location makes a statement that the program is institution based and driven by learning outcomes, whereas a location in the community may say more about the role of the community in the service-learning partnership. A community location may not be ideal for a number of reasons, but consideration of this option can initiate an interesting dialogue about program goals and priorities.

Human and Financial Resources

Adequate staffing from the beginning is key to long-term program success. The person responsible for program coordination, management, and quality should have an understanding of how higher education institutions and communities function. Other important qualities for a program coordinator include credibility among academicians, students, staff, and community members; organizational and planning skills; an understanding of best practices of service-learning; budget experience; and knowledge of evaluation and assessment. Also beneficial are knowledge of grant writing, theories of student learning and development, organizational dynamics, strategic planning, and community development. The coordinator should report to an administrator or faculty member who can open doors, gain access to resources, garner additional support, lend credibility, and advocate on behalf of the program and service-learning. In developing a position description for the service-learning coordinator, gathering such descriptions from other institutions eliminates the need to start from scratch.

Regardless of institution size, the service-learning program should ideally begin with a minimum of a full-time staff or faculty member and a full-time administrative assistant. Although this type of staffing may not always be realistic, it demonstrates institutional commitment and makes high-quality initiatives more likely. Recognizing that this approach may not be possible, there are multiple staffing alternatives that have proved successful, among them a graduate assistant supervised by a faculty member, an administrator dedicating a portion of time to the program with the aid of interns, and Volunteers in Service to America or AmeriCorps participants.

Establishing an advisory committee can be of great value in providing direction for a new service-learning program. Prior to forming such a body, much thought must be given to its purpose, scope of responsibility, and membership. The advisory committee can assist in developing a mission and vision statement, setting long-range goals and short-range objectives, selecting a location for the service-learning program, identifying initial community service partners, and procuring start-up funding for the program.

In addition to human resources, financial resources need to be located and allocated to the program. One-time start-up costs may include office renovation, a telephone, a computer, file cabinets, and furnishings. Much of this equipment can often be found within the institution or donated by the community or local companies. Ongoing program support needs include salaries and benefits, supplies, monthly telephone expenses, printing and mailings, promotional material, transportation to service sites, orientation and training costs, data collection and dissemination, subscriptions, and conference attendance.

Most programs begin with some institutional funds supplemented by seed monies from local foundations, private donors, federal or state programs, student activity fees, or national and state organizations. Obtaining a stable institutional funding base is essential to developing a sustainable program, however. Among the many and varied potential sources of initial institutional funding are the trustees, the president's office, student affairs and academic affairs officers, academic departments, student activities offices, student government, residential life, and career centers. In a creative example, Allegheny College in Pennsylvania, the University of California at Los Angeles, and California Polytechnic University–San Luis Obispo have placed a negative checkoff box on tuition invoices so that students can earmark tuition dollars for the service-learning program. Developing a service-learning program provides a unique opportunity for campus-wide collaboration.

Many service-learning programs supplement their institutional start-up funds with federal, foundation, or corporate grants. A first step in identifying sources of grants is contacting the institutional research, development, or grant office for help with researching available grants, preparing proposals, and providing advice on details such as budget, overhead costs, and letters of support. To assist the service-learning program at Hope College in Michigan, a faculty member who teaches grant writing had her students develop actual proposals for service-learning grants.

Community partners can play a critical role in garnering financial support for starting a service-learning program. Community-based foundations and local government agencies may provide support if the service-learning program's activities can help achieve their goals. Corporations often have mandates to invest in the communities in which they reside and may be willing to lend their support. The program may be able to connect with the local United Way and receive funding as an affiliated agency. Many school districts have developed partnerships with colleges and universities and pay to some extent for the assistance they receive.

Beginning Program Implementation

Once the programmatic framework has been established, materials that describe the program's philosophy, goals, and focus can be developed. Guidance and assistance from the public relations and graphic design departments can be useful in creating logos, brochures, and other materials. Student interns seeking experience in marketing can be valuable resources. Faculty, staff, and students with computer expertise can help to create ways to make program information available on the Internet and the World Wide Web.

It is essential to remember that a program does not sell itself. There needs to be a concerted marketing effort that clearly and professionally publicizes the mission, goals, and components of the program. A marketing strategy should be developed to promote the program both on and off campus to current and prospective students, faculty, staff, parents, alumni, community residents and organizations, and potential funders. The public relations, development, and alumni offices already have mechanisms to promote institutional resources and are in a position to help.

Whether the program's focus is curricular, cocurricular, or both, raising students' awareness of the service-learning opportunities available to them is essential. General recruitment strategies include use of electronic and real bulletin boards, announcements through campus and community media, presentations to classes and groups, direct mail, table tents in campus eateries and study areas, and volunteer fairs. Course catalogs and schedules should identify courses that include service-learning. One-time opportunities, described in Chapter Five, are also effective in introducing students—as well as faculty and staff—to service-learning.

In some cases, students may need to go through a formal application process in order to participate in a service-learning program. For one-time events, it may or may not be necessary to register students in advance. The application process needs to reflect the intensity and duration of the service experience and the skills required. It should complement the level of commitment necessary for the program but not be so daunting as to cause interested students to walk away in frustration. The legal affairs department can assist in creating forms that students can sign to demonstrate their understanding of risk and potential liability.

Developing a sustainable service-learning program requires that an effective student intake, placement, and tracking system be put in place. Career centers, internship offices, or cooperative education programs on campus may already have systems that can be adapted. At a minimum, effective record keeping enables the coordinator to answer administrators' questions about the numbers of students involved. At all times the means for identifying the status of a student (placed, on a waiting list) should be easily accessible. Ongoing channels for supervision need to be established. The faculty or staff who are coordinating service-learning placements need to monitor what is going on at the service site so that they are aware of the level of the students' and organization's satisfaction with the day-to-day and overall experience.

Prior to student placement, applicants' essential skills, knowledge, and sensitivities need to be identified. Students need structured training that addresses their role at the program site; responsibilities and limitations; potential risks; knowledge of the issues, dynamics, and culture they will find at the site; appropriate attitude, behavior, and attire; appreciation of the dignity and worth of persons being served; and reciprocity. For long-term placements, ongoing training may be appropriate and necessary to refine student skills and abilities.

Reflection is the key element that connects service and learning. Without reflection, service is simply that: service. Reflection on service experiences allows students to make cognitive and affective connections to learning, create linkages to prior learning and experiences, and make new sense of the world. (Reflection strategies appropriate to a wide range of service-learning experiences are contained in Chapters Five through Nine.)

Recognition is critical in acknowledging program and individual accomplishments and in providing closure to students' service-learning experiences. The third week of April, traditionally National Volunteer Week, is an excellent time to create opportunities to celebrate and reflect on accomplishments of the academic year. Recognition can include student awards or scholarships for outstanding contributions, dinners or receptions, features in the campus and local newspapers, a special designation on robes at graduation, transcript notation, letters of appreciation from the president, certificates or proclamations from local officials, and faculty awards for superior service-learning courses and fellowships for research involving service-learning.

Building in Evaluation Strategies from the Outset

From the very conception of a service-learning program, evaluation needs to be made part of the overall framework. If done with intentionality, thoughtful design, and even simple techniques, evaluation should yield data that will assist in building the case for program sustainability and enhancement. Often program coordinators shy away from doing comprehensive assessments and evaluation because of inexperience, a perceived lack of expertise, little time, or scarce resources. However, institutions of higher education and communities are excellent sources of knowledge and experience in this area. The program coordinator, together with the advisory committee, should establish initial predictors of program success, desired outcomes, and target areas to be monitored. Outcomes should be evaluated from the perspectives of the students, the communities, and the institution. Evaluation design should also allow for unanticipated successes, concerns, and outcomes to be captured in the data.

Evaluation can be formal or informal, qualitative or quantitative. Informal sources of qualitative evaluation include student reflection sessions, journals, papers, and portfolios. More formal qualitative methods include focus groups and structured interviews of both students and community representatives.

Quantitative evaluation can provide statistical evidence about numbers of people involved and affected. It can also indicate whether programs are resulting in a higher demand for services or services no longer needed. Spending time obtaining quantitative data can reap long-term dividends in credibility for program efforts.

Continuous quality improvement or Total Quality Management may be beneficial in shaping service-learning programs. This approach to ongoing evaluation is a way of thinking that allows the program to assess, critique, and improve constantly. There are four basic steps to continuous improvement strategies: identify stakeholders and their needs, set continuous improvement goals, check how the program is doing, and take action to improve (Office of Evaluation, Corporation for National Service, 1995). Institutional planning offices and business departments are likely to be able to provide advice and assistance.

A service-learning program should create an annual report that highlights accomplishments, strengths, areas of concerns, partnerships, placements, course offerings, results of program evaluations, and long-term goals. Maintaining a file of media clippings about the service-learning program makes it easy to include highlights in the report. The annual report should be distributed to the president, all partners (faculty, staff, students, and community representatives), funders, and prospective allies or new partners. Whenever possible, the accomplishments of the service-learning program should be highlighted in the institution's annual report.

Another important kind of program evaluation is reflection by its coordinators on its successes and setbacks. Starting a service-learning program is both challenging and rewarding. Dealing with community needs and problems can be overwhelming; grant proposals may be rejected; and supportive presidents, faculty members, and student leaders can move on. On the other hand, program expansion can happen quickly if grant funding is secured or if a new president arrives and establishes a comprehensive service-learning center. Successful programs sometimes find themselves in a tug-of-war between institutional power builders or faced with increased demands from the community. Building in time to reflect on change as it occurs will go a long way to sustain hardworking program coordinators.

Conclusion

Because each institution is unique, no two service-learning programs start in exactly the same way. Nevertheless, the principles in which they are grounded, their core elements, and their basic strategies are similar. From what is known about programs that have flourished over time, it is clear that initial efforts to situate a program comfortably within its institutional and community contexts, develop a sound programmatic framework, implement initiatives strategically, and conduct regular evaluation are essential. Putting these pieces into place at the outset establishes a foundation that will sustain the program into the future and provide guidance for its development.

References

Delve, C. I., Mintz, S. D., and Stewart, G. M. "Promoting Values Development Through Community Service: A Design." In C. I. Delve, S. D. Mintz, and G. M. Stewart (eds.), *Community Service as Values Education,* New Directions for Student Services, no. 50. San Francisco: Jossey-Bass, 1990.

Office of Evaluation, Corporation for National Service. *Handbook for Continuous Improvement.* Washington, D.C.: Corporation for National Service, 1995.

Chapter Eleven

Administering Successful Service-Learning Programs

Penny Rue

The success and sustainability of service-learning programs depend on effective administration. Service-learning may be pursued for all the right reasons, but without attention to key administrative concerns, it is likely to become another educational fad and another failed social program. This chapter covers issues that affect all types of service-learning programs, whether they are new or mature, curricular or cocurricular, or led by students or service-learning educators. It addresses the inherent complexities of managing service-learning programs, the human resource issues that must be considered, the challenges involved in different kinds of service-learning programs, and the pragmatic considerations that keep programs running effectively.

The administration of service-learning programs is especially complex because these programs can cross every conceivable departmental line and organizational boundary. A host of college and university officials—academic administrators, student activities staff, volunteer services coordinators, campus ministry personnel, external affairs liaisons, and residence life staff—will likely be engaged at some point in the administration of service-learning programs. These officials also need to work closely with faculty members who teach service-learning courses and student leaders who organize service projects. Their work will involve risk managers, motor pool coordinators, and development officers. Campus-based staff will coordinate their efforts with members of the community, including citizens, community-based organization staff, government officials, elected representatives, police, and school principals. In addition, productive relationships must be established with funding sources, including federal, state, and local government agencies, as well as private and nonprofit organizations.

A variety of administrative structures are currently in place to manage service-learning programs. Some institutions have comprehensive service-learning centers with several staff members; some provide coordination out of a student affairs or academic administration unit. At others individual faculty members or campus ministers are primarily responsible. Regardless of the model, administrative issues are vital to the success of the enterprise.

Challenges of Administering Service-Learning Programs

A number of challenges face service-learning administrators as a result of the multiple contexts within which service-learning operates. The student, faculty, and community cultures each have their own political realities that shape the environment for service-learning. Effective administration necessitates understanding these political realities and building key relationships and partnerships. Planning and coordination are absolutely essential in laying the foundation for successful service-learning. Decisions affecting the establishment and continuation of programs require clear goals and sound evaluation procedures. This section explores the political and contextual realities of administering service-learning programs.

Working Within the Institutional and Community Contexts of Service-Learning

Service-learning administrators must start with a thorough understanding of the community, including its resources, challenges, key constituencies, and political dynamics. They need to balance this understanding with the institution's focus on the learning and developmental outcomes of the service-learning experience for the students involved. Administrators must also continually balance the natural tensions between education and administration. They need to mediate between differing institutional subcultures, reconciling faculty autonomy with administrative accountability and the theory orientation of the academic world with the action orientation of the public service world.

The initial administrative challenges vary depending on the driving force for program development. It is optimal if service-learning has the support of key college or university administrators and faculty, community members, and students. If all of these constituencies are not involved in the initial impetus, first steps should focus on securing the participation and support of the others. If service-learning is initiated by faculty or administrators for reasons social, practical, or pedagogical, community assessment and developing student involvement should be the next steps. If members of the community request the institution's involvement, it is important to determine if there is a match between community needs and institutional resources. When students initiate a community relationship, administrators can help determine what services students are realistically able to deliver and assess what other institutional resources may be required. Despite the compelling nature of students' enthusiasm, it is advisable to determine how much control and accountability administrators can and should exert. Commitments made by students on behalf of the college or university may be interpreted by community members as having full institutional support. (Additional issues related to the importance of assessing institutional and community contexts when starting a service-learning program are discussed in Chapter Ten.)

Planning and Goal Setting

Strategic planning (Bryson, 1988) can provide a useful framework for program development. It offers a systematic method for clarifying organizational mandates and mission and a framework for identifying internal strengths and weaknesses and external threats and opportunities. The mission and strategic analysis lead to the development of a strategy and long-term objectives, linking the *what* and *why* to the *where, when,* and *how* (Below, Morrisey, and Acomb,

1987). Students who participate in the systematic strategic planning process will have a meaningful experiential learning opportunity, and community members will learn about a powerful framework that can be applied to other neighborhood planning efforts.

The many participants in the program development process are likely to have various ideas about where college or university energies can best be used. Neither agency personnel nor community representatives speak for all community members, and many will assign different priorities to the existing challenges. Although it is difficult, it is advisable in the early planning stages to have as many voices at the table as possible to determine program direction and forestall political problems.

Goal setting is important for a variety of reasons. It can help a planning group seek consensus among competing commitments or constituencies at the program planning phase. It establishes priorities for the use of scarce resources of time, space, and money. It allows the institution to be clear about what will *not* be accomplished if a program is not developed (Barr and Cuyjet, 1991). Perhaps the most important reason to clarify goals in the planning process relates to accountability. It is impossible to be held accountable for the kind of vague and well-meaning goals that often underlie an institution's interest in the community, for example, "to improve the lives of young people" or "to strengthen the family." Measurable goals set expectations that are clear from the beginning and give focus to a particular program. Rather than a vague goal of "to improve the students' education," a measurable goal might be to "increase the percentage of students who read at grade level from the current 22 percent to 35 percent in a six-month period." Of course, much research, thought, and planning rests behind such a carefully crafted goal, and that kind of planning is what is likely to yield a successful service-learning program. Measurable goals allow for a clear indication of a program's success or failure and more systematic decision making about continued funding or program termination. Specific learning goals for the participating college students should also be part of the goal-setting process. Such goals can include focus on cognitive, personal, and career development, as well as knowledge related to specific course content.

Campus Coordination

Campus coordination is a fundamental element in administering service-learning programs. Since individual initiatives often arise on campuses without knowledge of what other initiatives exist, inefficiencies, overlaps, and lost opportunities may result. Centralized authority over service-learning may not be necessary or desirable, but coordination clearly is.

The potential benefits of coordination are significant. The most obvious is the ability to share resources. Coordination may also allow campus leaders to share important community contacts. Another significant benefit is exchanging knowledge of advancements in the field of service-learning from both the student affairs and academic perspectives. There is still relatively little on service-learning in academic journals, nor is there a large body of information available at disciplinary conferences. Coordination allows the sharing of existing and evolving information that can contribute to the development of service-learning programs.

The costs of failing to coordinate efforts are compelling. As budgets come under scrutiny, duplication of resources is a prime target for cuts. Programs that appear to use resources inefficiently may be cut entirely rather than merely face the elimination of duplication. The most serious cost associated with failing to coordinate campus efforts may be the loss of credibility within the community. Community members will certainly expect that different representatives of the institution are working together, or at least know of each other's activities. An institution that appears to be unaware of what is going on within its own walls will probably be viewed skeptically by community members.

If a high-level college or university official can be persuaded to initiate coordination, diverse units may participate more willingly. If such leadership is not possible, a service-learning administrator attempting to encourage coordination should do so in an open and informal manner. Campus coordination should include all those offering service opportunities, such as academic units, campus ministry, residence life, fraternities and sororities, and student community-service organizations. Faculty involvement, including both direct service and research activities, should be represented. Coordination should also include federal work-study program administrators, as work-study becomes an entry into community service for more and more students; alumni services staff, who are often supporting alumni community service activities near campus and across the country; and career services staff, who may promote postgraduation service opportunities or careers in nonprofit and community agencies. Internship coordinators, who may be centralized or departmentally based, should be included because internships may take place in community agencies and nonprofit organizations. External relations staff may have a particular interest in being aware of the work the institution is doing in the community and may be willing to gather and disseminate information.

A service-learning advisory board can provide both coordination and strategic planning. Such a board ideally includes rotating representation from faculty, students, and community members, with support from service-learning administrators. Coordination also occurs through a service-learning curriculum committee that approves new service-learning-related courses and identifies areas of the curriculum that could be targeted for the development of additional service-learning courses. Some institutions may benefit from a centralized steering committee that establishes strategic direction for service-learning developments. Another type of coordination could be developed to ensure that community organization contacts are made in a coherent way. A process for reconciling competing interests and turf concerns needs to be developed if coordination is to serve a useful function.

Developing Community Partnerships

The success of service-learning programs will rest in part on the strength of the relationships between the college or university and the community. The history and imperative for such relationships vary with institutional type, location, mission, and tradition. Administrators with responsibility for service-learning programs should find out as much as possible about the nature of the relationship between the institution and its surrounding community. For example, does the president sit on any local governing boards or councils? Such memberships indicate a potential institutional focus as well as possible key relationships with other board members. Does the institution have a high-level official responsible for community relations? If so, it is important to understand the nature of this individual's work and the sources of support or criticism from within the community. Do faculty members have research or service connections to the community? Such connections can lead to opportunities to involve students in related service-learning experiences. On the other hand, if relationships are few, service-learning may be a way to begin to build a more cooperative relationship with the community.

A critical administrative challenge for college- and university-based service-learning programs is how to minimize the disruption caused by the academic year cycle. This issue is one of the most difficult stumbling blocks to substantive community involvement and one that student leaders rarely consider. The typical campus-based service-learning program involves students for a few hours a week over a semester or quarter. At the end of the term, the students' participation may end but the community realities remain. In the case of children's programs—the most frequent venue for service-learning—the cyclical nature of the volunteers' participation may become a source of profound disappointment for children. Developing special projects designed to be implemented over the semester breaks, creating pen-pal relationships that continue over the summer, and broadening the college or university's involvement in the program beyond that of the individual tutor or mentor can help smooth out the cyclical transitions. Twelve-month staff or paid student workers may be able to fill in the gaps created by loss of volunteers over the summer.

Program Evaluation

Action-oriented program administrators seldom feel they can take time away from the demanding requirements of their administrative duties in order to assess the impact of their efforts in a manner systematic enough to be reliable. The *Research Agenda for Combining Service and Learning in the 1990s* notes the lack of research on the effects of service-learning on student learning and development and on the communities in which they serve (Giles, Porter Honnet, and Migliore, 1991). Cronbach (1980) argues that regarding the efficacy of social programs, "there is a need for exchanges more energetic than the typical academic discussions and more responsible than debate among partisans" (p. 10). One of the side benefits of external funding sources is their emphasis on evaluation and accountability, so that the field of service-learning may be motivated to move beyond anecdote to a clear understanding of what works and what does not.

Both evaluation and research may be involved in assessing service-learning activities since they serve different purposes. Evaluation is performed to assess worth and assist decision making; research is performed to test hypotheses and find the truth (Brown, 1979). Weiss (1972) states that "the purpose of evaluation research is to measure the effects of a program against the goals it set out to accomplish as a means of contributing to subsequent decision making about the program and improving future programming" (p. 4). She further clarifies the distinction between evaluation and research: "Evaluation is intended for use. Where basic research puts the emphasis on the production of knowledge and leaves its use to the natural processes of dissemination and application, evaluation starts out with use in mind" (p. 6).

Investigations need to grapple with the dual purposes of service-learning. Some evaluation projects may be aimed at determining whether the service students provide is effective from the community's perspective, while others may be more concerned about the efficacy of service-learning as a vehicle for student learning and development. The goal-setting process will point toward what aspects of the service should be evaluated and what outcomes should be measured.

According to Maryann Jacobi Gray, associate behavioral scientist with the Rand Corporation and study director for the Corporation for National Service's Learn and Serve America: Higher Education program, it is useful to clarify whether evaluation is aimed at making internal program improvements or establishing external credibility and providing evidence that the outcomes of service-learning justify the investment. A project aimed at providing proof should strive to adhere to the principles of experimental or quasi-experimental design through the use of a control or comparison group; research aimed at program improvement may not require the same level of rigor in design. Without this kind of rigor, investigators cannot be sure that changes found are due to the program and not some other external factor. The national evaluation for the Learn and Serve America: Higher Education program is aimed at establishing normative data about community service practices that individual campuses can use for comparison and for identifying best practices that can serve as models for other campuses (M. Gray, personal communication, 1995). A small body of research (see Chapters Seven and Fourteen) describes various outcomes of service-learning for students involved.

Brown (1979, pp. 29–30) identifies seven common pitfalls of evaluation projects: poor planning, too complex an evaluation design, lack of attention to the details of data collection, inexperience on the part of evaluators, failure to use the collected data, a focus on program protection rather than program improvement, and poor presentation of results. Thoughtful yet realistic planning, with the full cooperation of all parties involved, is the key to avoiding most of these common pitfalls. In addition, evaluation should be directly linked to program goals and desired outcomes.

Program Termination

One of the most difficult decisions facing a service-learning administrator is deciding when to terminate a program. Such a decision should rest on the same criteria used in developing programs: the capacity of the program to meet community challenges given available resources and the congruence of desired student learning outcomes with community benefits. If student interest in the program wanes and cannot be revived, or if community participants dwindle, then the match between challenge and resources probably no longer exists, and terminating a program may be appropriate. Also problematic is when evaluation results show little or no program impact, even though the program is a popular one. Unless program costs are modest and justified by the goodwill gained, administrators cannot afford to ignore information that shows that institutional resources are not being used effectively. It is not advisable to let a program simply drift out of existence. For the sake of the long-term relationship with the community, the program should be given a proper burial, including correspondence or a meeting of all involved and an assessment of what factors contributed to the demise of the program.

More troubling is when program funding dries up, and there are no resources to continue. Most successful programs are constantly seeking resources to avoid this situation, and the link between effective program evaluation and the fundraising process is strong. Should funding disappear, administrators should meet with community members to determine what is feasible to accomplish without dedicated funds. It may be possible for volunteer community members to assume responsibility for certain administrative tasks if students can continue to volunteer as well.

Developing and Managing Human Resources

Service-learning administrators must attend to several different kinds of human resource issues. They must consider students as both learners and service providers and ensure that students have adequate preparation and training. They need to seek help from and offer help to faculty and other campus personnel, and at the same time they should be involved with community members in a reciprocal way. Approaches to conflict resolution must be considered. If service-learning is to be sustained, an ongoing approach to the development of student, faculty, and community leadership must be created. It is also important to develop methods of recognizing and rewarding participation and leadership.

Recruitment and Training of Students

Service-learning initiatives have a continuing need for new participants since students graduate or move on for other reasons. Recruitment efforts should be built into the infrastructure of the overall program. Curricular service-learning relies on those enrolled in service-learning courses. Faculty may need to pay special attention to attracting students to service-learning courses, but they may be unfamiliar with the techniques of promoting opportunities to students. Administrators can help, perhaps through placing announcements of academic service-learning opportunities in newsletters, distributing announcements to student groups, or publishing a booklet highlighting service-learning courses and other opportunities.

Individual service-learning projects can and should do their own recruitment, but campus-wide efforts, such as volunteer recruitment fairs and volunteer clearinghouses, can help. An innovative way to develop student and faculty interest simultaneously is to offer "substitute teacher" programs: When faculty members must miss a class, they can schedule a presentation on service-learning to be made during their absence. Another way to introduce students to service-learning is through the kinds of one-time programs described in Chapter Five.

Some service-learning projects may require little in the way of specialized training for students, while others require more in-depth preparation. Assessment with both the volunteers and the community or agency can pinpoint training requirements. As budgets of service agencies are cut, the volunteer coordinator functions may be spread among a variety of agency personnel, making preparation more difficult for them. The campus program administrator must then assume a greater role in understanding the training needs of the agency and in preparing students for service, including determining any prerequisites for the service experience and providing a preservice program that orients them to the general and unique challenges of the service environment. Prior volunteers can be a valuable resource. They can use their own journals or early reflections to recall what they needed to succeed at a site, and the experience of instructing others can reinforce their own learning from the experience.

Administrative preparation efforts should be coordinated with those of faculty. Faculty will expect high-quality reflection on the service experience in order to meet the learning goals of service-learning courses. In certain kinds of programs, faculty expertise may be imperative preparation for a service-learning experience. For example, health care projects or tutoring programs that use a special technique or methodology might require greater preparation before volunteers are ready to be placed.

Student Leadership Development

Institutions with well-developed service-learning programs, particularly in the cocurricular realm, pay attention to student leadership development by taking advantage of existing leadership programs, as well as creating specific programs for service-learning student leaders. One successful model is that of the intensive preorientation service-learning program for new students. This program uses experienced student leaders to introduce incoming first-year students to service-learning in the context of the institution and its community. New students elected to participate usually have community service experience, and this program allows them to begin their involvement in collegiate service-learning immediately. Because of their early start, these students often become program leaders more quickly than they otherwise might.

An informal but effective method of supporting student leaders is the leadership roundtable, where service-learning project leaders come together to discuss issues they face. They can help each other develop strategies to overcome potential obstacles and increase opportunities for reflection. Assessment of challenges common to several student leaders may highlight a need for a specialized workshop series on topics such as preparation, reflection, recruitment, or marketing. If sufficient resources exist, group retreats can be a powerful learning experience. There is also a growing number of national and regional conferences that students can attend, help plan, and participate in by facilitating workshops and making presentations. The focus of the meetings organized by the Campus Opportunity Outreach League (COOL) is on student leadership development, and some states have formed coalitions of student leaders from several institutions. Another way to nurture greater student leadership is by providing a capstone service-learning seminar in which experienced students, guided by faculty, facilitate discussions and training sessions for less experienced students as part of their responsibilities. Enabling students to provide leadership development opportunities for other students has the capacity to expand significantly their own learning about community, service, and citizenship.

Many institutions rely on paraprofessionals in the delivery of key student services, and service-learning programs are no exception. Providing leadership for service-learning programs through existing paraprofessionals such as resident assistants and orientation leaders can support service-learning programs significantly. Some of the best campus service-learning programs pay student coordinators to provide continuity and commitment. For a relatively small amount of money, especially if student coordinators are eligible for federal work-study, an institution can ensure the commitment of talented student leaders. Some of these students might otherwise not be able to participate in service-learning because of a financial need to work, and federal work-study regulations now require that 5 percent of work-study funds be allocated to work that addresses community needs.

A typical stress point of student-organized service-learning programs arrives when the student founders or leaders graduate or move on to other projects. Programs resting on the shoulders of one dynamic personality are also vulnerable. The use of individual program advisory boards can be useful in anticipating and managing transitions, and administrators can take an active approach to helping groups anticipate and navigate personnel transitions. A goal common to all service-learning programs is to be able to weather the loss of a key individual.

Recruitment of Faculty and Faculty Leadership Development

Most institutions use several strategies to develop faculty involvement in service-learning. A useful first approach is to identify faculty who are involved in community service independent of their professional life. Surprisingly these faculty may not know how they can integrate their vocation and avocation. Participation by service-learning administrators in new-faculty orientation programs can be an excellent way to provide information on service-learning opportunities. Campus-wide mailings or Internet messages can reach the widest audience. Asking faculty already involved in service-learning to bring a colleague to a roundtable discussion can also help broaden the network. An effective way for service-learning administrators to excite faculty is to assist students to make the connections between their service experience and their course work through reflection and to share them with their professors. Faculty are likely to be genuinely interested in an overture from motivated students who are actively applying their classroom experience to the world around them. Students can then draw their professors into a campus symposium, seminar, or information session about service-learning.

For service-learning to become central to rather than marginal at institutions of higher education, it will need to be embraced by faculty who will provide leadership for its continuing development. Administrators may be reluctant to relinquish control of service-learning, but without faculty leadership it is likely to remain marginalized at most institutions. Fortunately academic discipline associations are beginning to establish service-learning tracks and interest groups and soliciting papers for conferences and journals on this topic. Organizations such as the American Association of Higher Education, the Council of Independent Colleges, and the Invisible College of Campus Compact are making the development of faculty leadership in service-learning a national reality. According to a recent survey by Campus Compact, one-third of member institutions consider service in tenure decisions, while approximately one-fourth include service-learning in faculty orientation, provide awards for service-related efforts, and give release time for faculty involvement in community service (Miller and Steele, 1995). (Chapter Twelve further addresses the issues related to faculty involvement in service-learning.)

Developing Community Leadership

A productive way to work toward a reciprocal relationship with members of the community is to provide technical assistance in the development of community leadership. Faculty and administrators with expertise in public policy, political science, business and management, sociology, or organizational behavior all can assist community members who wish, for example, to develop grass-roots political organizations that can advance neighborhood concerns. Beginning with groups such as the local parent-teacher association, neighborhood watch program, civic associations, and church organizations, a leadership council can be formed to help develop the institution-community partnership. A leadership retreat can be conducted that focuses on resource and problem assessment, goal setting, effective advocacy, and developing the best means of participation in the political process. Identification of local funding sources available from government to community organizations can be part of the process, so that community members can bring financial as well as other assets to the partnership. The community organizations thus developed are then able and prepared to provide support for other improvement programs in their neighborhood.

In addition to working with community members and leaders, service-learning administrators should develop relationships with community agencies. Identifying specific agency staff members to serve as liaisons to the service-learning program can provide a valuable resource. On a regular basis, faculty and service-learning administrators can offer training sessions for agency volunteer coordinators to enable them to understand the potential of service-learning for college student learning and development. Other issues to be covered might include how to work most effectively with college students and concerns students may bring into the community setting. Agency representatives can also be invited to campus to meet faculty and staff and to hear from students about the impacts of their service-learning experiences.

Resolving Conflicts Between Students and Community

Despite efforts to provide preparation and training, conflicts between student volunteers and community members, leaders, or agencies inevitably will arise. Perhaps community members or agency staff do not understand the volunteers' role or they resent their intrusion, or perhaps a student oversteps the bounds of the volunteer role or makes inappropriate remarks to an agency client. Service-learning administrators should encourage students and agency staff to pursue the resolution of such conflicts as soon as they arise. According to Meg Stoltzfus, service-learning coordinator at the Feinstein Institute for Public Service at Providence College in Rhode Island, administrators should be prepared to play a mediating role when necessary. They have a vested interest in maintaining a positive relationship with the community and in having the conflict situation become a learning experience for the student(s) involved (personal communication, 1995). Without administrative involvement, the student may withdraw from the experience, or the community might harbor resentment toward the institution as a result of the unresolved conflict.

Recognition of Student and Faculty Involvement in Service-Learning

Developing appropriate recognition for student and faculty involvement and achievement in service-learning is different from and more complex than recognition for involvement in other volunteer service. Appropriate student recognition might include opportunities and funding to attend and make a presentation at a national conference, to copresent significant developments with faculty and community partners at campus or local symposia, or to coauthor a scholarly article with a faculty member. At commencement, special notation in the program booklet or a piece of regalia denoting substantial involvement in service-learning are options.

Faculty recognition is more challenging. Tenure-track faculty are quite clear that the only recognition that really counts is for service-learning to be taken seriously in tenure and promotion decisions. Symbolic efforts to recognize faculty cannot take the place of that more central acknowledgment, but they can be a positive statement on the part of the institution. Types of faculty recognition might include awards, an article in the faculty-staff newspaper, mini-grants for curriculum development, a course release, or the provision of a teaching or research assistant.

Special Administrative Considerations

Most service-learning programs have numerous facets, each presenting particular administrative challenges. This section will cover the variety of administrative considerations inherent in student-run service programs, service-learning as a graduation requirement, judicially mandated service-learning, and service-learning programs that are distant from campus.

Student Organizations and Student-Run Projects

The most difficult challenge in advising student organizations and student-run service-learning projects is achieving the appropriate balance between accountability and autonomy. Essential elements of accountability include safety and security, commitments made to others, and use of institutional resources. Autonomy matters because the student-run organizations and projects provide students with opportunities to make decisions and to develop leadership skills. Erring on the side of too much accountability can discourage student leadership; erring on the side of too much autonomy can result in inadequate standards or perhaps even harm to community members and students. Experienced student leaders and student activities professionals can inform other administrators about the prevailing leadership culture on the campus and identify advising strategies that work best.

One way to strike the balance is to establish broad parameters within which students can exercise autonomy. For example, program standards can state that reflection is mandatory but leave the group free to choose from a variety of reflection options or create its own. Standards might dictate that in order to be eligible for funding, groups must identify the risks involved in their project and submit plans for minimizing those risks. It is important to acknowledge the reality of risks, for students may assume the strategy most likely to win approval is to minimize or discount any risks. Another useful approach is to require student groups to have a faculty or graduate adviser. Faculty members and graduate students can be perceived as less threatening than administrators and at the same time can reinforce the educational aspects of the service-learning experience. It is worthwhile to provide a context within which the students and the adviser can establish a meaningful relationship. This may involve educating student leaders about the kinds of roles that advisers can play and then allowing them to negotiate specific roles with their advisers. It is possible that faculty members may take a heavy-handed approach in advising a student-run project; administrators may need to support students' rights to determine their program's goals and direction.

Often students resist leadership roles in service-learning programs because they want to spend their time performing service, not dealing with administrative and bureaucratic concerns. At the same time, student groups often embrace nonhierarchical forms of governance. These factors can lead to a diffusion of responsibility, which may result in the neglect of important tasks. Advisers can encourage student groups to develop a rotating leadership model to spread out administrative responsibility. This model can be challenging to establish but can result in smoothly functioning groups and powerful learning about leadership and organizations. Administrators can also encourage students to interview service providers and organizers in the community to appreciate the role of administrative detail in providing quality service.

One of the most perplexing challenges in advising student groups is determining how best to assist in the leadership transition. Seasoned leaders are often most sensitive to administrator overinvolvement and most confident in their own abilities as they complete their leadership term. Unfortunately the typical end-of-term turmoil leaves little time for succession planning, and failure to provide an appropriate process for selecting and training leadership successors can leave a program ill equipped to continue. An effective strategy can be to focus leadership development activities on those involved students who think they might be interested in leadership roles, placing more responsibility for succession planning on those who will remain rather than those who will leave.

Service-Learning as a Graduation Requirement

Requiring service-learning can be an exemplary way to build it into the infrastructure of the institution, making a clear statement about its centrality to the educational mission. There are many administrative issues involved in the decision to require service-learning for graduation. The educational power of the service-learning experience may be undermined for some students if it is mandated; indeed the lessons learned by a resentful participant can be reinforcement of stereotypes, cynicism about the rights and responsibilities of citizenship, or other potentially negative outcomes. In addition the college or university must be sensitive to the impact of negative attitudes of unwilling volunteers on clients, staff, and other volunteers at service sites. On a pragmatic note, an institution must determine whether it can develop and monitor sufficient placements for all students. The use of indirect service, which involves participants in activities away from the agency and its clients, or nondirect service, which takes place at the service site but not in direct contact with clients (Delve, Mintz, and Stewart,

1990), should be considered as ways to place reluctant volunteers and develop sufficient placements.

Depending on the manner in which mandatory service-learning is implemented, the administrative staff time required to track and certify completion of the requirements can be time-consuming and costly. If students are required to enroll in a designated service-learning course, the faculty members teaching the course may need assistance in tracking students' service hours. In the case of a course requirement, the credit and possibly the grade earned can be certified on the official transcript like other graduation requirements. Software can be purchased or developed to track students' service hours and generate reports.

Required service also carries with it a heightened liability concern since the concept of assumption of risk may not apply if service is mandated rather than voluntary.

Judicially Mandated Service-Learning

Some colleges and universities see service-learning as a powerful educational experience for students who have committed judicial infractions, as well as a way to provide a form of restitution to the community for inappropriate behaviors. Although service-learning sanctions can be beneficial to students and communities, both community concerns and student learning objectives must be considered in the decision to mandate these sanctions. Respect for an agency's clients dictates sensitivity in placing students who have been judicially sanctioned. Some agencies welcome such students and are able to find appropriate roles for then. Many are used to relying on court-mandated service providers and find judicially sanctioned students no more challenging. Judicially mandated students with negative attitudes about their service-learning requirement should be referred to indirect or nondirect options. Anecdotal evidence of students who continue to engage in service-learning after completing their sanction and go on to become campus leaders of service projects attests to the potential impact of judicially mandated service. As with other forms of service-learning, it is vital to build structured reflection into the sanction rather than to assume that performing service will in itself result in the desired learning.

Programs Distant from the Campus

One way of deepening institutional commitment to service-learning is to develop and support intensive service-learning programs, such as the increasingly popular alternative break programs and domestic and international summer or semester-long immersions. The administration of these programs, usually operated at a distance from campus, is especially complex, and the variety of options within these types of programs complicates the administrative issues to be considered: site development and selection of student participants (covered in Chapter Eight), finances, travel, housing, food, supplies, climate, communication, health, and liability issues.

Intensive programs are costly since most require travel and housing. In many cases volunteers must pay the expenses associated with their participation, perhaps with scholarships available for those who cannot afford it. Other programs may be funded by mini-grants from Break Away or by private benefactors. Individual participants may be required to recruit sponsors for support, or they may join together for a group fundraising project to support the trip. Students can also take advantage of in-kind services, such as housing in local churches and donated vans or other supplies.

Travel is often the most expensive item associated with intensive service-learning programs. International travel is especially costly and complex. Travel arrangements should be made as far in advance as possible; advance fares are less expensive, and it may be possible to solicit competitive bids and arrange group discounts. In one case, for a group of Georgetown University volunteers in a year-long program in South Africa, the airline from which they had purchased their round-trip tickets went bankrupt prior to their return, necessitating the purchase of a new set of return tickets. Surface travel can also be complicated because many service sites are located in remote regions underserved by public transportation. Administrators working with government officials or community agency staff at the site can help collect information that can be provided to students before their departure that can minimize their confusion on arrival.

International sites may necessitate obtaining visas for volunteers, a process that should be initiated well in advance of departure. Many bureaucratic snafus can be encountered in trying to obtain visas, especially for travel to developing nations, and building in extra time for stumbling blocks is wise. In addition, travel to some areas requires immunizations that necessitate advance planning.

Among the housing options for volunteers at distant sites, one possibility is to house and feed the students individually or in pairs with members of the community. This model provides a more authentic interaction with local residents but gives much less control over the arrangements and requires goodwill on the part of the community and flexibility on the part of the students. Another option is to house volunteers together in an institutional setting, such as a church, school, or religious community. For other sites it may be appropriate to have volunteers bring and pitch their own tents. The communal living experience can be a strong building block for relationships among the students and facilitates group reflection.

Food can be a challenging aspect of distant placements, and it is important to give students an accurate picture of what to expect well in advance of their trip. In a group living situation with access to cooking facilities, the volunteers can share responsibility on a rotating basis for preparing, serving, and cleaning up after meals. Menus can be developed in advance that rely on readily available ingredients or prepackaged foods. In more remote locations or those with very different cultures, students will need to be flexible about their meals, especially if staying with a local resident or family. The nature of the food, quantity available per person, and dining arrangements may be dramatically different from what students are accustomed to. Vegetarians, for example, may have difficulty in areas where few fresh vegetables are available, and those used to a meat-centered diet may find that little or no meat is served in some areas.

Climate is a factor that deserves consideration. Volunteers should know precisely what to prepare for, given both the weather and the local resources, such as availability of heat and hot water. These factors, combined with an awareness of the types of projects they will be engaged in, can help students pack wisely. Often baggage limits are imposed by travel and housing providers.

Health matters are usually one of the most troubling aspects of distant service sites, which are likely to be without hospital facilities and where local water supplies may be contaminated. Preparing students to maintain their own health is important. The book *Where There Is No Doctor: A Village Health Care Handbook* (Werner, 1985) can be a valuable self-help resource, for it covers a wide range of issues, including prevention, first aid, and determining when more serious attention is needed. It is wise to provide volunteers with the names of local English-speaking doctors, if possible, and to have an evacuation policy with guidelines for deciding when someone must return home and establishing how that will be accomplished. An emergency fund can be set aside for such an eventuality.

Another program detail to consider in advance is the availability of supplies needed for the service projects. Activities such as painting a building and putting on a new roof require both tools and supplies, and it is important to be clear about who will secure and pay for any needed items. Books and training materials may not be readily available, so it is important to consider these needs as part of the preparation process.

A critical policy issue is the use of alcohol and other drugs at a distant site. Local laws may differ from those at the college or university, and volunteers should be aware of them, as well as any policies in existence at potential or selected sites. Students and administrators must decide if they wish the program to be drug and alcohol free and what penalties to impose for failure to comply with program policy. Alternative break programs should strongly consider an alcohol-free policy, given the beer-soaked stereotype of the typical spring break that these programs seek to counter. Since student volunteers are institutional representatives in an unfamiliar setting, it is prudent to consider establishing such a ground rule.

Liability concerns require considerable attention in distant settings. Often students are unaccompanied by any college or university staff, and full responsibility for decision making that can affect the safety of the group will rest with them. Liability associated with travel, alcohol use, equipment use, and the inherent dangers of specific projects must all be considered. In general the best way to limit liability is to minimize risks by providing thorough orientation and training to the specific dangers of a given project and allowing the volunteers to exercise informed consent, so that they are aware of the risks they are facing and are accepting them willingly.

Nuts and Bolts

Several very practical considerations contribute to the success or failure of service-learning programs. Despite the numerous campus partners in the development of service-learning, these nuts-and-bolts concerns will usually fall to the service-learning administrator to manage. This final section focuses on the pragmatic concerns related to service-learning opportunity data banks, transportation, fiscal management, and risk management.

Service-Learning Opportunity Data Banks

A key step in sustaining both curricular and cocurricular service-learning is the development and maintenance of listings of service-learning opportunities for students. At many institutions service-learning administrators provide this type of service to faculty, student organizations, and individual students. In the ideal situation, faculty develop their own community relationships that relate to their research interests and lead to service-learning opportunities for their students; more typically, however, faculty rely on service-learning administrators to develop community relationships and provide data banks of service-learning opportunities that they and their students can use. Such data banks have a variety of administrative homes, including service-learning centers, student activities offices, campus ministries, or student organizations. Recent innovations include the University of Colorado at Colorado Springs's Service Link, a computer bulletin board, and the University of Rhode Island's use of e-mail to promote service opportunities.

As institutions make the transition from volunteer service to service-learning opportunities, the nature of the data bank requires increased administrative attention. Unlike routine volunteer openings that can be listed without expressed consideration for learning outcomes, service-learning opportunities require that the potential for significant learning exists for students. Feedback from students on placements should be sought to help identify inappropriate service-learning sites—those that provide poor or nonexistent training or orientation, do not allow students to exercise judgment, have volunteers perform only clerical tasks, require too much time or not have enough hours available, treat clients abusively, or provide no context for helping students understand the importance of the role that they play. Administrators should develop a rational plan for eliminating inappropriate service sites from the data bank, including communication with the sites.

The most effective way to maintain a data bank is with database software that organizes data and generates reports. Rockhurst College in Missouri uses Microsoft Office and its Access Database, which allows staff to produce both individual student transcripts and a variety of reports of student participation in service. At the University of Texas at Austin, Filemaker Pro is used to list 220 agencies with 600 individual volunteer job descriptions, as well as to maintain a database on involved individuals and student organizations. Bethany College in West Virginia uses SAM Volunteer Information Software to track demographic information, training, volunteer assignments, and recognition, as well as to generate customized reports. Servus software, which was developed specifically to track volunteer efforts, also includes a library of inspirational quotations about service. Recent upgrades have made Servus a quicker and more useful package. Librarians and campus computer programmers can be excellent partners in developing customized software.

In addition to site and placement information, data banks can include a variety of information of interest to students and other community members involved in service. They can contain material on grants and application processes, service-learning scholarships, paid opportunities in the nonprofit sector, and information about upcoming seminars or conferences on service-learning or relevant public policy issues. Depending on the nature and extent of the career center's offerings, the task of collecting and disseminating information about postcollege service opportunities may fall to the service-learning administrator.

Transportation

Depending on the location of a college or university, transportation to service sites can be a challenge. Urban institutions may be able to rely on public transportation, but even in cities service sites are often not well served by public transportation. Access to an institutional pool of vehicles can be the lifeblood of a program, and the needs of many different users can be met by the same vehicles. Risks can be managed through driver certification programs that limit driving privileges to those who have successfully completed a driver safety course and training in emergency procedures. Some institutions implement a driving records check with local law enforcement agencies to screen out risky drivers.

Grant or private funds, often unavailable for staff salaries, may be available to purchase or lease twelve- to fifteen-passenger vans that could be dedicated for use in service-learning activities or become part of a pool available to other campus users. Athletics, residence life, dining services, physical plant, and other campus departments often own numerous vehicles and may be willing to support service-learning programs through an in-kind contribution of vehicle use.

It may be worthwhile to ask local transit authorities to donate tokens to students involved in service-learning programs. Student activities funds can also help support transportation, and at some institutions, student-run or contract transit services can assist. Funding from the community may be available to transport children to the campus for programs or tutoring. Some institutions have received the loan of vehicles from local automobile dealerships or have negotiated the use of school buses for evening or weekend activities. Many service-learning programs rely on carpooling with students who have cars, while others concentrate on agencies within walking distance to campus. It is important to decide under what circumstances it is or is not appropriate to use personal vehicles, including whether volunteers may transport children and what kind of safety precautions are necessary. The use of institutional vehicles is already governed by policies that may need to be adapted for volunteer use. Policies should include penalties for vehicle misuse and emergency procedures.

A comprehensive transportation policy should be developed that covers a range of issues. When possible, the policy should encourage the use of public transit and consider the circumstances under which students or others will be reimbursed for out-of-pocket transportation costs, including the necessity of receipts.

Fiscal Management

Service-learning administrators may feel that they have little time to spare on fiscal management given the many pressing human and programmatic issues, but proper financial management needs to be a priority so that the overall success of the project is not jeopardized by sloppy finances. Since service-learning projects often start up with external funding, administrators may need to coordinate program management with campus foundation staff for private gifts and with sponsored programs staff for government grants. Grant requirements vary but usually are quite strict about the conditions under which funds can be spent. Federal grants require very specific accounting procedures, and even with private gifts, documenting in writing the intended use of funds and monitoring their actual use is prudent.

Assistance with fiscal management may be available from a number of sources. Most institutions employ a contract administrator to track the use of federal funds granted to the institution, as well as indirect costs and matching funds associated with the grants. Campus offices with full-time budget managers may be willing to make a contribution of staff assistance to support the service-learning program, or an advanced student in accounting or financial management may be available at minimum wage or as a practicum placement to keep track of the program's budget.

Risk Management

There are risks involved in service-learning programs, and risk-averse administrators may seek to avoid involvement in these activities. Nevertheless, risk is inherent in any student activity, and supportive administrators speak of risk management, not risk avoidance. Indeed there is probably less risk in service-learning activities than in student athletic programs. If an activity cannot be performed safely, however, because of lack of expertise, training, or proper equipment, avoidance is the appropriate risk management strategy (Tremper and Rypkema, 1994). There are two primary elements of risk in volunteer programs: risk of harm from volunteers and risk of harm to volunteers.

Some states have enacted volunteer protection laws designed to release volunteers from liability for harm they may cause while volunteering with established charitable organizations. These laws vary from state to state, but most cover a volunteer's conduct unless it meets a standard of gross negligence, recklessness, or willful and wanton misconduct (Tremper and Perry, 1994). Volunteers may also be covered by workers' compensation from the organization they work with. The Nonprofit Risk Management Center (1001 Connecticut Avenue, N.W., Suite 900, Washington, D.C. 20036–5504; telephone 202/785–3891) offers informative publications and institutes on various aspects of insurance, legal liability, and risk management for nonprofit organizations and volunteer programs.

It is often said that safety is everybody's business, but that kind of shared responsibility can have a downside, "because no one really knows what to do for safety. So, safety gets assigned to the four winds—in the hope that since everyone is responsible, no one can be blamed for accidents" (Grose, 1987, p. 89). Successful service-learning administrators identify allies within their institutions, such as risk management staff, insurance administrators, and legal counsel to assist in the proper management of risk. They form a partnership with institutional colleagues and community leaders to identify potential sources of risk and take all reasonable and necessary precautions—for example, effective volunteer education, proper volunteer and service site selection, appropriate service site management, and the judicious use of waivers.

Waivers can be helpful in limiting liability and educating volunteers when used appropriately. They can demonstrate after the fact that proper caution was exercised, that the students were aware of the risks inherent in a particular situation, and that precautionary measures were clearly articulated. Blanket waivers that seek to release the institution or individual administrator from any unnamed risk are no protection against the failure to exercise due care in the administration of a program. Courts have not upheld waivers in such cases. Their use may give uninformed leaders a false sense of security that they have taken care of any legal liability. Moreover, the best way to limit legal liability is to exercise appropriate caution in managing the program so that risks are minimal.

Volunteer education regarding risks will generally be a shared responsibility between the service-learning administrator and the agency volunteer coordinator. Traditional-age college students often consider themselves invulnerable and may be naive about the risks posed by challenging locations; any student new to an environment may be unfamiliar with its hazards. Basic personal safety workshops can provide volunteers with heightened awareness as well as simple techniques that can prevent them from becoming victims. It may be necessary to discuss inappropriate dress with students, including provocative clothing or ostentatious jewelry that can draw attention to volunteers as potential crime targets. Students should be informed how to react and respond if a violent incident, vehicle accident, or serious injury should occur. They should be advised not to attempt to handle such problems on their own and to preserve essential facts and physical evidence until these can be provided to the campus risk manager (Madsen and Walker, 1983).

In neighborhoods with high crime rates, risk can be minimized by students' traveling in vans clearly marked with institutional identification, working in groups, and wearing program T-shirts, caps, or the like. Administrators should be sure that community members and leaders are aware and supportive of the presence of student volunteers. A neighborhood watch program active near a volunteer site can be an excellent reciprocal program within the community. It is important not to pay undue attention to safety, however. If community members interpret concern for volunteer safety to take precedence over the concern for the residents, the institution-community relationship could be jeopardized.

Conclusion

Service-learning program administrators must possess a range of sophisticated skills to coordinate successful programs. They must provide consistent, focused attention to the desired learning and developmental outcomes for the students involved, as well as to the needs and interests of the community. In addition to these cornerstones, they must attend to a host of management concerns with little margin for error, for service-learning programs are often in the media spotlight.

Service-learning operates across the boundaries between education and administration, spanning historical and structural divisions on campuses. Well-administered service-learning programs provide one of the best opportunities for building alliances across campus and among disparate academic departments, creating relationships among people who otherwise would have little reason to work together. Facing collective problems along with community partners not only strengthens relationships between the institution and the community but can also enhance the sense of community within an institution, as colleagues from different administrative divisions work together. As any service-learning administrator will attest, although service-learning programs are challenging to administer, they can be the most rewarding programs to manage as well.

References

Barr, M. J., and Cuyjet, M. J. "Program Development and Implementation." In T. K. Miller and R. B. Winston (eds.), *Administration and Leadership in Student Affairs: Actualizing Student Development in Higher Education.* (2nd ed.) Muncie, Ind.: Accelerated Development, 1991.

Below, P. J., Morrisey, G. L., and Acomb, B. L. *The Executive Guide to Strategic Planning.* San Francisco: Jossey-Bass, 1987.

Brown, R. D. "Key Issues in Evaluating Student Affairs Programs." In G. Kuh (ed.), *Evaluation in Student Affairs.* Cincinnati: American College Personnel Association, 1979.

Bryson, J. M. *Strategic Planning for Public and Nonprofit Organizations: A Guide to Strengthening and Sustaining Organizational Achievement.* San Francisco: Jossey-Bass, 1988.

Cronbach, L. J., and Associates. *Toward Reform of Program Evaluation.* San Francisco: Jossey-Bass, 1980.

Delve, C. I., Mintz, S. D., and Stewart, G. M. "Promoting Values Development Through Community Service: A Design." In C. I. Delve, S. D. Mintz, and G. M. Stewart (eds.), *Community Service as Values Education.* New Directions for Student Services, no. 50. San Francisco: Jossey-Bass, 1990.

Giles, D., Porter Honnet, E., and Migliore, S. *Research Agenda for Combining Service and Learning in the 1990s.* Raleigh, N.C.: National Society for Experiential Education, 1991.

Grose, V. L. *Managing Risk: Systematic Loss Prevention for Executives.* Englewood Cliffs, N.J.: Prentice Hall, 1987.

Madsen, C., and Walker, J. H. *Risk Management and Insurance: A Handbook of Fundamentals.* Washington, D.C.: National Association of College and University Business Officers, 1983.

Miller, M., and Steele, L. *Service Counts: Lessons from the Field of Service and Higher Education.* Providence, R.I.: Campus Compact, 1995.

Tremper, C., and Perry, J. "Volunteer Protection Varies State to State." *Leadership,* Oct.–Dec. 1994.

Tremper, C., and Rypkema, P. "A Look at the Heart of Risk Management." *Leadership,* Oct.–Dec. 1994.

Weiss, C. H. *Evaluation Research: Methods for Assessing Program Effectiveness.* Englewood Cliffs, N.J.: Prentice Hall, 1972.

Werner, D. *Where There Is No Doctor: A Village Health Care Handbook.* Palo Alto, Calif.: Hesperian Foundation, 1985.

Chapter Twelve

Issues Related to Integrating Service-Learning into the Curriculum

Keith Morton

Faculty who seek to integrate service-learning into their teaching face a number of critical decisions, some particular to service-learning and others that arise anytime careful attention is given to the art and craft of teaching. The research suggests that curricular service-learning can improve student learning (Markus, Howard, and Peterson, 1993; Boss, 1994; Cohen and Kinsey, 1994). The gains often come with some costs to faculty, however, such as time spent mastering a new pedagogy, anxiety associated with what may feel like less control over the direction of a course, and the increased logistical complexity of incorporating community partners into the teaching process. Finally, although some individual faculty can and do manage to integrate service-learning into their teaching successfully, most find it difficult or impossible to begin or to sustain this effort without institutional support.

Note: The assistance of Sandra L. Enos and Marie L. Troppe with the section entitled "Structuring Opportunities for Student Reflection" is acknowledged and appreciated.

Deciding to Include Service-Learning in a Course

Generally there are two fundamental types of service-learning courses: those designed to assist students in reflecting on and learning from the service in which they are already engaged (service-centered courses) and those that have discipline and content objectives that can be more effectively reached by the inclusion of service (content-centered courses). It helps to distinguish these two types of courses because they differ in significant ways both pedagogically and institutionally.

Service-centered courses are designed to integrate learning with service. At their best, these courses are empirical and inductive and begin with the assumption that learning is a process of transforming experience into knowledge. Service is treated as an experience that students individually and collectively transform into knowledge through their participation in structured reflection. Such courses can also be consciously designed to reconnect the subjective and objective dimensions of "knowing" in more holistic and authentic ways. Knowing, writes Parker Palmer (1993), "is a dance between the subjective and objective in which we need both distance and intimacy with the known" (p. 17). Courses built around service experiences often evolve out of student interest and requests, with students who are heavily engaged in service seeking opportunities for formal reflection. For a number of years, Robert Coles has taught a course at Harvard titled The Literature of Social Reflection. Several discussion sessions are reserved for students involved in community service, who use the assigned readings as a basis for reflection on their service experiences (Coles, 1993).

Service-centered courses also arise out of institutional efforts to create integrative educational experiences such as first-year seminars or senior capstone courses. Institutionally driven service-based courses often have broad liberal education objectives, such as civic or social consciousness, critical thinking, awareness of and comfort with diversity, collaborative problem solving, and conflict resolution. Such courses often combine overt learning objectives—exploring concepts of citizenship or justice raised by the service experience, for example—with covert objectives, such as improvement of retention and graduation rates.

Content-based service-learning courses integrate service in order to achieve preexisting course outcomes. Faculty who are teaching courses with discipline-based, content-driven learning objectives sometimes elect to integrate service-learning as a way to build in liberal education objectives, but they more often do so as a way to achieve particular content outcomes. Lee Shulman (1991), a close observer of teaching, has suggested that "public service activity can be thought of as the missing clinical component of the liberal arts and sciences" (p. 1). Sociologist Jim Ostrow (personal communication, 1993) gives as his primary reason for incorporating service-learning into an introductory course that he wants his students "to *do* sociology." The service his students do with homeless people is a first step in this direction. Service, from this perspective, is integrated into courses to illustrate or provide a context for particular lessons or learning objectives. A history or political science course on immigration may have students tutor recent immigrants in English as a second language, develop oral histories with immigrants, or help at a community center in a predominantly immigrant neighborhood. A biochemistry course may assay and search for sources of heavy metals in soil or water, and a poetry course may pair college students with members of a senior center to write poetry. The distinguishing mark of this type of service-learning is that the service is intended to enhance the knowledge and skills determined to be important within an academic discipline.

Comparing service-centered and content-centered service-learning courses raises the question of purpose: What are the underlying reasons for combining service and learning in a particular course? The clearer the faculty member is about his or her reasons, the more likely it is that service and learning outcomes will be successful. Edward Zlotkowski (1993) of Bentley College describes his process for consulting with faculty new to service-learning as beginning with the questions, "What are the goals of your course? How could service help you to achieve them?" The answer to the first question should be independent of issues of methodology and should focus on the fundamental purpose of the course by selecting two or three lessons that students successfully completing the course will take away. The purpose of a history course surveying the years 1890 through 1920, for example, might be to acquire content knowledge of the key events of the period and to puzzle over the paradoxes of time and progress. In an introductory chemistry course, the purpose might be mastering the fundamental principles of the periodic table and grasping the practical and philosophical meanings of the term *conservation of energy*. The answer to the second question, regarding the potential role of service, forces faculty to consider how they will know if their purpose is achieved: How will I know if the students "get it"? For content-based courses, faculty grapple with choosing among teaching methodologies. What is most effective: lecture, demonstration, case study, or service-learning? The challenge is to determine whether service-learning is a more effective vehicle for teaching a body of material than other methods.

Faculty used to content-based teaching often tend to mistrust inductive, process-based teaching—the cycle of action and reflection—that characterizes service-learning, arguing that it is appropriate for cocurricular activities but not rigorous enough to be considered as a pedagogy. Hearing (or sharing) this perspective, faculty considering teaching a service-centered course or integrating service into a course may fear that they will be viewed by colleagues as diluting their discipline, replacing rigorous intellectual analysis with affective, shallow opinion based on limited, idiosyncratic experience. Experience-based teaching and learning runs counter to the predominant, deductive modes of teaching on college campuses, which move from theory to practice, teach theory only, or, in Paulo Freire's (1970) analogy, treat students as passive "banks" into which the teacher "deposits" information (pp. 57–59). Because they place students' interpretations of experience at the center of teaching, service-learning courses are, in essence, countercultural, and faculty seeking institutional permission and legitimacy or collegial and institutional support must acknowledge this in deciding whether to engage in service-learning. In addition, faculty teaching courses that involve substantial community outcomes may find themselves charged with compromising learning, at odds with the educational mission of their institution, or in an unfavorable position in the promotion and tenure process.

Another important issue is how to weigh and balance the learning and service objectives. Although creative tension between these objectives is appropriate and synergy may be an ideal product of that tension, on balance the primary purpose of colleges and universities is education, and the integration of service into the curriculum is appropriate only as it contributes to this end. At its best, service can be a way of making the learning real and concrete, increasing the perceived value of the knowledge that is transmitted, introducing accountability for doing the work of the class (reading, participating in discussions, turning assignments in on time), and provoking the curiosity that drives critical thinking.

This is not to say that potential community impacts, both positive and negative, are not of pressing concern. Rather it is to suggest that a healthy service-learning curriculum requires strong community partnerships that are committed to both community impact and student learning. Only when the community partners clearly understand course purposes can faculty feel comfortable focusing on learning. In fact, students' deeper engagement with the content of the course can lead to higher-quality service and even to outcomes that have a significant, long-term effect on an agency or a community.

Key Decisions in Developing Service-Learning Courses

Once a faculty member decides to engage in service-learning, a sequence of other decisions needs to be addressed, ranging from the philosophical, such as how to define service, to the practical, such as how to monitor and evaluate students' service.

What Is Service?

Service is a complicated and contested concept. An individual's conception of service is based on a range of factors and experiences, including family and class background, socioeconomic status, race or ethnicity, faith and religion, communities one has lived in, and previous experiences as one who has served those in need or has been served as one in need (Fitch, 1987; Koppi, 1992; Winniford, Carpenter, and Grider, 1995).

Service can be viewed as either a continuum or a set of paradigms, each containing three elements: charity, project management, and social change (Morton, 1995). Often as faculty (and students) become more involved in service and in reflection about its meaning, they come to understand it as a continuum that begins with individual acts of compassion or charity and culminates in commitment to social change, with a midpoint of project management (Morton, 1995). Movement along the continuum can be measured on two axes: degree of investment in relationships with those served, and commitment to seeking and addressing the root causes of the issues that affect the quality of life in a community. As one moves along the continuum, one becomes more and more deeply involved in relationships with people and organizations and commits greater amounts of energy to digging deeper and deeper in the search for the root causes of individual or systemic problems. One purpose of integrating service into a course, from this point of view, would be to move students along the continuum from acts of charity to commitment to social justice.

As attractive and logical as the image of a continuum may be, it is not the only way to understand service. An alternative is to conceptualize service as a set of three paradigms—charity, project management and social change—and to acknowledge that each type of service can be done with varying degrees of integrity, ranging from "thin," or having little integrity, to "thick," or having great integrity. The thick versions of each paradigm, to adapt the language of anthropologist Clifford Geertz (1973), are grounded in deeply held, internally coherent values; match means and ends; describe a primary way of interpreting and relating to the world; offer a way of defining problems and solutions; and suggest a vision of what a transformed world might look like. Thin versions of service are full of internal contradictions and irony: means and ends are inconsistent, responsibility for the long-term (or unanticipated) consequences of the service are avoided or ignored, and any vision of a transformed world is deferred or absent.

The different paradigms can be equally committed to sustaining and deepening relationships over time but may differ significantly in how they define problems to be addressed and in the strategies they hold to be effective in addressing them. Thick charity, deeply grounded in one's faith or personal concept of social responsibility and sustained over time, can lead to personal and systemic transformation. The project management approach emphasizes the practical creation of organizations that "make it happen"—educating children, building homes, cleaning up neighborhoods—rather than the abstractions of charity or social justice. Thick versions of project management have to do with community identification of capacity and need, shared authority and power, and constancy and consistency of effort. Thickness of the social change paradigm involves educating people to act in their own interest and empowering those who have been socially disenfranchised, while thin versions of social change establish narrow political positions, place the locus of control in the hands of others, and can tend to suborn people to ideas. A learning objective from this paradigmatic perspective might be to help students identify the paradigm of service that fits best for them and to challenge them to practice it with increasing integrity.

How one understands service thus has direct implications for how one teaches. Whether one envisions service as a continuum, as a set of paradigms, or in another coherent, consistent way, coming to grips with one's understanding of service is an important step in selecting the types of service that will match the purpose of a given course, defining the impacts one expects service to have, and determining the criteria by which success or failure will be measured.

Service as Text

In considering how to integrate service into a course, it can be useful to think of service in the sense of a "text" for the course. Service certainly is not a text in a traditional sense (most significant, it is "written" concurrently with the course), but thinking of it in this way has a number of practical benefits. First, it suggests that service is equal to written work in its learning potential. Second, the analogy of text implies that faculty must decide what texts are appropriate for the course and whether they are required or optional. Service as text also indicates that faculty should provide structures in which students read, analyze, and discuss the text. Finally, faculty need to evaluate how well students have learned from the text.

Based on course purpose and the faculty member's definition of service, decisions can be made about the types of service that can appropriately serve as text for the course. For example, must service activities be direct, that is, involving face-to-face interaction with those served? Can they be nondirect, where students are in the environment of the population being served but not in direct contact with the client population, or indirect, where students are physically distant from the service site and the individuals being served (Delve, Mintz, and Stewart, 1990)? Is serving meals in a soup kitchen appropriate as text? What about designing a marketing survey for a children's museum or collecting oral histories from the residents of a nursing home? A growing body of literature can assist faculty to answer these questions (Howard, 1993; Campus Compact, 1994; Jackson, 1994; Kraft and Swadener, 1994; Troppe, 1995). The one consistent characteristic of efforts to clarify the type of service is clarity about the purpose of the course.

Service: At the Center or the Periphery? Required or Optional?

Once service is selected as a course text, multiple issues of how to include it in a course must be addressed. As with any traditional text, service can be more or less central, and more or less class time can be given to studying it. The more central that service is to a course, the more it will direct the structure of the course; the greater the amount of time that is dedicated to learning from the service, the less time there is available for other content. This is not an issue specific to service; the trade-off between breadth and depth is an issue inherent in teaching any course. The intent of service-learning, especially in service-centered courses, is to focus more on unpacking the various layers of meaning embedded in the service experience and to use less external material. Service, from this perspective, is the central text, to be read together by students and teachers throughout the course. Additional texts are employed as they help provide context for the service experience and help students to reflect on it.

For content-centered courses, the issue is somewhat different, because service is typically one of several texts. Among the first decisions to be made is whether the service will be optional or required. Service has generally been used as a course option in one of three ways: as extra credit within a fixed grading system, as an alternative for another assignment, or as a means of earning additional course credit in what has become known as the fourth-credit option, in which students have the option of adding an extra credit to a regular course if a negotiated amount of service and reflection is completed. Making service optional has these basic merits: it recognizes that not all students choose to learn in this way, it makes fewer demands for time in a course syllabus, and it requires fewer service sites and less faculty supervision time.

On the other hand, optional service, especially a rigorous fourth-credit option, can leave faculty who do not have staff support feeling that they are supervising a large number of independent study projects in addition to teaching the basic course. Further, if the service is not required, it is equivalent to making a text optional—of having only a percentage of a class read it. This makes it more difficult to incorporate the service experience into class discussions and will likely lead to greater reliance on learning vehicles that are more individual, such as journals and papers. In addition, many faculty comment that the service experiences of their students are powerful enough that limiting discussion of service once it is opened up can be difficult and that the differential in experience and point of view between those doing service and those who are not can create a rift among the students in a class.

Alternatively, service can be a course requirement. Requiring service generally means that it will consume a significant amount of the effort students put into the course and that the format of the class should be structured to facilitate discussion and reflection. In addition, requiring service may increase the logistical complexity of a course by increasing the number of sites needed for placement, requiring more meetings and more supervision time, and raising the likelihood that problems will occur (for example, students not doing their service, conflict between a student and a site supervisor).

How Much Service Is Enough?

The next question is how much service, required or optional, should be asked of students. Faculty—especially those working with commuter, adult, part-time, or low-income students—do not want to place additional burdens on their students. They are concerned that the time students spend in service is time taken from family, work, or other responsibilities. It is helpful once again to consider service as the learning equivalent of a text in a course and to consider service requirements by the same standards as other out-of-class requirements. If, for example, a three-credit course meets three times per week for fifty minutes, a typical expectation might be that each class hour is matched by two to three hours of out-of-class work. If three hours of service are required each week, this leaves three to six hours for other out-of-class work, including reading, research, and writing. It is important to note that no empirical data exist on the optimum amount or intensity of service that is required to support learning outcomes (Giles and Eyler, 1994), although Dwight Gyles and Janet Eyler of Vanderbilt University are midway through a research project designed to isolate duration and intensity of service as variables that affect learning outcomes.

The time commitment and duration of service experiences can vary widely depending on the role of service in a particular course. It can be very appropriate for an introductory women's studies course, for example, to structure four one-time service experiences—at a crisis center, a homeless shelter, a political advocacy organization, and an arts center, all focusing on women—if the goal is exposure to a set of issues and to the people directly affected by those issues. This approach can underscore the importance of firsthand experience in research or policymaking. Conversely, it can be appropriate for such a course to require each student to serve three hours per week at one of the organizations for the duration of the course and use class discussion to draw out the similarities and differences among the four organizations. Exposure over time offers different lessons, trading scope of experience for depth of experience. Given that students lead busy lives, service options should be available that accommodate a wide range of schedules and lifestyles. A student without a car may need a site close to campus or on a bus line; a single parent may need a project that can be carried out while children are in day care, in the evenings at home, or at a site where children are welcome.

Structuring Opportunities for Student Reflection

Hutchings and Wutzdorff (1988) define reflection as "the ability to step back and ponder one's own experience, to abstract from it some meaning or knowledge relevant to other experiences" (p. 15). "The capacity for reflection," they conclude, "is what transforms experience into learning" (p. 15). No matter what the role of service is in a course, no matter whether a course is service based or content based, reflection is central to achieve student learning and developmental outcomes.

Reflection can occur through class discussions or on an individual basis. Class discussions offer faculty opportunities to challenge and support students as they process their experiences and to help students see the connections between their service and course objectives, be they discipline oriented or not. Class time can also be used for student presentations of their research findings, applications of theory to practice in the service setting, or projects they have completed at the service site.

Journals are a commonly used form of reflection, often focusing on affective responses to the service experience. A journal is a safe arena in which students can examine the emotions and challenges to their values that may arise from service. Some faculty specify double-entry journal writing, which requires reflections on the service experience as text and on other course readings. This approach helps students move from focusing on themselves and their emotional reactions to contemplating the larger issues of the root causes of social problems, social justice and injustice, and how academic disciplines relate to real-world issues.

In addition to journals, faculty often require papers linking academic content with service experiences. Such papers provide opportunities for critical thinking, but some students need considerable direction in making meaningful connections between theory and practice, in moving from simplistic, unidimensional analyses of situations to complex, multifaceted ones.

Evaluation and Grading

The service-as-text analogy is also useful in thinking about evaluation and grading. Faculty are often concerned that because they have little opportunity to observe the service directly, they do not have the time or relationships necessary to pursue formative evaluations of student performance with community-based supervisors, and they recognize that factors contributing to the successes or failures of a service experience are often beyond the control of students. Although these concerns are real and important, the service-as-text analogy suggests that student evaluation and grad-ing are not based on the experience itself but on the learning that comes from the experience. Students are not graded for how well they read a text but for demonstrating what they have learned from it, how they can apply what they have learned to problem solving, or how they integrate ideas from the text with other ideas. In short, the issue is how to construct appropriate measures for evaluating learning, an issue that is not at all unique to service-learning.

A growing literature on evaluation, assessment, and grad-ing describes a number of options that may work well in service-learning courses: case studies, portfolios, self-assessment, team-based learning, and learning communities. In their recent book, *Class-room Assessment Techniques* (1993), Patricia Cross and Thomas Angelo report on the research they did on classroom assessment and describe in detail a number of very useful techniques that can help determine how much and how well students are learning. Richard Kraft and James Krug's essay, "Review of Research and Evaluation on Service Learning in Public and Higher Education" (1994), does a good job of summarizing the assessment and evaluation litera-ture particular to service-learning, and Campus Compact's *Con-necting Cognition and Action: Evaluation of Student Performance in Service Learning Courses* (Troppe, 1995) further explores some of the issues that are peculiar to service-learning courses. Similarly, the rich lit-erature on program assessment techniques is relevant in assessing the service outcomes of service-learning. Particularly useful resources are *Evaluating Service-Learning Programs: A Guide for Pro-gram Coordinators* (ACTION, 1978), *Doing Self-directed Study for Ser-vice-Learning* (Shumer and Berkas, 1992), and *Evaluation: The Key to Improving Service-Learning Programs* (Neal and others, 1994). Com-mon themes throughout the literature on evaluation are that it requires clarity about what it is one is attempting to evaluate, care in using measures that will generate relevant and useful data, and willingness to act on what is learned.

In the context of evaluation and grading, the service-as-text analogy has some immediate limitations. First, it is a different matter for students not to read a conventional text than it is for them to skip their service commitments. Failing to meet a service commitment can leave immediate community needs unmet, waste community resources, threaten institutional relationships with the community, and generally leave a situation worse than if nothing had been expected. It is therefore necessary to develop some way of ensuring that service is performed and that absences or schedule changes are arranged ahead of time. Some faculty address this issue by assigning a certain percentage of a course grade (say twenty out of one hundred points) to the performance of the service as a base. This base can be lost if service is not performed (generally on a rapidly increasing scale). Other faculty have tried a "necessary and sufficient conditions" approach, stating in their syllabus that a necessary condition for passing a course is completion of the service requirement. Information on the fulfillment of a service commitment can be gathered by student self-reporting, telephone calls to site supervisors, or more formal means, such as written reports or time sheets signed by students and site supervisors. Another option is to have other students—as teaching assistants or as community-based work-study employees— supervise the placement and tracking of the student service at a site. Student absences, disappointments with the quality of their service, and other potential issues at the service site can be minimized by good advance communication with students and with the site supervisor.

Institutional Support for Curricular Service-Learning

Institutional support of service-learning by department chairs, deans, and academic vice presidents is necessary for three basic reasons: providing professional development for faculty who practice, or want to practice, service-learning; providing assistance to faculty in developing service sites and administering service; and establishing policies that support service-learning and ensure its academic credibility.

The early work of Presidents Donald Kennedy of Stanford University and David Warren of Ohio Wesleyan, in a survey of Campus Compact institutions, proposed five principal roles for faculty and administrators in service-learning: the importance of faculty as advisers, participants, and role models actively supporting and promoting student participation in public and community service; the need for students to connect their service experiences with their studies; the recognition of the academic curriculum as the principal means for developing in students an understanding of the importance, traditions, and critical issues related to social responsibility; the importance of administrative support, recognition, rewards, and incentives for faculty who participate in and support students who engage in public and community service, particularly the integration of service with study; and advocation by the leadership of institutions, that is, presidents and chief academic officers, of the faculty's role in public and community service (Stanton, 1990). Subsequent work strongly supports the importance of these five roles.

College and university student community service initiatives have historically fallen within the jurisdiction of student affairs or campus ministry, and because these offices have experience in supporting student service activities, they often provide initial support to academic service-learning efforts. As academically based efforts increase, however, tensions can develop: the resources of student affairs can be unfairly taxed; the interests of student affairs and academic affairs may diverge; faculty involvement may change the dynamic of previously established community relationships; and, at worst, faculty critical of service-learning may see an alliance with a nonacademic area as "evidence" that service-learning lacks rigor. All of this suggests the need for a careful and politic decision about where to base institutional support for integrating service into the curriculum.

Some institutions have succeeded with student affairs (or campus ministries) continuing to play a lead role; others have chosen to make academic affairs the lead office; and a larger number report a joint effort with shared resources (Morton and Troppe, 1996). Indiana University–Purdue University Indianapolis, with support from the academic vice president, has established a service-learning office led by a tenured faculty member and a staff person in a newly created position that supports faculty work. Calvin College in Michigan has released both faculty and student development staff time to create a jointly run service-learning office. Regardless of the organizational structure that is adopted, it is critical that faculty engaged in service-learning view the administration as supporting their work. As Lynn Montrose of Regis University in

Colorado points out, "The lifeblood of a service learning program is strong faculty commitment. Faculty tend to take ownership of service learning programs that they perceive as integral to the academic curriculum of the college" (1994, p. 17).

Faculty Development

Among the common strategies for identifying and educating faculty interested in service-learning are faculty convocations, speaker series, workshops, and seminars. These short-term efforts are most successful, however, when combined with intensive activities, such as summer service-learning institutes and regular meetings with colleagues involved in service-learning. Encouraging and supporting faculty participation in such national meetings as Campus Compact's Invisible College, a network of selected faculty who practice service-learning, and the annual meetings of the American Association of Higher Education and the National Society for Experiential Education is also useful.

What constitutes an effective strategy for faculty development will vary from campus to campus. Generally, however, such efforts are most effective when they are faculty driven. A committee composed largely of faculty will understand the cultural and political terrain of the campus and have a good sense of how to address the competing interests that define much of what it means to be a faculty member: balancing involvement in their discipline, their department, and their institution; and balancing teaching, research, and service. Faculty will also have a good sense of the key questions their colleagues have regarding service-learning: How does service-learning fit with our institutional mission? Will our students learn more if we introduce service into the curriculum? What do we mean by service? What kinds of research would be effective in addressing pressing community issues?

A resource collection is another effective faculty development tool. Collecting in one location books, manuals, sample syllabi, assessment tools, articles (especially those related to service-learning within the disciplines), journals, research questions, and models is a good starting point for providing technical assistance, and the simple mass of the collected resources can be reassuring to faculty concerned about academic respectability. Campus librarians are often willing to help collect and house such resources. Bibliographies compiled (and regularly updated) by the National Society for Experiential Education and Campus Compact provide a good starting point for creating a resource collection.

Faculty Assistance

Integrating service into a course can place extra demands on the time of faculty members, especially time dedicated to developing community partnerships, supervising and monitoring student service, and dealing with administrative issues. Strong support in any or all of these areas can significantly reduce the amount of time and effort it takes to integrate service into a course successfully, enabling faculty to concentrate on achieving student learning outcomes. Providing assistance to faculty in identifying service sites is an ideal way for student affairs–based service-learning centers to support faculty efforts to integrate service with academic study. Faculty also need guidance regarding institutional policies related to transportation and risk management. Without this support, faculty often feel that they are stealing time from other professional demands such as teaching, research, writing, and committee work. Support can be provided by professional staff, graduate or undergraduate teaching assistants, or students experienced in service-learning, who may or may not be paid a stipend. Several institutions have established mini-grant programs that allow faculty to devote their summers to curriculum development or provide released time from some of their teaching or administrative responsibilities.

Policies Supporting Service-Learning

Policies that support faculty involvement in service-learning generally take three forms: those designed to meet the immediate needs of faculty, those that deal with issues likely to come up as faculty interest in service-learning increases, and those that support service-learning over the longer term. The immediate issues include developing guidelines for service-learning courses (see Chapters Two and Seven), establishing service-learning course designations, and creating credit options, such as the fourth-credit option.

Midrange policy issues include educating curriculum committees and other academic policymakers about the value of service-learning. In addition to the formal decisions they make about courses that may or may not be taught, curriculum committees and similar policy bodies often play the role of opinion leader in establishing a positive or negative climate for new academic initiatives. Climate is an important factor in determining whether an initiative will receive ongoing institutional support. Educating curriculum committees about service-learning—often with stress on its academic rigor—can go a long way toward establishing a positive climate and smoothing the approval process for new or significantly modified courses.

The long-term issues are linked to promotion and tenure policies. According to findings of Campus Compact, "The surest indicator that service-learning has been effectively institutionalized . . . is a faculty reward system that recognizes service in its promotion and tenure-granting policies" (Kupiec, 1993, p. 21). Faculty engaged in service-learning are only one of many constituencies interested in redefining research, teaching, and service and the methods of assessing them. Participatory action research, for example, can be supported by creating mechanisms that recognize whether research is used or is of service to a community (Harkavy and Benson, 1991; Penas and Porpora, 1993; Troppe, 1994); evaluations of teaching can be expanded to include multiple ways of measuring learning outcomes; and definitions of faculty service can be broadened to include work that improves the quality of life in the surrounding communities. The potential also exists for developing sabbatical programs that allow faculty to spend their time in service to a particular community or studying issues related to some aspect of community development. Changing or expanding promotion and tenure policies is equivalent to changing the faculty culture of a campus and is therefore typically a difficult and incremental process. It is encouraging that the American Association of Higher Education, building on the work of Boyer (1990), Lynton (1995), and others, and the New England Resource Center for Higher Education have recently begun serious discussions about the relationship of service-learning to the redefinition of teaching, research, and service.

Conclusion

Among the great attractions of service-learning for faculty appear to be that it provides an opportunity for engaging in a deeper intellectual discourse and for exploring the ethical implications of that discourse. It also invites the broader community to help bring this discourse and these implications to the surface.

It speaks highly of service-learning that it is enjoying increasing faculty interest in a period of general discontent and austerity in higher education. Competition for institutional resources is fierce, and however compelling the promise of service-learning, it is competing with a dominant culture in a relatively hostile environment. On the other hand, service-learning is a viable vehicle for achieving broad and specific educational goals and helps to focus the energies of students and faculty on problems that are community and national priorities.

In addition to requiring resources for logistical and technical support for faculty, the growth of service-learning will require that executive officers, from department chairs to presidents, find ways to recognize and reward different teaching styles, assign equitable teaching loads, assess student learning in richer ways, support faculty research agendas that grow out of local community needs, expand the meaning of service in rank and tenure from committee work to community work, and otherwise protect and promote the careers of faculty who wish to commit to the integration of service and learning. What makes these efforts worthwhile is that service-learning offers a renewed vision of the college or university as a community of scholars united by the quest for and application of knowledge that will lead to a more just world. In the long run, service-learning will be judged by its contribution to this vision.

References

ACTION: National Student Volunteer Program. *Evaluating Service-Learning Programs: A Guide for Program Coordinators.* Pamphlet no. 4300.7. Washington, D.C.: ACTION, 1978.

Boss, J. "The Effect of Community Service Work on the Moral Development of College Students." *Journal of Moral Education,* 1994, *23*(2), 183–198.

Boyer, E. L. *Scholarship Reconsidered: Priorities of the Professoriate.* Princeton, N.J.: Carnegie Foundation for the Advancement of Teaching, 1990.

Campus Compact. *Fourteen Findings: Experiences of Teams Attending the 1991, 1992, and 1993 Summer Institutes on Integrating Service with Academic Study.* Providence, R.I.: Campus Compact, 1994.

Cohen, J., and Kinsey, D. "'Doing Good' and Scholarship: A Service Learning Study." *Journalism Educator,* 1994, *48*(4), 4–14.

Coles, R. *The Call of Service: A Witness to Idealism.* Boston: Houghton Mifflin, 1993.

Cross, P., and Angelo, T. *Classroom Assessment Techniques: A Handbook for Faculty.* Ann Arbor, Mich.: National Center for Research to Improve Postsecondary Teaching and Learning, 1993.

Delve, C. I., Mintz, S. D., and Stewart, G. M. "Promoting Values Development Through Community Service: A Design." In C. I. Delve, S. D. Mintz, and G. M. Stewart (eds.), *Community Service as Values Education.* New Directions for Student Services, no. 50. San Francisco: Jossey-Bass, 1990.

Fitch, R. T. "Characteristics and Motivations of College Students Volunteering for Community Service." *Journal of College Student Development,* 1987, *28*(5), 424–431.

Freire, P. *Pedagogy of the Oppressed.* (M. B. Ramos, trans.) New York: Herder and Herder, 1970.

Geertz, C. *The Interpretation of Cultures.* New York: Basic Books, 1973.

Giles, D. E., and Eyler, J. "The Impact of a College Community Service Laboratory on Students' Personal, Social and Cognitive Outcomes." *Journal of Adolescence,* 1994, *17,* 327–339.

Harkavy, I., and Benson, L. "Progressing Beyond the Welfare State." *Universities and Community Schools,* 1991, *2*(1–2), 2–27.

Howard, J. (ed.). *Praxis I: A Faculty Casebook on Community Service Learning.* Ann Arbor: OCSL Press, 1993.

Hutchings, P., and Wutzdorff, A. "Experiential Learning Across the Curriculum: Assumptions and Principles." In P. Hutchings and A. Wutzdorff (eds.), *Knowing and Doing: Learning Through Experience.* New Directions for Teaching and Learning, no. 35. San Francisco: Jossey-Bass, 1988.

Jackson, K. (ed.). *Redesigning Curricula: Models of Service Learning Syllabi.* Providence, R.I.: Campus Compact, 1994.

Koppi, S. R. "The Relationship Between Community Service Orientation, Gender, Sociopolitical Attitudes, and Demographic Characteristics of Newly Enrolled Students." Unpublished master's thesis, University of Maryland at College Park, 1992.

Kraft, R., and Krug, J. "Review of Research and Evaluation on Service Learning in Public and Higher Education." In R. Kraft and M. Swadener (eds.), *Building Community: Service Learning in the Academic Disciplines.* Denver: Colorado Campus Compact, 1994.

Kraft, R., and Swadener, M. (eds.). *Building Community Service Learning in the Academic Disciplines.* Denver: Colorado Campus Compact, 1994.

Kupiec, T. Y. (ed.). *Rethinking Tradition: Integrating Service with Academic Study on College Campuses.* Providence, R.I.: Campus Compact, 1993.

Lynton, E. A. *Making the Case for Professional Service.* Washington, D.C.: American Association for Higher Education, 1995.

Markus, G., Howard, J.P.F., and Peterson, M. "Instruction Enhances Learning: Results from an Experiment." *Educational Evaluation and Policy Analysis,* 1993, *15*(4), 410–419.

Montrose, L. "Planning for a Service Learning Center on Campus." In R. Kraft and M. Swadener (eds.), *Building Community: Service Learning in the Academic Disciplines.* Denver: Colorado Campus Compact, 1994.

Morton, K. "The Irony of Service: Charity, Project and Social Change in Service Learning." *Michigan Journal of Community Service Learning,* 1995, *2*(1), 19–32.

Morton, K., and Troppe, M. "From the Margin to the Mainstream: Campus Compact's Project on Integrating Service with Academic Study." *Journal of Business Ethics,* 1996, *15*(1), 21–32.

Neal, M., and others. *Evaluation: The Key to Improving Service-Learning Programs.* Minneapolis: University of Minnesota, Center for Experiential Education and Service Learning, 1994.

Palmer, P. "Is Service Learning for Everyone? On the Identity and Integrity of the Teacher." In T. Y. Kupiec (ed.), *Rethinking Tradition: Integrating Service with Academic Study on College Campuses.* Providence, R.I.: Campus Compact, 1993.

Penas, N., and Porpora, D. "Participatory Research: Three Models and an Analysis." *American Sociologist,* Nov.–Dec. 1993, pp. 107–126.

Shulman, L. "Professing the Liberal Arts." Presentation at Campus Compact's 1991 Institute on Integrating Service with Academic Study, Stanford, Calif., July 1991. Text available from Campus Compact.

Shumer, R., and Berkas, T. *Doing Self-Directed Study for Service-Learning.* Minneapolis: University of Minnesota, Center for Experiential Learning and Service Learning, 1992.

Stanton, T. *Integrating Public Service with Academic Study: The Faculty Role.* Providence, R.I.: Campus Compact, 1990.

Troppe, M. *Participatory Action Research: Merging the Community and Scholarly Agendas.* Providence, R.I.: Campus Compact, 1994.

Troppe, M. (ed.). *Connecting Cognition and Action: Evaluation of Student Performance in Service Learning Courses.* Providence, R.I.: Campus Compact, 1995.

Winniford, J. C., Carpenter, D. S., and Grider, C. "An Analysis of the Traits and Motivations of College Students Involved in Service Organizations." *Journal of College Student Development,* 1995, *36*(1), 27–37.

Zlotkowski, E. Untitled presentation at 1993 Campus Compact Institute on Integrating Service with Academic Study, Providence, R.I., July 1993.

Zlotkowski, E. "Service Learning as Campus Culture." In T. Y. Kupiec (ed.), *Rethinking Tradition: Integrating Service with Academic Study on College Campuses.* Providence, R.I.: Campus Compact, 1993.

Chapter Thirteen

Institutionalizing Service-Learning

Sharon Rubin

In the 1960s and 1970s, when volunteer and social action programs like the University Year for ACTION involved many college students in community service, colleges and universities expected that federal funding and social relevance would ensure the continuation and growth of such programs. Ten years later most of these programs had disappeared, victims of changed national priorities and their own self-confidence.

Current service-learning initiatives tend to be more modest and more focused, as administrators have learned to be wary of investing in programs that are weak administratively, tangential to the educational mission, or of questionable service to the community. They also seek assurance that service-learning programs will survive even if the outstanding volunteer coordinator takes a new job, the committed faculty member assumes another campus role, the community agency reorganizes, or the energetic student leader graduates.

Fortunately, there are institutions throughout the nation whose service-learning programs have been firmly embedded for years, are central to their missions, and make a significant contribution to the communities in which they are located. They are so different from one another in terms of their operation that they seem at first glance to have little in common other than their commitment to combining service and learning and their belief in the reciprocal relationship between those serving and those served. Nevertheless, there are some useful generalizations about the shared characteristics of programs that have become integral to their institutions.

Programs that are central rather than marginal grow out of institutional mission and culture and develop from or are included in institutional planning. They enjoy a high level of both student and faculty interest, as well as top administrator validation. Depending on institutional strengths and structures, their organizational home may vary, but all are involved with many different campus constituencies. Strong programs receive the respect of community agencies and organizations because of the collaborative planning they are willing to do and the long-term investment in the community they are willing to make. They connect service to the curriculum and the cocurriculum in a variety of creative ways, and they define learning and developmental outcomes clearly. They have dependable core funding but are entrepreneurial in seeking additional resources. Finally, they are learning organizations, constantly assessing outcomes and evaluating program policies and practices in order to improve their effectiveness.

Fit with Institutional Mission, Culture, and Planning

One would expect service-learning to fit comfortably into colleges and universities with religious affiliation and mission, and this is the case in numerous examples. For instance, the motto of Augsburg College in Minneapolis, a Lutheran institution, is "Education for Service," so a recent institutional plan for integrating service and academic study drew on core institutional values: "Service learning reflects and gives students opportunities to practice Christian values of service to others and of stewardship. Service learning is a form of faith in practice" (*Augsburg College Plan for Integrating Service Learning and Academic Study,* 1993, p. 2). At Providence College in Rhode Island, which has a Catholic affiliation, the Feinstein Institute for Public Service has as its mission "strengthening communities by integrating public and community service into the liberal arts curriculum. Believing that service bears witness to religious and ethical values central to the college's mission . . . the institute provides an environment for research and reflection on the meaning of public and community service" (*Feinstein Institute for Public Service,* n.d.).

Public institutions and private institutions without religious affiliation also include public service in their varied missions. Spelman College in Atlanta commits itself to instilling in students "an appreciation for the multicultural communities of the world in which they live and a sense of responsibility for bringing about positive change in those communities" (Catalog, 1992, p. 12). The University of North Dakota "encourages students to . . . commit themselves to lifelong learning and the service of others, to share responsibility both for their own communities and for the world" (Catalog, 1992, p. 2). Mankato State University is even more specific: "Many of the values we have committed ourselves to demand action in the world. We will continue our commitment to service to our community through service projects; cultural, intellectual and artistic opportunities; dedication of professional expertise to regional and community development and to health care; and responsible citizenship. We will be responsible social critics and contribute to the building of a good and just society. We expect members of the Mankato State University community to serve others as one means of enlivening learning" (Catalog, 1992, p. 2).

Colleges and universities may fit readily into Carnegie classifications and have similar-sounding missions, but beneath their superficial similarities, each is unique in culture and self-concept. Their walls may be ivy-covered brick or modern glass; across the road may be a cornfield or urban sprawl. At some the students go home every night to family farms or low-income inner-city neighborhoods; at others most students live in dormitories with every amenity. The faculty may enjoy international reputations or piece together a livelihood by teaching courses at several institutions. An institution may focus on training underprepared students for entry into the labor force or educating leaders whose ideas will shape the future of the world.

Effective service-learning models must complement the particular culture and environment, as well as mission, of their institutions. Southern University and A&M College, a historically black institution in Baton Rouge, Louisiana, has had a graduation requirement of sixty hours of community service since 1991. Although a primary purpose of the requirement is to address social problems in the community through a partnership between the college and community, the Center for Service Learning also notes three advantages for students: practical experience, job opportunities and placement, and personal accomplishment (*Southern University and A&M College Center for Service Learning*, n.d.). Brevard Community College in Florida offers more than 220 academic courses with service-learning components. As a college preparing students for work as well as for transfer to four-year institutions, Brevard emphasizes the value of service-learning experiences to help students develop personally, academically, and occupationally. (*Brevard Community College Center for Service-Learning*, n.d.). On the other hand, liberal arts colleges often emphasize leadership or citizenship skill enhancement as a major service-learning goal for students. Tusculum College in Tennessee calls its service-learning program "The Civic Arts Project," and the Jepson School of Leadership at the University of Richmond requires service-learning as an important component of leadership development.

Many colleges and universities are involved in regular strategic planning processes; others have ongoing Total Quality Management or continuous improvement programs. At still others, program reviews and assessment of student outcomes undergird institutional planning efforts. Institutions with strong service-learning programs have realized that service-learning has much to offer institutional planners as a powerful means of achieving a wide range of educational outcomes and, at the same time, fulfilling institutional service missions.

Ramapo College of New Jersey is an example of a public institution whose mission, culture, and planning processes support service-learning. A twenty-six-year-old liberal arts college, Ramapo has had a strong commitment to experiential learning since its founding; its mission statement highlights experiential learning as one of four pillars of the college's mission. With strong internship, fieldwork, cooperative education, and campus employment programs already in place, service-learning was readily adopted as another effective way of linking learning and practice. The service-learning program was nurtured by Experiential Learning Programs, the umbrella unit within the Office of Student Affairs for career planning and curriculum-connected work experience. The program started modestly with grants and is now directed by a staff member funded through the institution's budget. In a campus culture where faculty were already used to sponsoring students involved in internships or cooperative education, it has not been difficult to interest faculty in service-learning. About twenty faculty each semester include service-learning in their courses, assisted by the staff member who coordinates placements. A literacy course, funded initially by the Student Literacy Corps program of the U.S. Department of Education, is now a regular part of a faculty member's teaching load.

Because experiential learning is a mission-driven priority, the needs of the service-learning program have been taken seriously in budgetary planning. When the grant for the service-learning coordinator's salary terminated, the senior administrators agreed that the position needed to be maintained, despite other compelling needs. And when the Department of Education grant program ended suddenly, the dean and vice president determined that the college would support the literacy course as part of the faculty member's course load. Each year the growth of student interest and faculty involvement leads to incremental progress, as additional courses and new community affiliations are supported by the institution's leadership.

Private institutions fulfill their commitment in other ways. For example, Stanford University's commitment to service arose from the combination of the desire of Stanford students to find meaningful ways to serve society and the vision of President Donald Kennedy, who established the public service center in 1985. Stanford, as an internationally ranked research university with ties not only to its California community but to scientific and intellectual communities worldwide, had to develop service-learning that supported its research mission and was also responsive to student and faculty interest in public service. Because of the generous endowment by the Haas family of San Francisco in 1989, the Haas Center for Public Service, under the division of Student Affairs, has become a major resource for service in the Palo Alto area and in distant sites as well. Currently "more than 3,000 students annually join staff, faculty, policy makers, and community members in local, national, and international voluntary efforts. The Center is home to varied student service organizations and university programs, among them a Public Service Opportunities Clearinghouse, the

Stanford Volunteer Network, the Community Service Writing Project, the Ravenswood Stanford Tutoring program, the East Palo Alto Stanford Summer Academy, and Upward Bound. Through the Center's 'study-service connections' initiative, staff work with faculty and students to connect service and study across the curriculum in 40 different courses" (*Haas Center for Public Service: An Introduction*, n.d., p. 1).

Any college or university can begin to develop a strong service-learning program by starting an ongoing dialogue on the potential of service-learning to support the mission of the institution and by choosing a program model that is consistent with institutional culture. Integration of service-learning into planning processes is also critical, so that its lines of responsibility, budget development, staffing, and role in the institution's vision of its future are understood and accepted by the entire campus community.

Developing and Building on Support from Varied Constituencies

Service-learning programs are housed in a variety of organizational locations and have many different reporting relationships. What successful programs have in common is that they intentionally develop strong ties with many other campus units and, in turn, receive the support of various constituencies.

In starting a service-learning program, it is important to find out where compatible efforts already exist on campus. Even at small institutions, it is not surprising to find a chaplain's office, the career center, student activities, and an academic department each working independently to develop service-learning programs. A faculty member may be trying to learn how to make community contacts, when the career center staff, the director of fieldwork for the social work program, the director of teacher education, the internship coordinator for the political science department, or the clinical director for the nursing program already have effective community outreach strategies and established community connections. The chaplain may be trying to develop curriculum when faculty in sociology, education, or philosophy already have courses that could be tied with ease to service-learning opportunities. Such duplication of effort wastes valuable resources. In addition, community organizations can become more annoyed than appreciative when contacted by the fifth program manager, and recruiting of students can become competitive rather than cooperative.

It is also worthwhile identifying and cultivating relationships with other internal constituencies. Strong service-learning programs meet the interests of many constituencies, and their goals become intertwined with the goals of those constituencies, benefiting all involved. For instance, the admissions office, seeking to attract students with community service experience, values strong service-learning programs as recruitment tools. The public relations office needs to know about student and faculty accomplishments to keep the name of the institution in the news. The student government supports programs that foster student involvement and satisfaction, the student newspaper wants interesting stories, and fraternities and sororities need meaningful service opportunities. The president and board of trustees value good community relationships.

Institutions as varied as the New Jersey Institute of Technology (NJIT), a public technical university in inner-city Newark, and Bentley College, a private business-oriented college outside Boston, have found ways to develop exemplary service-learning programs based on existing institutional structures and relationships. NJIT has always had partnerships with businesses and nonprofit organizations in the Newark area based on its technological expertise. Numerous faculty research projects and student internship and cooperative education placements have created many affiliations with the campus. Rather than starting a parallel program, NJIT's Office of Community and Public Service has built on the institution's relationships with community agencies, as well as on student and faculty technical expertise, connecting their abilities with community development. NJIT's service-learning programs enable students to develop social responsibility and leadership while strengthening their preparation for a competitive job market. In a senior architecture studio, groups of students have worked with a local nonprofit organization to design housing for mothers and children with AIDS. Computer science students helped design a computer system for the New Jersey Performing

Arts Center. Management students assisted in the creation of the first teen business camp on the campus, and premedical honors students developed databases for patient surveys for a major hospital.

Students undertake these projects through credit-bearing experiential education courses, federal work-study, housing scholarships (which enable students to work full-time during the summer on low-cost and affordable housing for community agencies), a volunteer clearinghouse, and special grant-funded programs. Numerous units work collaboratively on service-learning at NJIT, and student involvement in the community is important at all levels of the university. The service-learning program is frequently highlighted in institutional publicity and recruitment materials and is prominent in the president's speeches and annual reports.

The service-learning program at Bentley College also receives support from all parts of the institution. The program has grown from an experiment by one faculty member in 1990 to a comprehensive program encompassing twenty courses per semester, involvement of over fifty full-time faculty members, and participation by over fifteen hundred students. Edward Zlotkowski, director of the Bentley Service Learning Project, describes the internal coordination that accounts for the success of the Bentley program:

> What, then, made it possible? The answer is complex and involved individual as well as institutional considerations, fortuitous as well as planned developments. Clearly, however, one of the single most important factors was the formulation from the start of a comprehensive vision—a vision of community involvement as a distinctive feature of a Bentley education. This vision, worked out by a truly inclusive campus-wide "committee" even before the Bentley Service Learning Project (BSLP) had officially begun to exist, has helped facilitate the design and development of all aspects of the program. . . . This has meant, among other things, the collaboration of student affairs with faculty affairs whenever possible; the organization of "learning communities"—courses from different departments linked by a community focus and a shared service assignment; the creation of interdisciplinary service internships; the granting of service scholarships to better connect the college with high school service leaders; the development of residence hall–community agency partnerships; and the participation of the whole college—secretaries and maintenance staff as well as deans

and vice-presidents—in the school's annual community service
week. By casting its net so wide, the BSLP has tried to ensure that
every campus group will feel at least some connection with it.
As a result, we regularly discover collaborative possibilities not
at all anticipated [Zlotkowski, 1993, pp. 47–48].

The service-learning programs at NJIT and Bentley have developed complex and valuable relationships with many internal constituencies by building on an institutional commitment and a few
existing relationships. Similarly, other institutions with strong
service-learning programs have cultivated the support of colleagues
from all corners of the campus, so that such events as the arrival
of a new president, provost, or vice president for student affairs;
the awarding of a grant; or a curriculum review or accreditation
self-study can become opportunities to make progress toward the
development of a stronger service-learning program.

Collaborating with Community Organizations

In the early days of the service-learning movement, college and
university administrators often assumed that any student community service activity was a good thing. In addition, all too many faculty or staff sending students into the community presumed they
knew what communities needed without consultation. Community
agencies were considered laboratories for student learning; those
that used the services of such agencies were sometimes viewed as
subjects for research rather than associates in service and learning.
For their part, community organizations sometimes failed to
acknowledge the important roles they could play in educating students, instead using students to do menial or repetitive tasks.

A good deal of education by community organizations and
reflection by service-learning educators has resulted in a more
sophisticated approach by colleges and universities to the development of reciprocal relationships with communities. For example, Mary Washington College, a public liberal arts college in
Virginia, has developed an educational and service partnership
with Germanna Community College, Orange County High School,
and many community organizations. The three educational institutions have received a grant from the Virginia Campus Outreach

Opportunity League (COOL) to create a culture of service-learning in Fredricksburg and in Spotsylvania, Orange, and Culpeper counties in Virginia. In addition to two hundred students assisting nearly one thousand community members during the course of the academic year, fifty teachers will also be involved. Representatives of twenty community partners, high school teachers, and faculty from both colleges will be trained together, enabling all of them to become more informed community leaders.

Institutions seeking to build service-learning programs work to establish long-term community partnerships at a number of levels. For example, at the practical level, program staff from both campus and community plan and implement programs together. At the executive level, college and university officials and organization executive directors meet to discuss broad policy issues and to plan mutually beneficial activities such as lobbying and fundraising. Boards of trustees are often kept informed of such reciprocal activities and may be invited to attend joint receptions and meetings as appropriate. (Chapter Four elaborates on how to develop and sustain reciprocal relationships between higher education institutions and communities.)

One way colleges and universities with strong service-learning programs have found to build partnerships with community organizations is through advisory boards. These boards take a wide variety of forms, depending on the goals of the service-learning program and the particular cultures of the campus and community. At James Madison University in Virginia, an advisory board includes community agency staff, faculty members, undergraduate and graduate students, representatives of the residence life and assessment offices, and service-learning coordinators. Western Montana College has a board of community members representing educational, environmental, public safety, and human needs; faculty representing various disciplines; and students. The University of Washington has a community advisory board of higher education, government, professional, corporate, and nonprofit leaders.

Some institutions have more than one board. NJIT has two boards: one consisting of faculty and students and one consisting of community agencies. The University of Dayton has three boards, each addressing a different sphere of service. A coalition of the presidents of the twenty-eight student service organizations meets monthly to discuss projects, other opportunities for service, and leadership development. An advisory board comprising faculty and students meets twice a year to consider ways to incorporate service-learning into curricular and cocurricular programs. And the Into the Streets Coalition, which consists of faculty, students, and community representatives, explores ways to improve the one-day Into the Streets program through orientation, training, reflection, and evaluation (Cha and Rothman, 1994).

Advisory boards can be effective only if their purposes are clear. They may be passive, serving primarily as hubs for communication, or actively engaged in overseeing service-learning efforts. If board members are expected to participate in fundraising, for example, they need to know from the outset that their role is going to be an active one. Additionally staff need to remember that faculty, students, and community partners expect that their advice will be heeded and followed when appropriate. And any board, no matter how active, does not take the place of ongoing relationships at many levels.

Integrating Service-Learning into the Curriculum and the Cocurriculum

Strong service-learning programs span all aspects of an institution's offerings, enabling students to participate whether they receive academic credit or not. Service-learning is characterized by its combination of action for the common good with its commitment to critical reflection and reciprocal relationships with the community. Although it is quite possible for service and learning to be combined in the cocurriculum if student learning and development outcomes are clearly defined and if reflection is designed and implemented to achieve those outcomes, the quality and extent of learning and development generally cannot be compared with the quality and extent of learning when service and reflection are integrated into the curriculum. It is clearly easier to implement reflection within the structure of a course and with the incentive of earning credit. In addition, students and private donors alike are more likely to believe service-learning is important to an institution if it is incorporated in the curriculum.

There are many examples of colleges and universities that have successfully integrated service-learning into both their curricular and cocurricular aspects. Brevard Community College's service-learning program, which operates on its campuses in Cocoa, Titusville, Melbourne, and Palm Bay, Florida, demonstrates how students can have multiple points of access to service-learning. Brevard's Center for Service-Learning coordinates noncredit volunteer opportunities, paid community service work, over 180 courses integrating service and academic study, and four courses that directly study service. Since 1988, 8,089 students have served about 279,000 hours in over 245 organizations or projects, with 75 percent receiving academic credit (*"Headlines" 1994–1995 Report,* p. 1).

Other institutions choose to ensure a central rather than marginal position for service-learning by making it a part of the core curriculum. At Waynesburg College in Pennsylvania, every student must fulfill a general education service requirement that includes thirty hours of service, weekly journal entries, seminar discussion, and a weekly paper. Students at Franklin and Marshall College, another small, private institution in Pennsylvania, have a three-step social responsibility experiential learning requirement, in which they identify an issue of concern, commit fifteen hours to address this issue, and write a paper focusing on their learning from the service experience. Chandler-Gilbert Community College in Arizona has incorporated service-learning into a required English course. In addition, a Career and Community course places students in service experiences related to their planned careers (Cha and Rothman, 1994). Edgewood College, a small Catholic college in Madison, Wisconsin, has had a core senior-level service-learning requirement for over twenty years.

Other colleges have institutionalized service-learning as part of a specialized degree program or an honors curriculum. At the University of California–Santa Cruz, Merrill College offers a community studies major, which prepares students to study community systems and how to change them. At Vanderbilt University, the interdisciplinary major in human and organizational development requires a number of experiential learning projects, including service-learning, throughout the major. Stanford's Public Service Scholars program supports students seeking to do honors research related to their public service experience. Illinois

State University requires service-learning as a component of the honors program.

While some institutions, like Chandler-Gilbert, have "jumped into the field of service-learning with both feet" (Cha and Rothman, 1994, p. 43), most choose the route of accumulating solid programmatic pieces, curricular and cocurricular, as means of institutionalizing service-learning. Both approaches can work, as long as a secure source of funding exists.

Core Funding and Entrepreneurship

Even administrators enthusiastic about the benefits of service-learning wonder how to build programs without additional resources. Federal funding cannot be relied on, and many institutions are heavily committed to cost containment and other budget reductions.

Funding for service-learning is necessary for faculty development and support, student financial assistance, and program staff and implementation. Although some individual faculty members design and teach service-learning courses as part of their regular course load or through supervising independent study, colleges and universities seeking to strengthen and increase service-learning find ways to provide faculty release time or additional pay. Faculty support in terms of professional development, recognition of service-learning in promotion and tenure policies, and technical assistance is also important.

Students of all socioeconomic classes deserve the opportunity to participate in service-learning. Although federal work-study funds can now be used for financial support of students working off campus in community service jobs, many middle-class students are not eligible for work-study and need to work to pay for college expenses. More and more institutions are seeking creative mechanisms to make it financially possible for students to become involved in service.

It is not unusual for admissions offices to work with service-learning centers to recruit and support students who have shown commitment to service and who will be expected to continue to do so in college. Bentley College offers six renewable scholarships of $5,000 each to students who have been involved in community service in high school. Youngstown State University in Ohio, Washington State University, and John Carroll University in Cleveland offer similar scholarships. Barry University in Miami allows students to turn loans into grants through community service; students can sign up for loans of $200 to $700 and then earn loan forgiveness through participation in service. The Feinstein Institute at Providence College is matching a number of AmeriCorps grants with scholarship aid. One of the oldest community service scholarship programs is the Cornell Tradition, funded by an anonymous gift of over $7 million in 1982. The program provides fellowships of up to $2,500 a year, as well as public service internships during the academic year and in the summer (Murphy and Mulugetta, 1994).

Funding of program staff and implementation expenses is another crucial element of strong service-learning efforts. Often service-learning programs that started out with grant-funded staff must turn to the administration to provide institutional funds for staff once the grant expires. Many service-learning programs bring faculty into temporary staff positions to evaluate programs and assess student outcomes, support student-initiated community partnerships, and work with other faculty in designing service-learning courses.

Bentley makes use of its scholarship students to staff service-learning projects. First-year students in the program work approximately ten hours a week at a community agency and participate in the Organizational and Interpersonal Skills Workshop Series, through which they learn time management, communication, and reflection facilitation skills. As students move through the program, they take on greater leadership roles on campus and in the community, working closely with faculty, serving as project managers and course coordinators, and facilitating the progress of specific service-learning projects. They also represent the BSLP at national and international conferences, make presentations, and facilitate reflection sessions. Students are strongly encouraged to develop their own service-learning initiatives, and during their third or fourth year in the program, they participate in internships (*Bentley College Service Learning Project Scholarship and Grant Opportunities,* n.d.). The development of student leadership through work for the service-learning program ensures continuity, dedication, and adequate staffing.

Program implementation requirements such as publicity, training materials, and transportation to service sites also cannot be overlooked. Chapters Ten and Eleven offer suggestions for obtaining funding for or covering these costs through in-kind contributions.

It is an unusual institutionalized service-learning program that receives funds from only one source. Sustainable programs, however, do require a stable institutional funding source. Campus Compact's 1993 survey of its members reveals that the number of service-learning programs receiving institutional funding jumped from less than 50 percent four years prior to the research to over 80 percent in 1993 (Cha and Rothman, 1994).

In addition to a stable funding base, strong programs find that they must be entrepreneurial in seeking funding from a variety of sources. At Tougaloo College in Mississippi, the president's office both directs college fundraising efforts toward the service-learning program and assists the program's own efforts to seek funds. The service-learning program at Frostburg State University in rural Maryland emphasizes collaboration with the office of contracts and grants in its mission statement. Loyola College in Maryland receives support from its development office, which has set a goal of a $1 million endowment for the Center for Values and Service, and from the students in its graduating class, whose class gift was a scholarship for students involved in service. And Albion College in Michigan turned to its student senate for funding (Cha and Rothman, 1994). Large private gifts created the basis for the service-learning centers at Stanford, the University of Utah, Providence College, and the University of Washington, which are financed through combinations of endowed and university funds, foundation support, and corporate and individual gifts.

Service-learning programs that enjoy both institutional support and strong relationships with community organizations are most effective in leveraging funds and applying for grants. For instance, Clark Atlanta University joined forces with Hands on Atlanta, the local chapter of City Cares of America, which provides training and placement of volunteer youth; the Atlanta Project, which provides networking with five community education sites; and the Greater Atlanta Conservation Corps. Through this collaboration, grant funding was obtained to create a fifty-member corps and ten fifteen-member education crews to work with at-risk youth in an inner-city elementary school. The education crews—each comprising college, high school, and middle-school students—receive substantial training before engaging in conflict resolution, educational enrichment, and programs for parents (Cha and Rothman, 1994).

In summary, strong service-learning programs coordinate their fundraising efforts with other priorities of their institutions rather than placing themselves in competition with them. Packaging funding from a variety of sources allows program flexibility and is vital for institutionalization to occur.

Service-Learning Programs as Learning Organizations

One of the major problems of grant-funded programs is that they have such short time lines for establishing operational programs that the grant often runs out before anyone has had time to do much thinking. Many Student Literacy Corps grantees, for example, spent their time placing students, doing paperwork, and writing proposals for renewal funding to such an extent that they could not answer the basic questions, "What are we doing, why are we doing it, and how well are we doing it?" Certainly service-learning programs are understaffed and underfunded, as are many other programs in higher education. Strong programs are distinguished by their continual quest for self-assessment and excellence. In a significant way, they go through the same reflective processes they urge on students to help them learn from their service experiences.

One of the most basic aspects of reflection is evaluation of program impacts on students and communities. Although almost every program occasionally highlights a student or a faculty member who is exceptional, consistent recognition and analysis of quality are crucial. For instance, faculty at Vanderbilt University continually evaluate course quality and effects on students. Internal studies such as "Evaluating the Freshman Community Service Laboratory" (Eyler, Giles, Schmiede, and Martin, 1995) and publications such as "The Impact of a College Community Service Laboratory on Students' Personal, Social, and Cognitive Outcomes" (Giles and Eyler, 1994) result. Stanford's Haas Center includes in its annual report a section entitled, "Evaluation and Reflection." As the report notes, "Haas Center program evaluation is designed to support and structure student and staff reflection on service activities. . . . In addition to informal, ongoing consultation with staff and students, the evaluation specialist is responsible for conducting more formal evaluations and data collection efforts as needs arise and resources permit" (*Haas Center for Public Service Annual Report,* 1994, p. 63).

Stanford and Vanderbilt are also participants in the first national, longitudinal study designed to investigate the impacts of different models of service-learning on postsecondary education, through a three-year research project funded by the Fund for the Improvement of Postsecondary Education. The University Internship Program and Madison House of the University of Virginia have recently undertaken a major study of the long-term effects of service-learning on college alumni. The Bentley Service Learning Project includes a faculty member who is principal researcher, responsible for conducting program assessment and experiential research in order to make recommendations concerning the quality of various initiatives and strategies for change.

Although it may seem difficult for a service-learning program to incorporate the kind of sophisticated research undertaken at Vanderbilt, Bentley, and Stanford, faculty and graduate students, and even undergraduates, can become active participants in critical reflection on program practices and outcomes. The *Research Agenda for Combining Service and Learning in the 1990s* offers thoughtful formulations of research questions that can be used as the beginning of local conversations (Giles, Porter Honnet, and Migliore, 1991). The principles discussed in Chapter Two are useful for benchmarking. Even the newest and smallest programs can begin to become learning organizations by keeping data and recording their own history. All programs can develop opportunities for students, faculty, and staff involved in service-learning to step back from their daily work to discuss larger issues and future directions.

Another characteristic of effective learning organizations is recognition and celebration of excellence in student, faculty, and community achievement. Individual awards to students who have distinguished themselves are the most common type of recognition in service-learning programs (Cha and Rothman, 1994). Some of these carry monetary awards. At the University of Maryland at College Park, the president sends personal letters of appreciation to participants in the You Can Make a Difference program, and the Community Service Programs office runs a series of advertisements in the student newspaper that picture and highlight the achievements of students involved in service. Faculty and staff, while equally deserving of recognition for the service they perform, receive it less often. At Spelman College, however, President Johnetta Cole created presidential awards for faculty and staff who perform outstanding service. The awards are presented at the college's annual convocation (Cha and Rothman, 1994).

Conclusion

The institutionalization of service-learning in American higher education is more likely now than in the 1960s and 1970s because many colleges and universities have learned from the past and have become more collaborative and creative in developing programs that are directly tied to the mission and the culture of their institutions. Colleges and universities are also developing service-learning in collaboration with communities and based on principles of good practice. They are integrating service-learning into all institutional offerings through the curriculum and the cocurriculum. Service-learning programs are gaining increasingly stable funding and engaging in reflective self-assessment and evaluation.

What makes the institutionalization of service-learning so crucial as the twenty-first century approaches is the part it plays in fostering student commitment to active participation in public life and civic processes. As citizens' cynicism about the possibility of achieving a just society grows, higher education must find ways to help students overcome their feelings of helplessness about making a difference and their withdrawal into private interests. In his essay "Reflective Citizen Participation," Fred M. Newmann describes five dimensions of reflective citizenship. He believes that educators must help students see the necessity to make decisions and take action in the face of pervasive uncertainty and ambiguity; gain the capacity to make moral choices about public policies and personal actions; define strategies in setting policy and action goals; clarify their personal commitments to increased effectiveness, integrity, and responsibility; and engage in honest and serious conversation about their role in the greater society (1990, p. 79).

It is difficult to imagine an institution of higher education that does not have as a goal to graduate citizens who will participate in public life with wisdom and dedication to democratic values. There is no more effective way for colleges and universities to demonstrate their commitment to these and other core values than through a strong, institutionalized service-learning program.

References

Augsburg College Plan for Integrating Service Learning and Academic Study. Minneapolis: Augsburg College, 1993.

Bentley College Service Learning Project Scholarship and Grant Opportunities. Waltham, Mass.: Bentley College, n.d.

Brevard Community College Center for Service-Learning. Cocoa, Fla.: Brevard Community College, n.d.

Cha, S., and Rothman, M. *Service Matters: A Sourcebook for Community Service in Higher Education.* Providence, R.I.: Campus Compact, 1994.

Eyler, J., Giles, D. E., Schmiede, A., and Martin, E. "Evaluating a Community Service Laboratory." In M. Smith (ed.), *Service Counts: Lessons from the Field of Service and Higher Education.* Providence, R.I.: Campus Compact, 1995.

Feinstein Institute for Public Service. Providence, R.I.: Providence College, n.d.

Giles, D. E., and Eyler, J. "The Impact of a College Community Service Laboratory on Students' Personal, Social, and Cognitive Outcomes." *Journal of Adolescence,* 1994, *17,* 327–339.

Giles, D., Porter Honnet, E., and Migliore, S. (eds.). *A Research Agenda for Combining Service and Learning in the 1990s.* Raleigh, N.C.: National Society for Experiential Education, 1991.

Haas Center for Public Service Annual Report. Stanford, Calif.: Stanford University, 1994.

Haas Center for Public Service: An Introduction. Stanford, Calif.: Stanford University, n.d

"Headlines" 1994–1995 Report. Cocoa, Fla: Brevard Community College Center for Service-Learning, 1995.

Mankato State University Catalog 1992–94. Mankato, Minn.: Mankato State University, 1992.

Murphy, S., and Mulugetta, Y. "Making a Difference: The Cornell Tradition." *College Board Review,* no. 173, Fall 1994.

Newmann, F. M. "Reflective Civic Participation." In J. C. Kendall (ed.), *Combining Service and Learning: A Resource Book for Community and Public Service,* Vol. 1. Raleigh, N.C.: National Society for Experiential Education, 1990.

Southern University and A&M College Center for Service Learning. Baton Rouge, La.: Southern University and A&M College, n.d.

Spelman College Catalog, 1992–93. Atlanta, Ga.: Spelman College, 1992.

University of North Dakota Catalog, 1992–94. Grand Forks: University of North Dakota, 1992.

Zlotkowksi, E. "Service Learning as Campus Culture." In T. Y. Kupiec (ed.), *Rethinking Tradition: Integrating Service with Academic Study on College Campuses.* Providence, R.I.: Campus Compact, 1993.

Chapter Fourteen

Securing the Future of Service-Learning in Higher Education

A Mandate for Action

Barbara Jacoby

The principal aim of this book is to provide a greater understanding of service-learning in higher education and how it can achieve significant outcomes in terms of both learning and development for students and enhancement and empowerment for communities. Previous chapters have discussed the foundations and principles on which high-quality service-learning courses and programs are built, examples of service-learning successes in a wide range of institutional and community settings, and administrative issues relevant to program development and sustainability. Service-learning is still a relatively new and evolving practice, however, so large issues remain that will determine its future. To survive and thrive in the long run, service-learning must be central rather than marginal, institutionalized rather than fragmented, and strong rather than weak. This chapter examines five major issues, or themes, that are germane to the future of service-learning in higher education. As advocates of service-learning, we must work to renew higher education's commitment to service, support changes in higher education, demonstrate service-learning's effectiveness, strengthen the relationship of elementary and secondary education with higher education, and institutionalize service-learning.

Taken together, these themes serve as a mandate for action to ensure that service-learning will continue to yield its substantial benefits for students, communities, and institutions.

Renew Higher Education's Commitment to Service

As social problems become more complex and more wrenching, higher education must renew its historic commitment to service and exercise its social responsibility vigorously. The need for new knowledge and its rapid and effective application is growing and intensifying. Greiner (1994) describes this phenomenon as a need to respond to "a chaos of cries for help, understanding, new frameworks and ideas and solutions" (p. 12). Higher education is logically in a position to respond to social needs because one of its key functions is the development and application of new knowledge. Further, as Plater (1995) asserts, "Communities now believe that universities and colleges not only have an obligation to apply their knowledge and expertise to the solution of problems, but they have to do so in a timely fashion with immediate and demonstrable results" (p. 32).

Chapter One indicates that higher education experts are calling for an expansion of the role of colleges and universities in addressing social problems (Bok, 1982, 1986; Ehrlich, 1995; Hackney, 1994; Newman, 1985; Wingspread Group on Higher Education, 1993). As president of the American Association for Higher Education (AAHE), Russell Edgerton (1994) announced that AAHE will pursue the theme of "The Engaged Campus": "By setting that course, we hope to signal a more vigorous interest in, and commitment to, this task of reconnecting higher education to the needs of the larger society" (p. 4). Edgerton realizes that pursuing this theme will "take AAHE into uncharted waters" because "The Engaged Campus is *not* a problem that is simply about outreach efforts and add-ons and the things faculty do 'other' than teaching and research" (p. 4). The traditional focus of faculty research has not been on society's needs. Similarly, the definition of faculty service has traditionally included service to the college or university, such as serving on a curriculum or planning committee, or to one's discipline through leadership roles in disciplinary associations, for example. Edgerton suggests that a starting point for thinking about "The Engaged Campus" is "to realize that *all* of the critical tasks we do—teaching, research, and professional outreach—need to change if we are truly to connect with the needs of the larger community. The challenge is not simply to do—at a higher level of quality, with more productivity and with more accountability—the tasks we have always done. We also need to rethink which tasks are most *essential* for us to perform" (p. 4).

In this vein, Boyer (1990) believes that higher education must redefine faculty scholarship: "What we urgently need today is a more inclusive view of what it means to be a scholar—a recognition that knowledge is acquired through research, through synthesis, through practice, and through teaching" (p. 24). He advocates a scholarship of application, a dynamic process that denies that "knowledge is first 'discovered' and then 'applied'": "The process we have in mind is far more dynamic. New intellectual understandings can arise out of the very act of application—whether in medical diagnosis, serving clients in psychotherapy, shaping public policy, creating an architectural design, or working with the public schools. In activities such as these, theory and practice vitally interact, and one renews the other" (p. 23). Boyer's definition of scholarship asks how knowledge can be applied to help individuals and institutions and, further, "Can social problems *themselves* define an agenda for scholarly investigation?" (p. 21).

Deborah Hirsch and Ernest Lynton (1995) call for a similar redefinition of faculty professional service to mean "work based on the faculty member's professional expertise which contributes to the outreach mission" of the institution (p. 10). They then take a major further step to conceptualize faculty professional service and outreach as a bridge between the worlds of service-learning and faculty scholarship. If faculty engagement in the scholarship of application described by Boyer creates opportunities to involve students in service-learning, then research, teaching, and service can become interconnected in ways that make each more vital and effective.

Such new definitions of faculty teaching, research, and service are necessary to provide fertile ground for the development and sustenance of service-learning. However, substantial revision of faculty roles, promotion and tenure policies, and other reward structures is also required. Institutions of higher education throughout the United States are involved in strategic planning, Total Quality Management, process redesign, and other restructuring efforts that may or may not fundamentally alter the way they do business. As proponents of service-learning, we would do well to use these opportunities to advocate for changes in faculty roles and rewards that favor service-learning. In addition, we should support the efforts of the national professional organizations such as AAHE that are invested in bringing about these changes. The future of service-learning depends in large part on whether the changes these efforts bring about support higher education's role in addressing societal problems and meeting community needs.

Support Changes in Higher Education

Both college students and institutions of higher education are changing dramatically and at a rapid pace. Traditional college students—those who are eighteen to twenty-two years old, attend full-time, and live in residence halls—constitute only 15 percent of all college students in the United States today. Adult students now make up higher education's new majority. Nearly one-half of all undergraduates attend part-time, and over 40 percent of bachelor's degrees are awarded each year to part-time students (Jacoby, 1996). Students are becoming more diverse in many ways, including race, ethnicity, and socioeconomic status. More and more students are subject to financial pressures while attending college as a result of rising college costs and declining federal student financial aid. Over two-thirds of college students work, many more than twenty hours per week and/or at more than one job. Changes in how students learn, in their preferred learning styles, have also been documented. Recent studies show that the largest group of college students consists of hands-on, active learners who learn best through concrete experiences that engage their senses, beginning with practice and ending with theory (Schroeder, 1993). Charles Schroeder (1993) points out that this preferred learning style is the opposite of the abstract, reflective style preferred by the vast majority of faculty, creating a growing disparity between teacher and learner.

Simultaneous with these changes in students are profound changes in the learning environment: "We are witnessing changes in *where* students learn. No longer confined exclusively to the classroom, credit-bearing learning now occurs in workplaces, from the office to the factory floor to submarines under the sea; in malls; in hotel rooms; and in the home. Enabled by the power of information technology, classroom learning now extends beyond a single campus to distant sites across the town, across the state, and across the country. How many of our institutions understand this profound shift away from the concept of the university as a place? How many of our faculty are thinking about new pedagogies that reach out to students, wherever they are?" (Twigg, 1995, pp. 4–5) In addition, existing and emerging technologies are powerful tools that provide ever-increasing access to and uses for information. Personal computers and computer networks are providing new capabilities for imagining, creating, analyzing, and communicating (Wilson, 1994).

Since students will have less need to travel to a campus to learn in the future, the role of faculty and of colleges and universities will change (Twigg, 1995; Wilson, 1994). Twigg (1995) posits: "Institutions of higher education will continue to assist students in organizing their learning experiences and linking them to appropriate instructional resources. . . . Faculties will continue to be important, but not as teachers: rather, as mentors, group project leaders, and designers of instructional experiences" (p. 10). Technology will become more and more of a teaching and learning tool; "electronic collaboration" will grow (p. 11).

The extent to which service-learning can enable higher education to cope with these challenges is a factor that will determine whether it will thrive in the future. Advocates should advance service-learning as a practical and effective means of addressing the changes in students and learning environments. For example, service-learning can be designed to take place in community and work settings where students are already engaged. Options for involvement in service-learning can be created to accommodate a variety of student lifestyles and schedules. It is a form of active learning that responds to the preferred learning style of increasing numbers of students, and it is compatible with the evolving role of faculty as group project leaders and designers of educational experiences. Electronic communication can be developed as a way to facilitate individual and group reflection.

Demonstrate Service-Learning's Effectiveness

When a group of educators, researchers, service-learning practitioners, foundation representatives, government officials, students, and staff members from national organizations gathered at the Johnson Foundation's Wingspread Conference Center in March 1991 to set a research agenda for service-learning for the 1990s, they found a "scarcity of replicable qualitative and quantitative research on the effects of service-learning on student learning and development, the communities in which students serve, on educational institutions and on society" (Giles, Porter Honnet, and Migliore, 1991, p. 5). Research on the effects of service-learning is challenging because few standardized instruments exist, variables are difficult to identify and define, service takes place in many different settings and involves many kinds of tasks, causality is difficult to determine, control or comparison groups are not readily available, and extensive longitudinal studies are necessary to measure effects over time. And, often feeling pressure to get programmatic efforts going, many practitioners simply do not take the time to establish measurable goals and objectives for either student or community outcomes.

It is generally agreed that the reported studies are of small scope and have limited potential for generalization; most of the research has focused on the personal, career, and social outcomes of service for the students involved; many of the data collected have been anecdotal and self-reported; the bulk of the research has emphasized out-of-class learning, with little attempt to measure academic and cognitive goals related to classroom learning; little attention has been focused on the effects of service-learning on the community providers or on development in the community itself; and the research tends to measure short-term effects or to use short-term, proximate predictors of long-term behavior (Boss, 1994; Giles and Eyler, 1994). The research results have also been hard to access because most have been available until recently only through conference presentations or unpublished reports.

Despite these problems, the existing research on service-learning, although much of it focuses on students at the elementary and secondary school levels, has been encouraging. Service-learning has been correlated with a higher grade-point average and improved academic performance (Greco, 1992; Hannah and Dworkowitz, 1992; Levinson and Felberbaum, 1993; Nelms, 1991). One study found that 90 percent of student volunteers reported that their service-learning was as valuable as or more valuable to them than classroom work (Krehbiel and MacKay, 1988). These results are supported by the research of Crowner (1992) and Miller (1994). Others indicate that community service enhances students' moral development (Boss, 1994; Boyd, 1980) and that it is effective in building students' self-esteem (Adams, 1993). And recent studies are beginning to suggest that service-learning that is connected to a specific course can increase students' learning of course content (Boss, 1994; Cohen and Kinsey, 1994; Markus, Howard, and King, 1993; Miller, 1994).

Other encouraging developments include a three-year national study of the impact of service-learning on college students' citizenship values, skills, attitudes, and understanding that is currently under way. Janet Eyler and Dwight E. Giles of Vanderbilt University are in the process of gathering and analyzing data from over fifteen hundred students at twenty colleges and universities. The study will examine not only whether students' participation in service-learning makes a difference but how differences among service-learning programs affect student outcomes (Eyler and Giles, 1995). It is also noteworthy that this comprehensive study is federally supported by the Fund for the Improvement of Post-secondary Education. Other public and private funding sources for service-learning programs, including the Corporation for National Service and the Lilly, Ford, and Kellogg foundations, are supporting research and requiring research and evaluation by grantees. In addition, more and more academic journals are publishing research on service-learning, including the *Journal of Moral Education, Liberal Education, English Journal, College Composition and Communication, Teaching Sociology, Journal of Research in Higher Education, American Educational Research Journal, Journal of Business Ethics,* and *Hispania.*

Much more research, however, is needed to enable service-learning proponents to justify its costs in terms of dollars, time, and effort. By its very nature, service-learning "combines a strong social purpose with acknowledgment of the significance of personal and intellectual growth in participants" (Giles, Porter Honnet, and

Migliore, 1991, p. 7). Service-learning's dual emphasis requires two broad areas of research, since, unlike some other forms of education, it necessarily takes place in a social context. Research addressing the effects of service-learning on individual learners is necessary but not sufficient. Because its outcomes have the potential to affect communities and individual community members profoundly in both positive and negative ways, it is essential to evaluate the quality and effectiveness of students' engagement with the community *from the perspective of the community*. Such evaluation must be carried out in true collaboration with the community so that the information gathered answers questions and addresses issues that will enable the community to move forward with its agendas.

The *Research Agenda for Combining Service and Learning in the 1990s* (Giles, Porter Honnet, and Migliore, 1991, pp. 9–11) proposes five categories of research questions about service-learning and its effects:

The Participant

What are the general effects of the service-learning experience on the individual student?

- What is the effect of service-learning on students as learners?

- What knowledge do students gain as a result of service-learning?

- Does participation in service-learning affect the participant's perception of self and others, prosocial attitudes and behaviors, and view of the world?

- What is the effect of service-learning on participants as citizens?

- Do learner characteristics, such as age, socio-economic status, developmental stage, and family background and support lead to different social developmental outcomes?

- Do different models of service-learning lead to different types of world views, value constructions, or skill development in participants?

The Educational Institution

What is the effect of service-learning on the improvement of the educational system and on specific types of educational institutions?

- What are the outcomes of service-learning which contribute to institutional missions?

- How can service-learning lead to the effective integration of teaching, research, and service?
- How can service-learning be used as a vehicle for reform in areas of teaching effectiveness, curriculum design, teacher training, school mission and structure, and practical use of theories of learning and development?
- How can traditional subjects be taught effectively by incorporating a service-learning component?

The Community

What is the effect of service-learning on community improvement?

- To what extent does service-learning promote multicultural understanding within institutions, communities, and society?
- Does service-learning result in the development of long-term habits of participation in the community?
- What are the benefits and costs for communities as a result of service-learning?
- How does service-learning contribute to the collaborative development of democratic community?

Theoretical Bases

How can service-learning research contribute to the development of theories that can further undergird and illuminate service-learning?

- How can service-learning research contribute to the development of more comprehensive theories of human development?
- How can service-learning research contribute to the development of more comprehensive theories of community development?
- How can service-learning research contribute to the development of more comprehensive theories of epistemology and learning?
- How can human development, community development, and learning theories be used to increase our understanding of effective service-learning?

Program Models

What are the components and outcomes of various models of service-learning?

- Is there a difference in impact on students between programs which use systematic reflection and those that don't?

- What program characteristics have enhanced or deterred the institutionalization of service-learning?

- What program characteristics, such as duration, intensity, content, and mandatory or voluntary participation, promote various outcomes?

- How can service-learning be incorporated effectively into the curriculum at a variety of grade levels and throughout the disciplines?

Service-learning educators must not only build research and evaluation into their programs from the outset but must also expand the pool of potential researchers to include faculty not necessarily directly engaged in service-learning, graduate and undergraduate students, teachers and students in elementary and secondary schools, community-based service providers and other civic and community organizations, national and international youth service organizations, and national educational associations. The questions generated in the research agenda provide a rich source of research topics that will do more than promote and justify the existence of service-learning. Answers to these questions will also contribute to our knowledge of how experiential education fosters individual learning and development and how higher education and communities can best collaborate to reach mutual goals.

Strengthen the Relationship of Elementary and Secondary Education with Higher Education

The future of service-learning in colleges and universities is closely tied to elementary and secondary education. Given the nationwide concern for the growing numbers of at-risk children and youth, the desire of many college students to work with this population, and higher education's natural interest in its potential future students, K–12 schools are perhaps the most logical settings for community service by college students. In addition, as service-learning is introduced in more and more elementary and secondary schools throughout the United States, it has become clear that the quality of students' experiences in their precollege years will, to a large extent, determine their attitudes toward collegiate service-learning. Thus it is critical that teacher preparation and in-service training include service-learning.

The statistics on at-risk children and youth in the United States are overwhelming: one in five children lives in poverty, seven in ten drop out of school in some cities, one in ten teenage girls becomes pregnant, and U.S. teens rank number one in the world for drug abuse (Kniseley and Beaird, 1993). Since 1985, the Education Commission of the States (ECS) has taken a leadership role in promoting greater understanding of the issues related to at-risk youth and in mobilizing political support for action in this area: "These statistics paint an alarming picture of America's youth and call educators, policy makers and national organizations to take immediate action to improve the prospects of youth in need of support and caring" (Kniseley and Beaird, 1993, p. 2). Campus Compact, a project of ECS, has funded and provided technical assistance to campus-based mentoring programs for at-risk youth and encouraged the collaboration of higher education institutions with local school systems, community organizations, and state policymakers to address their needs. Many other such programs and collaborations exist, and many more are needed.

Institutions of higher education have numerous compelling reasons for involvement in elementary and secondary education. In addition to benefits for at-risk children and youth, developing service-learning programs in partnership with local schools yields opportunities for increased public support, grants and contracts, recruitment of historically underrepresented students, and heightened college student learning through teaching. Thus advocates of service-learning would do well to encourage institutions to focus both curricular and cocurricular service-learning on at-risk youth in K–12 settings.

Every year more schools, school systems, and states are making service-learning part of the elementary curriculum and requiring it for high school graduation. As a result increasing numbers of students are coming to college with impressions of service-learning, either positive or negative: "To the extent that they perceive their service and reflection activities attractive and valuable, students will seek opportunities to continue service when they enter higher education. Hence, students may 'vote with their feet' in favor of institutions with well-developed service-learning programs. . . . To the extent that service-learning becomes institutionalized in K–12 education, then, colleges and universities will encounter a steady stream of students seeking service-learning as part of their postsecondary educational experience" (Droge, 1995, p. 2).

If colleges and universities are to be successful in developing citizenship and social responsibility, it is important that students begin to develop an understanding of participatory democracy and of social issues in the K–12 years. Advocates of service-learning should encourage higher education institutions to support elementary and secondary schools' efforts in this area. Institutions that have teacher preparation programs should train both prospective and current K–12 teachers in the principles and practice of service-learning. They should follow the example of South Carolina, where all major colleges of education offer a service-learning education program (O'Neill, 1995). In addition, service-learning supporters should encourage faculty and students to conduct research to assess the outcomes of elementary and secondary service-learning on students, communities, and schools.

Institutionalize Service-Learning

Service-learning must be fully integrated into the mission, policies, and practices of individual institutions of higher education if it is to remain viable. A fundamental element of an institutionalized service-learning program is a secure funding base. Stable funding derives from a variety of sources rather than a single source. While federal funding, either direct or through support of students through federal work-study or programs such as AmeriCorps, should certainly be sought, it is politically volatile. As this book goes to press, the viability of the Corporation for National Service and its programs is the subject of much debate, and the Fund for Improvement of Postsecondary Education has discontinued its grants for community service in higher education, at least for the present.

The support of the nonprofit sector is important in several ways. Although the ability of community-based organizations to provide direct financial support is limited, they can offer valuable in-kind contributions, including training and supervision of student volunteers, information about issues, data about populations, and physical facilities. Community organizations can also be effective in working with colleges and universities to raise money for joint projects and scholarships for students involved in service-learning. Developing partnerships between institutions and community agencies enables access to funding opportunities that are not available to higher education institutions alone. Partnerships between institutions of higher education and community organizations are currently eligible for funding through the federal Departments of Housing and Urban Development, Education, and Labor, among others.

Because of the limitations on federal and nonprofit sector support, private sector support of service-learning is important. It can take many forms, including direct support of students through service-learning scholarships and awards, support of institutional service-learning programs, and support of collaborative ventures with communities. Service-learning advocates should work to make private individual and corporate funding of service-learning initiatives a focus of the development office agenda.

Faculty involvement in and leadership of service-learning is also essential to sustain service-learning on an institutional level. Service-learning will become central only if it is embedded in the curriculum across disciplines. As a student in Levine's (1994) study of undergraduate student community service said about a particular institution: "'Service isn't important. If it were, it would be part of the curriculum'" (p. 5). Service-learning must therefore be supported by changes in the tenure, review, and promotion process that validate faculty involvement in service-learning.

Such changes will be hard-fought but are already under way. In a 1995 test case at Florida Atlantic University, a faculty member won tenure solely on the strength of her community service and teaching. At the time of her tenure review, she had helped start three service organizations for migrant farmworkers, worked with autistic children and their parents, and conducted action research in the community but had produced no publications (Cage, 1995). According to the *Chronicle of Higher Education,* some observers predict that Florida's public institutions will soon offer a two-track path to tenure: one track would continue to require a balance of research, teaching, and service, and the other would be a less-traditional track for those who would be promoted on the basis of their teaching and service (Cage, 1995). As supporters of service-learning, we should follow such developments and promote those that are appropriate for our institutions.

In addition, faculty engagement in service-learning depends on a variety of supports, both institutional and disciplinary. Key institutional resources are course development funds or released time to design or redesign courses, assistance with site development and student placement, and opportunities to develop expertise in service-learning pedagogy. Discipline-based resources, also critical, include sample syllabi and other course materials, successful teaching and student evaluation strategies, and published research on student and community outcomes. It is extremely encouraging that in addition to increased attention in disciplinary associations and journals, AAHE and the Invisible College of Campus Compact have begun a major project to produce a series of monographs on service-learning in individual disciplines. Under the leadership of Edward Zlotkowski of Bentley College, the first volumes are scheduled for publication in 1996 and 1997. Each volume is being written by faculty in a particular discipline and will cover the history and theoretical perspectives of the discipline's relationship with the community; pedagogical essays, including samples of course material and student work; an annotated bibliography of readings; and a resource listing of national and regional organizations, opportunities for presenting strategies and findings, and individuals working in service-learning in the discipline (Zlotkowski, 1995).

Advocates of service-learning in the curriculum should strive to create institutional resources for faculty by working with centers for teaching and learning, curriculum transformation projects, academic administrators, and student affairs professionals on our campuses. In addition, we should support the development of national resources by AAHE, Campus Compact, and the National Society for Experiential Education, as well as those of disciplinary associations.

Besides strengthening its role within the traditional academic disciplines, efforts to institutionalize service-learning will be bolstered by the development of interdisciplinary connections. Community issues and social problems rarely fit neatly into any one discipline. In fact, most are complex and multifaceted, requiring perspectives, knowledge, and approaches from a wide range of disciplines to unravel their causes and consider solutions. The practice of service-learning can lead to the creation and sustenance of interdisciplinary connections through collaborative research, team teaching of courses and seminars, and projects that involve faculty and students across departments in working with communities to enhance services or address needs. Service-learning advocates can and should encourage interdisciplinary outreach and engage in interdisciplinary work ourselves.

Another level of collaboration within institutions that can be both a result of and a contribution to service-learning is the collaboration between academic affairs and student affairs. Traditionally working in functional silos as isolated from each other as faculty in different disciplines, academic and student affairs personnel on more and more campuses are finding that working together helps to institutionalize service-learning and that we have much to learn from one another. Faculty can benefit from student affairs professionals' knowledge of theories and models of college student learning and development, expertise in program planning and implementation, and administrative experience and acumen. Student affairs professionals can learn from faculty colleagues about curriculum development, research and teaching strategies, and student performance in the classroom.

If service-learning is to be truly institutionalized, it must become integral to all aspects of a college's or university's programs, practices, and policies—in both the curricular *and* cocurricular realms. Student affairs and academic affairs personnel must work together to make this happen. Those of us who seek to establish the permanent presence of service-learning at our institutions, no matter whether our reporting line is to academic or student affairs, must reach out to colleagues throughout the institution to share information and resources and to work in a concerted fashion to develop mutually beneficial relationships with communities.

As several chapters in this book have emphasized, colleges and universities that enter into service-learning relationships with communities must do so in a responsible, reciprocal, and sustainable manner. In order to enable the kind of commitment that brings human and other resources from throughout the institution to a community partnership, service-learning must be institutionalized. When an institution attempts to enter into a relationship with a community in a piecemeal, half-hearted way, negative outcomes for individuals and communities are likely to result, and communities will learn to fear and resist subsequent institutional outreach, even if unrelated to past failures. Unfortunate service-learning endeavors can have the effect of hindering community relationships for a long time to come, even if changes in institutional leadership or commitment favor the development of high-quality service-learning partnerships. Thus the future of efforts to institutionalize service-learning can be seriously jeopardized by weak and ill-supported earlier attempts at community involvement. It is essential that we who believe in service-learning do all we can to prevent this situation from arising by strongly discouraging premature, irresponsible, or nonsustainable service-learning initiatives.

In effect, service-learning will become central to and sustained by institutions to the extent that it benefits the institutions that support it: "I think we [service-learning educators] may be seeing the end of our support as a creative way of supplying community services and may be entering a phase where we are sustained for what we bring to our institutions" (Richard E. Cone, personal communication, 1995). These benefits include student learning and development outcomes, opportunities for faculty to revitalize teaching and research, and more favorable public opinion and stronger support. As a result, in addition to working to develop a secure financial base and faculty ownership and involvement, advocates of service-learning should identify, document, and promote its benefits within our institutions.

Conclusion

Will service-learning continue to grow in breadth and depth into the twenty-first century? Optimism is justified by the number of both recently developed and classic resources to support it and the many examples of outstanding service-learning programs, some of them described in this book. Many of the building blocks necessary to construct a firm foundation for the continuing development of service-learning are in place.

Higher education is taking major steps toward reaffirming its key role in responding to growing social needs. Service-learning educators recognize and have begun to address how service-learning will anticipate and respond to current and future changes in students and educational environments. Both researchers and practitioners are involved in studying the effects of service-learning on students, communities, and institutions. More and stronger connections are developing between K–12 and higher education. And service-learning is in the process of becoming institutionalized at colleges and universities throughout the country. Indeed, models of successful institutionalization exist to encourage those of us who are working to reach this goal.

Service-learning will survive and thrive because the powerful combination of service and learning will always inspire educators, students, community members and advocates, and public and corporate leaders to come together in the spirit of collaboration and concern for the common good. Democracy depends on the development of active citizens and participation in the life of our communities. Effective programs that fully involve participants in service-learning will develop individuals who will go on to use the important lessons they have learned to create and sustain institutions and environments that, in turn, will lead future generations of citizens to seek solutions to social problems and opportunities to engage in service and learning.

References

Adams, L. B. "How One School Builds Self-Esteem and Serves the Community." *Middle School Journal,* 1993, *24*(5), 53–55.

Bok, D. *Beyond the Ivory Tower: Social Responsibilities of the Modern University.* Cambridge, Mass.: Harvard University Press, 1982.

Bok, D. *Higher Learning.* Cambridge, Mass.: Harvard University Press, 1986.

Boss, J. "The Effect of Community Service Work on the Moral Development of College Ethics Students." *Journal of Moral Education,* 1994, *23*(2), 183–198.

Boyd, D. "The Condition of Sophomoritis and Its Educational Cure." *Journal of Moral Education,* 1980, *10*(1), 24–39.

Boyer, E. L. *Scholarship Reconsidered: Priorities of the Professoriate.* Princeton, N.J.: Carnegie Foundation for the Advancement of Teaching, 1990.

Cage, M. C. "A Test Case for Tenure." *Chronicle of Higher Education,* Dec. 8, 1995, pp. 17–18.

Cohen, J., and Kinsey, D. "'Doing Good' and Scholarship: A Service Learning Study." *Journalism Educator,* 1994, *4.*

Crowner, D. "The Effects of Service Learning on Student Participants." Paper presented at the National Society for Experiential Education Conference, Newport, R.I., Nov. 1992.

Droge, D. "Thoughts on the Future of Service-Learning in Higher Education in the United States." Unpublished paper, 1995.

Edgerton, R. "The Engaged Campus: Organizing to Serve Society's Needs." *AAHE Bulletin,* 1994, *47*(1), 3–4.

Ehrlich, T. "Taking Service Seriously." *American Association of Higher Education Bulletin,* 1995, *47*(7), 8–10.

Eyler, J., and Giles, D. "Summary of Preliminary Results and Analysis of Selected Data from FIPSE Comparing Models of Service-Learning Research Project." Paper presented at the National Society for Experiential Education Conference, New Orleans, La., Nov. 1995.

Giles, D. E., and Eyler, J. "The Impact of a College Community Service Laboratory on Students' Personal, Social and Cognitive Outcomes." *Journal of Adolescence,* 1994, *17,* 327–339.

Giles, D., Porter Honnet, E., and Migliore, S. *Research Agenda for Combining Service and Learning in the 1990s.* Raleigh, N.C.: National Society for Experiential Education, 1991.

Greco, N. "Critical Literacy and Community Service: Reading and Writing the World." *English Journal,* 1992, *81*(5), 83–85.

Greiner, W. R. "'In the Total of All These Acts': How Can American Universities Address the Urban Agenda?" *Universities and Community Schools,* 1994, *1–2,* 12–15.

Hackney, S. "The Roles and Responsibilities of Urban Universities in Their Communities: Five University Presidents Call for Action." *Universities and Community Schools,* 1994, *1–2,* 9–11.

Hannah, S., and Dworkowitz, B. *Queens Tri-School Confederation, 1991–1992 Evaluation Report.* Brooklyn: New York City Board of Education, 1992.

Hirsch, D., and Lynton, E. "Bridging Two Worlds." *NSEE Quarterly,* 1995, *20*(4), 10–11, 28.

Jacoby, B. "Making Commuter Students Matter." *About Campus,* Mar./Apr. 1996, pp. 31–32.

Kniseley, M., and Beaird, B. *Linking College Students and At-Risk Students.* Providence, R.I.: Campus Compact, 1993.

Krehbiel, L. E., and MacKay, K. *Volunteer Work by Undergraduates.* Washington, D.C.: ERIC Clearinghouse on Higher Education, 1988.

Levine, A. "Service on Campus." *Change,* July–Aug. 1994, pp. 4–5.

Levinson, J. L., and Felberbaum, L. "Work Experience Programs for At-Risk Adolescents: A Comprehensive Evaluation of 'Earn and Learn.'" Paper presented at the American Educational Research Association annual meeting, Atlanta, Ga., Apr. 1993.

Markus, G. B., Howard, J.P.F., and King, D. C. "Integrating Community Service and Classroom Instruction Enhances Learning: Results from an Experiment." *Educational Evaluation and Policy Analysis,* 1993, *15*(4), 410–419.

Miller, J. "Linking Traditional and Service-Learning Courses: Outcome Evaluations Utilizing Two Pedagogically Distinct Models." *Michigan Journal of Community Service Learning,* 1994, *1*(1), 29–36.

Nelms, B. F. (ed.). "Community Service Projects and Communication Skills—The Round Table." *English Journal,* 1991, *80*(6), 89–91.

Newman, F. *Higher Education and the American Resurgence.* Princeton, N.J.: Carnegie Foundation for the Advancement of Teaching, 1985.

O'Neill, M. A. Letter to colleagues of the Maryland Student Service Alliance, Dec. 1, 1995.

Plater, W. M. "Future Work: Faculty Time in the 21st Century." *Change,* May–June 1995, pp. 22–33.

Schroeder, C. C. "New Students—New Learning Styles." *Change,* Sept.–Oct. 1993, pp. 21–26.

Twigg, C. A. *The Need for a National Learning Infrastructure.* Washington, D.C.: Educom, 1995.

Wilson, B. J. "Technology and Higher Education: In Search of Progress in Human Learning." *Educational Record,* Summer 1994, pp. 9–16.

Wingspread Group on Higher Education. *An American Imperative: Higher Expectations for Higher Education.* Racine, Wisc.: Johnson Foundation, 1993.

Zlotkowski, E. Presentation at the National Society for Experiential Education Conference, New Orleans, La., Nov. 1995.

Appendix A

National Organizations That Support Service-Learning

Alliance for Service Learning in Education Reform (ASLER)
c/o Close Up Foundation
44 Canal Center Plaza
Alexandria, VA 22314–1592
phone: (703) 706–3640
fax: (703) 706–0001
Internet address: cufmail@ixnetcom.com

An alliance of individuals and organizations seeking to promote educational reform through service-learning, primarily in K–12 settings. Publishes "Standards of Quality for School-Based and Community-Based Service-Learning."

Alpha Phi Omega National Service Fraternity
14901 East 42nd Street
Independence, MO 64055
phone: (816) 373–8667

A national collegiate service fraternity with chapters on more than three hundred college and university campuses. Membership includes sixteen thousand active members who provide service to campus, community, state, and nation.

American Association of Community Colleges (AACC)
Service Learning Clearinghouse
One Dupont Circle, N.W., Suite 410

Washington, DC 20036–1176
phone: (202) 728–0200
fax: (202) 833–2467
Internet address: aacc@aacc.nche.edu

Provides information and sample materials and links community colleges interested in starting service-learning programs with others that have programs underway.

American Association for Higher Education (AAHE)
One Dupont Circle, N.W., Suite 360
Washington, DC 20036
phone: (202) 293–6440
fax: (202) 293–0073
Internet address: aahela@gwuvm

A national organization of 8,500 individuals dedicated to improving the quality of higher education, with a strong commitment to helping service-learning attain a stronger, lasting place in the academy. Service-learning figures prominently in its National Conference on Higher Education. Also publishes *Change* magazine and a monthly newsletter.

American College Personnel Association (ACPA)
One Dupont Circle, N.W., Suite 300
Washington, DC 20036–1110
phone: (202) 835–2272
fax: (202) 296–3286
Internet Address: info@acpa.nche.edu

Addresses issues and trends affecting student affairs in higher education and provides professional development through conferences and publications. Service-learning has become a focus of its professional development efforts.

American Friends Service Committee (AFSC)
1501 Cherry Street
Philadelphia, PA 19102–1479
phone: (215) 241–7295
Internet address: afscid@apc.org

Sponsors international and domestic service programs focused on social justice and community development. During AFSC workshops in Mexico, groups of ten to twelve participants spend the summer in small villages engaged in projects that range from digging irrigation ditches to building houses for local teachers.

ASPIRA Association, Inc.
1444 I Street, N.W., Suite 800
Washington, DC 20005
phone: (202) 835–3600
fax: (202) 835–3613
Internet address: aspiral@aol.com

The only national nonprofit organization solely devoted to developing the leadership and educational potential of Latino and Latina youth. ASPIRA works with more than one hundred high school youth clubs and a variety of leadership and educational programs.

Best Buddies International
100 S.E. 2nd Street, Suite 1990
Miami, FL 33131
phone: (305) 374–2233
fax: (305) 374–5305
Internet address: bestbud@gate.net

Provides information and support for creating one-to-one mentoring programs for people with developmental disabilities, including conferences, seed funding, training in fundraising, and campus-based chapters.

Big Brothers/Big Sisters of America
230 North 13th Street
Philadelphia, PA 19107–1510
phone: (215) 567–7000
fax: (215) 567–0394

A national youth service organization providing one-to-one mentoring relationships between adult volunteers and children. Works through more than five hundred agencies throughout the United States. Publications describe mentoring practices.

Bonner Foundation
22 Chambers Street
P.O. Box 712
Princeton, NJ 08542
phone: (609) 924–6663
fax: (609) 683–4626

Provides colleges and universities with funding for financial aid packages to incoming students who commit to engage in community service. The foundation also supplies technical assistance and training to help institutions of higher education create and maintain a service ethic.

Break Away: The Alternative Break Connection
6026 Station B
Nashville, TN 37235
phone: (615) 343–0385 x3
fax: (615) 343–3255
Internet address: http://www.vanderbilt.edu/breakaway

A national network of colleges, universities, and community organizations to promote local, regional, national, and international service through academic break programs. It offers resource guides, a database of potential work sites, consultation, regional conferences, summer training sessions, mini-grants, and a newsletter.

Campus Compact: The Project for Public and Community Service
c/o Brown University
Box 1975
Providence, RI 02912
phone: (401) 863–1119
fax: (401) 863–3779
Internet address: campus@compact.org

A coalition of more than five hundred college and university presidents who believe that institutions of higher education have a primary responsibility to foster students' sense of civic responsibility and contribute to the welfare of their communities. Campus Compact works on a national level to cultivate discourse and support for public and community service; develop resource materials, grant programs, workshops, and institutes; and support a network of state and specialized offices to provide targeted assistance for institutions. In addition to sixteen state compacts, it includes the Center for Community Colleges and the Historically Black Colleges and Universities Network. Campus Compact administers programs to recognize outstanding students and faculty, and its wide range of publications is available to members and nonmembers. The Project on Integrating Service with Academic Study provides training and technical assistance to member institutions, as well as to individual faculty seeking to incorporate community service into teaching and research.

Campus Ecology
National Wildlife Federation
1400 Sixteenth Street, N.W.
Washington, DC 20036
phone: (703) 790–4317
fax: (202) 797–6646
Internet address: http://www.nwf.org/nwf/prog/campus.html

Promotes leadership and action to establish environmentally sound practices on college campuses, and provides resources, organizational assistance, and recognition of outstanding projects.

Campus Outreach Opportunity League (COOL)
1511 K Street, N.W., Suite 307
Washington, DC 20005
phone: (202) 637–7004
fax: (202) 637–7021
Internet address: homeoffice@cool2serve.org

Works with hundreds of colleges and universities to start, strengthen, and expand community service programs. COOL supports college student community service through campus-based training and consulting, conferences, publications, and the national Into the Streets program.

Center for Democracy and Citizenship
Hubert H. Humphrey Institute of Public Affairs
301 19th Avenue South

Minneapolis, MN 55455
phone: (612) 625–0142
fax: (612) 625–3513
Internet address: tsheldon@hhh.umn.edu

A national civic and political initiative focused on promoting democracy and strengthening citizenship and civic education within a variety of settings. The center's youth-focused programs include outreach, teaching, and research projects to strengthen community and civic capacities.

Constitutional Rights Foundation (CRF)
601 South Kingsley Drive
Los Angeles, CA 90005
phone: (213) 487–5590
fax: (213) 386–0459

A nonprofit, nonpartisan, community-based organization dedicated to educating young people to become active and responsible citizens. Its materials and programs, including *Learn and Serve in Urban Settings,* focus on civic participation and community building.

Corporation for National and Community Service
1201 New York Avenue, N.W.
Washington, DC 20525
phone: (202) 606–5000
fax: (202) 565–2781

Created by the 1993 National and Community Service Trust Act to administer and distribute federal funds to engage people of all ages and backgrounds in local, community-based service. The corporation's work includes AmeriCorps, the National Senior Corps, and Learn and Serve America. Its publications are useful for program design and evaluation.

Council of Independent Colleges (CIC)
One Dupont Circle, N.W., Suite 320
Washington, DC 20036–1110
phone: (202) 466–7230
fax: (202) 466–7238

A national association of four hundred private colleges and universities that assists institutions in improving leadership expertise, educational programs, administrative and financial performance, and institutional visibility. A current initiative in service-learning involves grants to thirty institutions to improve institutional capacity to conduct service-learning, a conference for campus teams from 175 institutions, publications, and grants to ten institutions for service-learning in teacher education programs.

Council on International Educational Exchange
205 East 42nd Street
New York, NY 10017
phone: (212) 661–1414, ext. 1139
fax: (212) 972–3231
Internet address: ivpbrochure@ciee.org

Sponsors international volunteer projects in twenty-three countries that bring volunteers from different countries together to work for two to four weeks on an environmental or community service project. Participants work and share accommodations and meals with local residents.

Do Something
423 West 55th Street, 8th Floor
New York, NY 10019
phone: (212) 523–1175
fax: (212) 582–1307
Internet address: dosomthng@aol.com

A national nonprofit organization that provides training, guidance, and financial resources to emerging youth leaders seeking to build their communities. Its mission emphasizes the belief that fundamental change occurs locally.

Foundation Center
1001 Connecticut Avenue, N.W., Suite 938
Washington, DC 20036
phone: (202) 331–1400
fax: (202) 331–1739
Internet address: http://www.fdncenter.org

Provides information on private and corporate philanthropy, fundraising, and nonprofit management. Its library is open to the public.

Giraffe Project
197 Second Street
P.O. Box 759
Langley, WA 98260
phone: (360) 221–7989
fax: (360) 221–7817
Internet address: giraffe@whidbey.com

Seeks through its mission to inspire people to "stick their necks out" to make the world a better place by telling their stories in schools and in the media. Its K–12 service-learning curriculum, *Standing Tall,* is used by the National Interfraternity Conference and others to teach courage, responsibility, and caring.

Habitat for Humanity International
121 Habitat Street
Americus, GA 31709
phone: (912) 924–6935
fax: (912) 924–6541

A nonprofit Christian ministry that works in partnership with low-income people to build or renovate homes, which are then sold at no profit and with low-interest mortgages. Campus chapters involve students directly in Habitat's work.

Higher Education Consortium for Urban Affairs (HECUA)
Hamline University
Mail #36
1536 Hewitt Avenue
St. Paul, MN 55104–1284
phone: (612) 646–8831
fax: (612) 659–9421
Internet address: hecua@alex.stkate.edu

Sponsors programs that guide students in linking theory with real-life experience through a combination of reading seminars, field-work, study-travel, and internships. Students are challenged to reflect on, analyze, and integrate their learning experiences. An interdisciplinary, global perspective and personal, local responsibility are emphasized in all programs.

INDEPENDENT SECTOR
1828 L Street, N.W., Suite 1200
Washington, DC 20036
phone: (202) 223–8100
fax: (202) 416–0580
Internet address: http://www.indepsec.org

A nonprofit coalition of more than eight hundred corporate, foundation, and voluntary organization members that promotes giving, volunteering, and the importance of the nonprofit sector. Publishes national statistics on nonprofit activity and the charitable behavior of Americans, as well as providing many other resources.

Mentoring Resource Centers (MRCs)

Located in California, Massachusetts, and Michigan, MRCs are part of a national program to encourage college students to serve as mentors to at-risk youth in their communities. MRCs offer literature, telephone consultation, workshops, and technical assistance on how to improve mentoring programs.

Boston University Mentoring Resource Center (serving Connecticut, Washington, D.C., Massachusetts, Maine, Maryland, New Hampshire, New Jersey, New York, eastern Pennsylvania, Rhode Island, Vermont, and West Virginia)
School of Education
605 Commonwealth Avenue
Boston, MA 02215
phone: (617) 353–3552
fax: (617) 353–3924

California Mentoring Resource Center (serving Arizona, California, Colorado, Nevada, Oregon, Utah, and Washington)
California Campus Compact
10920 Wilshire Blvd., Suite 1840
Los Angeles, CA 90024–6520
phone: (310) 794–8638

fax: (310) 794–8643
Internet address: ejc8jhk@mvs.oac.ucla.edu

Michigan Mentoring Resource Center (serving Illinois, Indiana, Kentucky, Michigan, Minnesota, Ohio, western Pennsylvania, and Wisconsin)
Michigan Campus Compact
31 Kellogg Center
East Lansing, MI 48824–1022
phone: (517) 373–9393
fax: (517) 355–3302
Internet address: hn2116@handsnet.org

National Association of Partners in Education, Inc. (NAPE)
209 Madison Street, Suite 401
Alexandria, VA 22314
phone: (703) 836–4880
fax: (703) 836–6941

Through its service-learning division, IDEALS, provides training and technical assistance to service-learning coordinators, educators, and representatives from businesses that are interested in partnering with schools and school districts to advance service-learning initiatives.

National Association for Public Interest Law (NAPIL)
1118 Twenty-second Street, N.W., Third Floor
Washington, DC 20037
phone: (202) 466–3686
fax: (202) 429–9766

A national coalition of student organizations at 133 law schools devoted to training the next generation of public service lawyers. NAPIL seeks to surmount, through a number of programs and publications, the obstacles that bar access to equal justice for poor and disadvantaged Americans.

National Association of Service and Conservation Corps (NASCC)
666 Eleventh Street, N.W., Suite 500

Washington, DC 20001
phone: (202) 737–6272
fax: (202) 737–6277

The membership organization for youth corps programs. It serves as an advocate, central reference point, and source of assistance for its members, with more than one hundred programs that employ more than twenty-six thousand young people nationwide. NASCC's primary mission is to strengthen the quality of existing youth corps and to promote the development of new ones.

National Association of Student Personnel Administrators (NASPA)
1875 Connecticut Avenue, N.W., Suite 418
Washington, DC 20009
phone: (202) 265–7500
fax: (202) 797–1157
Internet address: office@naspa.org

Provides professional growth opportunities for chief student affairs officers and other professionals who consider higher education and student affairs issues from an institutional perspective. Publications and conferences address service-learning.

National Coalition for the Homeless
1612 K Street, N.W., Suite 1004
Washington, DC 20006
phone: (202) 775–1322
fax: (202) 775–1316
Internet address: http://nch.ari.net

A national network working to end homelessness through education, policy advocacy, and grass-roots organizing. Offers a wide range of related publications.

National Helpers Network
245 Fifth Avenue, Suite 1705
New York, NY 10016–8728
phone: (800) 646–4623
fax: (212) 679–7461

Offers technical assistance, training, program development, resource materials, and other services for educators, practitioners, students, policymakers, and others interested in service learning.

National Interfraternity Conference (NIC)
3901 West 86th Street, Suite 340
Indianapolis, IN 46268–1791
phone: (317) 872–1112
fax: (317) 872–1134
Internet address: nicindy@eworld.com

Provides numerous resources and services to fraternities and institutions of higher education. It advocates for the enrichment of the fraternity experience. NIC's Adopt-a-School Program involves college students at 185 institutions in hands-on service in local schools.

National Service-Learning Cooperative/Clearinghouse
c/o University of Minnesota
R-290 VoTech Ed Building
1954 Buford Avenue
St. Paul, MN 55108
phone: (800) 808–7378
fax: (612) 625–6277
Internet address: serve@maroon.tc.umn.edu

Provides support and technical assistance regarding K–12 service-learning. Services include a national database of programs and resources, an electronic bulletin board, referrals to training, and peer consultants.

National Society for Experiential Education (NSEE)
3509 Haworth Drive, Suite 207
Raleigh, NC 27609–7229
phone: (919) 787–3263
fax: (919) 787–3381
Internet address: info@nsee.pdial.interpath.net

An association of more than fifteen hundred individuals, institutions, and organizations that supports the use of learning through experience for intellectual development, civic and social responsibility, career exploration, cross-cultural and global awareness, and ethical and leadership development. In addition to the National Resource Center for Experiential and Service Learning, NSEE offers the *NSEE Quarterly,* books, papers, consulting services, an annual conference, and regional meetings. NSEE's membership includes both individuals and institutions, and its publications are available to both members and nonmembers.

National Student Campaign Against Hunger and Homelessness (NSCAHH)
11965 Venice Boulevard, #408
Los Angeles, CA 90066
phone: (310) 397–5270, ext. 324
fax: (310) 391–0053

Provides training, telephone consultation, and project manuals for a variety of advocacy, education, and service projects to end hunger and homelessness. NSCAHH is also a national information clearinghouse and holds an annual national conference. Six hundred campuses in forty-five states are in its network.

National Youth Leadership Council (NYLC)
1910 West County Road B
Roseville, MN 55113
phone: (612) 631–3672
fax: (612) 631–2955
Internet address: nylcusa@aol.com

Develops service-oriented youth leaders by supporting individuals, organizations, and communities that encourage youth service and leadership. NYLC publishes a variety of resources, including the *Generator,* a biannual magazine, and *Update,* which focuses on policy issues.

Neighborhood Reinvestment
1325 G Street, N.W., Suite 800
Washington, DC 20005
phone: (202) 376–2400
fax: (202) 376–2600

Creates and strengthens resident-led partnerships to revitalize older urban neighborhoods. Established by an act of Congress in 1978.

One to One
2806 M Street, N.W.
Washington, DC 20008
phone: (202) 338–3844
fax: (202) 338–1642

Dedicated to bringing mentoring to children to help them reach their full potential. Toward that end, One to One promotes school-based team mentoring, which matches a group of three adults—a businessperson, a teacher, and a college student—with a group of ten to twelve middle-school students.

Oxfam America
26 West Street
Boston, MA 02111
phone: (617) 482–1211
fax: (617) 728–2594
Internet address: oxfamusa@igc.apc.org

An international agency that funds self-help development projects and disaster relief in Africa, Asia, the Caribbean, and the Americas, including the United States. Oxfam also distributes educational materials on hunger and on the annual Fast for a World Harvest, which colleges and universities can use as a fundraising and awareness-raising event.

Partnership for Service Learning
815 Second Avenue, Suite 315
New York, NY 10017–4594
phone: (212) 986–4594
fax: (212) 986–5039
Internet address: pslny@aol.com

Offers international and intercultural programs uniting formal studies with substantive community service in eleven locations around the world, including the United States. Since 1982, more than two thousand undergraduates and graduates from approximately 180 U.S. and Canadian colleges and universities have participated. The partnership holds an annual conference, publishes a newsletter and other materials, offers consultant services, and houses the Alec and Mora Dickson Resource Library for Service-Learning.

Points of Light Foundation
1737 H Street, N.W.
Washington, DC 20006
phone: (202) 223–9186, ext. 113
fax: (202) 223–9256

A nonprofit, nonpartisan organization that seeks to engage more people more effectively in community service to address serious social problems. Its Youth and Education Outreach program focuses on young people and schools. The foundation offers numerous resources.

Public Allies
1511 K Street, N.W., Suite 330
Washington, DC 20005
phone: (202) 638–3300
fax: (202) 638–3477
Internet address: panational@aol.com

A multicultural organization founded in 1991 by young leaders and community advisers to provide young people with opportunities to take leadership for solving pressing social problems. It recruits, places, trains, and supports young people in jobs in both the public and nonprofit sectors.

Service-Learning List

An active listserv discussion group of approximately eight hundred subscribers. To subscribe, send the command

SUB SERVICE-LEARNING First name Last name

to

listproc@csf.colorado.edu

Extensive service-learning files can be accessed at:

http://csf/colorado.edu/sl

Student Coalition for Action in Literacy Education (SCALE)
140½ East Franklin Street
University of North Carolina at Chapel Hill
CB3505
Chapel Hill, NC 27599–3505
phone: (919) 962–1542
fax: (919) 962–1533
Internet address: scale@unc.edu

A national network of college and university students, faculty, and administrators that mobilizes college student involvement in increasing literacy in the United States. SCALE supports new and existing campus-based literacy programs. Its publications are designed to serve as tools to assist college students in providing literacy education in their communities.

Student Environmental Action Coalition (SEAC)
P.O. Box 116
Chapel Hill, NC 27514–1168
phone: (919) 967–4600
fax: (919) 967–4648
Internet address: seac@igc.apc.org

A national student-led grass-roots organization dedicated to building power among students and youth involved in environmental and social justice action. It has seventeen regional coordinating groups and publishes a monthly magazine.

Student Pugwash USA (SPUSA)
815 Fifteenth Street, N.W., Suite 814
Washington, DC 20005
phone: (202) 393–6555
fax: (202) 393–6550
Internet address: uspugwash@igc.org

Inspires commitment among students and young professionals to solve global problems through the responsible use of science and technology. SPUSA provides a variety of educational activities that enable current and future leaders to examine critical social and global issues, and publishes a quarterly newsletter.

United Negro College Fund (UNCF)
8260 Willow Oaks Corporate Drive
Fairfax, VA 22031–4511
phone: (703) 205–3400
fax: (703) 205–3574

Provides support to its member colleges and universities. It has a major service-learning initiative underway.

YMCA of the USA
101 North Wacker Drive
Chicago, IL 60606
phone: (800) 872–9622
fax: (312) 977–9063

The largest nonprofit community service organization in the United States. At the heart of community life in neighborhoods across the nation, Y's are for people of all faiths, races, abilities, ages, and incomes. They work to strengthen families and to help people develop values and behaviors that are consistent with Christian principles.

Youth Service America (YSA)
1101 Fifteenth Street, N.W., Suite 200
Washington, DC 20005
phone: (202) 296–2992, ext. 21
fax: (202) 296–4030
Internet address: ysal@aol.com

To promote a unified, nonpartisan national youth service movement, provides leadership development, technical assistance, and training for community service programs in schools, colleges, universities, and community organizations. Services include the weekly National Service Briefing, other publications, and a national conference.

Programs and Resources Useful in Helping Students Make Postcollege Service and Career Choices

Selected National and International Service Programs

AmeriCorps

AmeriCorps, administered through state commissions on national service and the Corporation for National Service, focuses on four national priorities: education, human needs, public safety, and the environment. Participants work with eligible entities, which include nonprofit organizations; institutions of higher education; school and police districts; local, state, and federal governments; and Indian tribes. They may, for example, rehabilitate overgrazed land, tutor in schools with large numbers of disadvantaged children, or teach English as a second language. The range of actual work responsibilities is very broad. Full-time participants earn a modest living allowance and a postservice award of $4,725 to help pay for higher education or vocational training. These funds can repay student loans or pay for future higher education costs. AmeriCorps members must be citizens or permanent residents of the United States and at least seventeen years of age. Interested applicants

Note: Appendix B was compiled and written by Irene S. Fisher.

should contact the Corporation for National Service or state commissions on national service for applications and information. State commission telephone numbers are available through the Corporation for National Service. Telephone: (800) 942–2677 or (202) 606–5000.

AmeriCorps*VISTA is a one-year, full-time service program through which men and women over the age of eighteen commit themselves to increasing the capability of low-income people to improve the conditions of their own lives. VISTA volunteers receive a subsistence allowance, health insurance, student loan deferment, travel expenses, and a stipend or education voucher on completion of service. VISTA On-LINE, a biweekly electronic bulletin, features immediate assignment openings, program updates, and items of interest to career centers, libraries, professional groups, and potential volunteers. To subscribe, e-mail a single-line message: SUBSCRIBE VISTA-L (your name) to listserv@american.edu.

Habitat for Humanity International

Habitat for Humanity offers both domestic and international service opportunities. The domestic Habitat programs serve as community partners for many college and university service-learning programs. International opportunities are quite varied. Some have very technical requirements; others ask for only broad knowledge and service experience. Pay depends on the area and requirements, and a variety of benefits is offered. Telephone: (912) 924–6935.

Jesuit Volunteers

Jesuit volunteers serve throughout the United States and in several developing countries. They work as teachers, counselors, social workers, nurses, youth ministers, coaches, and community organizers. Volunteers must be at least twenty-one years old and have a bachelor's degree or equivalent work experience. The length of service is one year in the United States and two years for those serving internationally. Participants receive room and board, a small monthly stipend, international travel expenses (transportation home for domestic volunteers), health insurance, student loan deferral, and retreats and workshops throughout the term of service. Applications are accepted to only one region at a time but are transferrable. Programs begin in August. Telephone: East (215) 232–0300; Midwest (313) 963–4112; Northwest (503) 335–8202; South (713) 756–5095; Southwest (510) 653–8564; International (202) 687–1132.

Lutheran Volunteer Corps

This program provides varied full-time service options in a non-profit setting working for social justice through the improvement of health care, public policy, and housing. Volunteers work in Washington, D.C., Baltimore, Chicago, Milwaukee, Minneapolis–St. Paul, Seattle, and Wilmington, Delaware. Participants must be at least twenty-one years old and make a one-year commitment (August to August). They receive a stipend that covers rent, food, and personal needs, plus travel assistance and health insurance. Telephone: (202) 387–3222.

Overseas Development Network

The Overseas Development Network (ODN) is a national student organization promoting education and action around global issues. ODN places young people in three- to twelve-month internships with its grass-roots partners. For those interested in working on global issues in the United States, ODN offers staff-level positions. Telephone: (415) 431–4204.

Peace Corps

The Peace Corps, perhaps the best known of a wide array of international service opportunities, is open to individuals with a bachelor's degree; some assignments also require three to five years of work experience or other qualifications. Peace Corps volunteers work in most areas of the world except North America, in a variety of fields such as health education, community development, engineering, and industrial arts. Benefits include a monthly allowance for housing, food, and clothing; free medical and dental care; transportation to the overseas site; and twenty-four vacation days each year. Educational deferment and partial loan cancellation are available. Telephone: (800) 424–8580.

Teach for America

This program is committed to improving education and the lives of public school students in particularly troubled educational settings in the United States. It seeks recent college graduates with leadership qualities, teaching abilities, an undergraduate grade-point average of at least 2.0, and U.S. citizenship. Selected participants commit to teaching for two years in a school district or area with large numbers of children who are at risk of school failure and face a multitude of other social problems. The program offers an eight-week summer training institute. Pay varies from district to district, with a general range of $17,000 to $31,000 annually. Telephone: (800) 832–1230.

World Teach

Similar in mission to Teach for America, this program offers opportunities to teach in areas as diverse as Costa Rica, Mexico, and China. Participants need a bachelor's degree and a minimum of twenty-five hours of experience in teaching English as a volunteer. There is no language requirement. Participants make a one-year commitment. They receive a predeparture fee of $3,500, plus a stipend on arrival. Travel, housing, and health care are provided as well. Telephone: (617) 495–5527.

Resources on Nonprofit and Public Sector Careers and Volunteer Service Opportunities

Career Information Center. (5th ed.). Vol. 11: Public and Community Services. New York: Macmillan, 1993.

A how-to guide on getting into public and community service. Contains publication listings and specialized and nonspecialized training tips.

Community Jobs: The National Employment Newspaper for the Non-profit Sector. New York: Access.

A monthly publication of full-time job listings by region. Contains overseas opportunities, internships, and profiles of nonprofit organizations.

Cowan, J. (ed.). *Good Works: A Guide to Careers in Social Change.* New York: Barricade Books, 1991.

A student-initiated directory aimed at people of all ages wishing to connect idealism with employment opportunities. Lists eight hundred social change groups with career opportunities.

Earth Work. Charlestown, N.H.: Student Conservation Association.

A monthly magazine for people who want to make protecting wildlife and the environment their life's work. Each issue features employment opportunities, profiles of "earth workers," graduate programs in environmental studies, and articles on trends in conservation work.

Eberts, M., and Gisler, M. *Careers for Good Samaritans and Other Humanitarian Types.* Lincolnwood, Ill.: VGM Career Horizons, 1992.

Contains opportunities to work in disaster relief, hunger, mental health, and homelessness. Appendixes are particularly useful: State Offices of Volunteerism, InterAction Member Agencies (a coalition of American private and voluntary organizations), and missionary organizations.

Everett, M. *Making a Living While Making a Difference.* New York: Bantam, 1995.

A self-help guide and practical approach for the idealistic job seeker in an imperfect world. Includes a useful section on questions to ask potential employers and other sources of information on corporate policies and practices. As the title suggests, taking charge of one's own career choice and creating a compatible workplace are addressed.

INDEPENDENT SECTOR. *Academic Centers and Programs Focusing on the Study of Philanthropy, Volunteerism, and Not-for-Profit Activity.* (3rd ed.) Washington, D.C.: INDEPENDENT SECTOR, 1993.

This publication describes as thoroughly as possible the programs identified in its title.

International Employment Hotline. P.O. Box 3030, Oakton, VA 22124.

A monthly subscription newsletter with information on international and private voluntary organizations, government jobs, and contract positions. Includes professional conferences and summer volunteer opportunities.

Lasky, V. (ed.). *New Careers Directory: Internships and Professional Opportunities in Technology and Social Change.* Washington, D.C.: Student Pugwash USA, 1993.

Addresses global issues and socially responsible professional opportunities. Lists the percentage of time organizations devote to social and ethical implications of science.

Lauger, D. *Non-Profits' Job Finder.* River Forest, Ill.: Planning/Communications, 1993.

Contains comprehensive listings of job, internship, and grant opportunities by state.

Lewis, W., and Milano, C. *Profitable Careers in Nonprofit.* New York: Wiley, 1987.

Matches readers' interests and values with nonprofit opportunities through discussion of intangible rewards and compatibility with personal values.

Morgan, B. J., and Palmisano, J. M. (eds.). *Public Administration Career Directory.* Washington, D.C.: Visible Ink Press, 1994.

Contains useful chapters on working in community affairs at the state level and in public works careers to serve people and communities.

Scheiber, C. (ed.). *Opportunities: The Annual Volunteer Service Handbook.* Berry Publishing Services, 448 Decatur St., Toledo, OH 43609; (419) 385–0355.

A new annual magazine on how to get started and what to expect of full-time voluntary service in the United States and abroad. Includes reflections on service experiences.

Transitions Abroad. *1995–96 Educational Travel Planner and Resource Guide: The Guide to Learning, Living, and Working Overseas.* Amherst, Mass.: Transitions Abroad Publishing, 1995.

Offers comprehensive and reliable listings on long- and short-term work abroad, international teaching opportunities, worldwide volunteer programs and internships, overseas job hunting, and starting a business abroad.

Index